Fishing the Great Lakes of the South

Fishing the Great Lakes of the South

——— An Angler's Guide to the TVA System

Don and Joann Kirk

Menasha Ridge Press
Birmingham, Alabama

Printed in the United States of America
Published by Menasha Ridge Press
First edition, first printing

Library of Congress Cataloging-in-Publication Data
Kirk, Don, 1952–
  Fishing the great lakes of the south.

  Includes index.
    1. Fishing—Tennessee Valley—Guide-books.
2. Fishes, Fresh-water—Tennessee Valley. 3. Lakes—
Tennessee Valley—Guide-books. I. Kirk, Joann.
II. Title.
SH464.T46K57   1988   799.1'1'09768   88-1768
ISBN 0-89732-043-3

Cover photograph of Bill Dance by Richard Simms,
  Tennessee Wildlife Resources Agency.
Cover design by Teresa Smith; book design by Barbara
  Williams
All photographs in this book are by Joann Kirk unless
  otherwise credited.

Menasha Ridge Press
Post Office Box 59257
Birmingham, Alabama 35259-9257

This book is dedicated to our three children, Jeffrey, Shae, and Stephanie. They endure seeing much of the country in the quest of outdoor adventure.

Contents

*Note: Each chapter in Parts II and III contains a section, "Fishing Information," which gives details on the specific angling conditions in that lake.

List of Maps

Foreword

Over the years, I have often admired—indeed, envied—those ardent outdoorsmen who are blessed with a knack for taking pen in hand and transcribing the details of their exploits afield so well that all who read their words can truly share, learn from, and enjoy their experiences.

For me, it takes a very special scribe to accomplish this; since I was a very small boy, I have spent most of my waking hours in pursuit of angling sports. Naturally, I want to be entertained when I read anything about fishing, but I especially like the writer to pass along every tidbit he can about the quarry, its habits and environment, and the area in which one can pursue it.

Don Kirk is such a writer. I was so impressed with his first work a few years ago that I have made sure to watch for every succeeding piece, and I have never been disappointed. Don's first book, *Smokey Mountains Trout Fishing Guide,* has been a real hit with trout fishermen everywhere and his enlightening articles have graced the pages of all the noteworthy outdoor magazines.

Now, here is his new book, written with Joann Kirk, *Fishing the Great Lakes of the South: An Angler's Guide to the TVA System,* and you can be sure it will become well-worn from tagging along in this fisherman's tackle box. I believe this sensational text is the best guide ever written to my favorite lakes and the fish that inhabit them, and it is written in the same concise style that my friend Don Kirk has become known for. It contains hundreds of hours of research on the who, what, when, where, why, and how of fishing for every species of fish that you'll find in our super TVA waterway system. Every time I pick it up, I learn something else new. It'll help you the same way. If you're as serious about your fishing as I am—especially on TVA waterways— "you won't leave home without it!"

Bill Dance
February 23, 1988

Acknowledgments

This book could never have become a reality without valuable help from several people. More than anyone else, long-time friend and fishing buddy, John Doty of the Tennessee Valley Authority, provided immeasurable help and technical assistance.

Scott Sieber, Gary Jenkins, and Rick Lowe at TVA's Land Between the Lakes preserve must also be thanked for their generous help. The folks at TVA's Map Division and many other field people also assisted in bringing this project to completion.

Tennessee Wildlife Resources Agency fishery biologist, Price Wilkins, and Doug Peterson were great help, along with TWRA Creel Clerk Sonny Poole. Literally hundreds of weekend fishermen added their two-cents worth, and, although it's impossible to thank them all individually, let us say thank you this way.

Lastly, I'd like to thank Bill Dance, the Tennessee River Valley's most famous fisherman, for his help.

Before You Go

This guidebook will give anglers a packet of useful information as they go fishing, camping or boating at a TVA lake. Before we start, however, there are a few general precautions and tips we should mention.

Safe conduct on the water is essential. On mainstream impoundments, where barge traffic can be quite heavy, special care is needed. Personal flotation devices are essential equipment everywhere, but must always be worn when fishing the system's extremely dangerous tailwater reaches. Unexpected water-level changes and turbine boils can overturn and sink a tied-off fishing boat in less than 20 seconds.

Boating safety rules are not just good sense; they're often state law. The lakes covered in this book are located in seven states, and each has its own boating regulations.

Seven states also mean seven different sets of fishing regulations. Creel limits, size restrictions and bait regulations vary widely from state to state. Several lakes are shared by two or more states, and on several of these reciprocal angling agreements are in place. Information on licenses, fishing regulations, and boating laws for these states can be obtained from the agencies listed at the end of this chapter.

Maps

Knowledgeable fishermen know that nothing is more important when going to a new lake than a good map of that body of water. Lake maps of all of the lakes in this book are available in one or more forms from TVA.

For lakes not maintained by TVA only USGS topographic quad maps are available (topo maps are available for TVA lakes as well.) These can be purchased through the TVA Map Sales Office for a couple of dollars each, but it may take four or more maps to cover even a small lake.

Recreation maps are the simplest and least expensive of the lake maps. These show the entire lake, as well as the locations of commercial docks, public boat-launch ramps, major highway and secondary road access routes, public-use areas and sometimes the locations of man-made fish attractors.

The quality of these maps varies considerably. The TVA mountain lake recreational maps from Georgia and North Carolina are of relatively poor quality. The newer Tims Ford and Tellico lake maps are superb, however, and even have topographic detail (the only "recreational" maps that have this addition). These were free until the federal budget crunch of the early eighties. Now they're available at a nominal fee.

Greater detail is available in the TVA navigational charts. These show detail very similar to that of the USGS topographical maps, but, unlike topos, they deal with specific bodies of water rather than arbitrary quad units. The largest navigational charts cover entire lakes (Cherokee and Douglas, for example); Kentucky Lake, on the other hand, requires over a dozen charts. These maps note shoals, topographic details, stump beds and other features which anglers find valuable. Even with this detail, though, the charts are relatively inexpensive.

All of these maps and charts, as well as a free map and chart catalog, are available from the TVA Map Sales Office, Haney Building, Chattanooga, TN 37401, or the TVA Map Sales Office, Union Building, Knoxville, TN 37902.

State Game and Fish Departments in the TVA System

Alabama Game & Fish Division
Department of Natural Resources
64 North Union Street
Montgomery, AL 36104

Georgia Game & Fish Division
Department of Natural Resources
270 Washington Street, SW
Atlanta, GA 30334

Kentucky Department of Fish & Wildlife Resources
State Office Building Annex
Frankfort, KY 40601

Mississippi Game & Fish Division
Game and Fish Building
402 High Street
P.O. Box 451
Jackson, MS 39205

North Carolina Wildlife Resources Commission
Albemarle Building
325 North Salisbury Street
Raleigh, NC 27611

Tennessee Wildlife Resources Agency
Ellington Agriculture Center
P.O. Box 40747
Nashville, TN 37220

Virginia Commission of Game and Inland Fisheries
4010 West Broad Street
P.O. Box 11104
Richmond, VA 23230

The lakes of the Tennessee River valley are nationally known for producing impressive, mixed-bag stringers of black bass.

PART ONE

Fish of the TVA Lakes

Smallmouth Bass

Ripping, cartwheeling surface antics are Mr. Smalljaw's calling card. This well-muscled fish's strength is overshadowed only by its courageous determination to be free and its no-nonsense, aggressive disposition.

The smallmouth bass *(Micropterus dolomieui)* is a member of the Centrarchidae family of sunfish. Among the thousands who identify themselves as "bass fishermen," this battler is their passion, the thing from which sweet dreams are made. The Tennessee River Valley is prime bronzeback country. Recognizing this, the legislature made the smallmouth bass the official fish of the state of Tennessee.

The TVA lakes include some of the finest smallie lakes in the country. Each year Watauga, Nottely, Norris, Watts Bar, Fontana, Cherokee, Tims Ford, South Holston, Wheeler and Fort Loudoun lakes produce loads of 5-to-7-pound bronzebacks. And we haven't even mentioned the nation's top spot for a wall-hanger—Pickwick Landing Lake.

The world record smallmouth bass, which weighed 11 pounds, 15 ounces, was caught in Dale Hollow Lake in Tennessee in 1955. Actually, the fish was caught so close to the Kentucky state line that both states claim it. Being a good Volunteer State resident, however, I'll go with the home team!

Alabama's state record bronzeback, which rocked the scales at 10 pounds, 8 ounces, was caught at Wheeler Dam in 1950. At the time this fish was caught, it was the world record holder. Georgia's number-one smallmouth bass weighs 7 pounds, 2 ounces; it was taken from Chatuge Lake in 1973. The Mississippi record bronzeback tipped the scales at 7 pounds, 5 ounces, and was caught from Pickwick Lake. North Carolina's top smallie weighed 10 pounds, 2 ounces and came from Hiwassee Lake in 1953. 'Nuff said?

Lunker smallmouth bass are found throughout most TVA lakes.

The smallmouth bass is a member of the black bass clan, the toughest branch of the scrappy sunfish family. They resemble their larger-growing cousins, the largemouth bass, as well as the Kentucky bass. The most notable differences are in body shape and coloration. Smallies are more streamlined and sport amber to bronze coloration. Their flanks have vertical bars, or "tiger stripes," and their eyes are reddish colored.

In Tennessee River system lakes all three bass usually coexist wherever the smalljaw is found. The balance can range from a near even, three-way split to total dominance by one of the three species. Habitat is usually the determining factor. Smalljaws require cool, clean lakes with gravel, rock and sand bottoms. Largemouth thrive in warmer abodes and do as well in soft, muddy-bottomed lakes as do flathead catfish. The Kentucky seems to do best in shared habitats.

Smallmouth bass spawn earlier than most sunfish. Water temperatures in the 60s beckon these fish to shoreline areas that have sloping gradients and gravel bottoms. This occurs in low-elevation lakes, such as Kentucky Lake, in late April and may be delayed in high-country impoundments, such as Hiwassee, until late May.

Adult smallmouth bass prefer rock- or gravel-bottom feeding stations.

Where there's good smallmouth bass fishing, expect to find a sizeable population of crayfish.

Crawfish are key diet items, along with shad, chubs and other small fish, spring lizards, and insects and other invertebrates.

Fishing specifically for smallmouth bass is a challenging sport, but their abundance in the TVA system makes it so worthwhile. One could easily devote an entire book to this subject, as the various techniques and awesome array of different fishing situations, from small mountain lakes to tailrace fishing to night fishing, take years to master.

Experienced smallie fishermen agree that more consistent results are obtained with light tackle and relatively small baits. I like 2-to-4-pound-test line, but some fishermen advocate the use of 6-to-8-pound test. On occasion, it's possible to get away with heavier line, but because big bronzebacks are such spooky varmints, the odds are stacked against success.

Favorite smallmouth baits include ⅛-to-⅜-ounce grubs, jigs, and bucktails, crawdad- and shad-style crankbaits, small spinnerbaits, 6-to-8-inch plastic worms, and 2-to-3-inch top-water plugs. Smoke, purple, brown, and black are effective leadhead dressing hues, while green, brown, silver, and red are good crankbait colors. Purple, red, motor oil, and blue are usually effective worm colors.

Live-bait fishermen probably nab more lunker smalljaws than the hardware casters. Point fishing the bottom with minnows is a favorite ploy among old-timers, and live crawdads staircased down a steep, rocky bank can get a shoulder dislocated. Hellgrammites, spring lizards,

Live crayfish are exceptional smallmouth bass baits, but artificial offerings, like these plastic crayfish, also work well.

grasshoppers, nightcrawlers and small frogs are also heady inducements for a bronzeback's strike.

Winter is a fine time to fish for brown bass. December water temperatures and normally abundant rainfall help keep these cool-natured fish active in most TVA lakes. Jigs and live minnows can't be beaten at this time. The fish are 10 to 20 feet down, and their metabolisms are slowed. Baits like plastic worms or jigs worked slowly over drop-offs, saddles and bars can bring surprising results. Even during the dead of winter smallie fishing can be excellent.

Around late February smallmouth bass begin getting active and wander. Point fishing with medium-to-deep-diving crankbaits can be good at this time. Bottom fishing sloping rock or shale points with several shinner-baited poles is an old-time tactic that still works.

March and April are exciting months for tangling with Tennessee River Valley brownies. In most lakes they can be found shallow in the headwaters of creeks and coves. Two-to-four-foot depths are not uncommon. Spinnerbaits tossed to the shoreline and retrieved at a brisk pace are met by violent strikes.

The fish often station in the shade of floating debris, a common sight in impoundments when water levels are rising. Bass under trash can be taken by using the spinnerbait techniques noted above or by flippin' grubs or spider jigs. This kind of action peaks in mid-April.

During this period, tailrace smallies like those below Pickwick

Some of the mountain lakes in Tennessee, North Carolina, and Georgia produce big stringers of brown bass, such as this one.

Landing and Watts Bar dams stay in water quite different from such backwater lairs. Spring smalljaw action is best during periods of upstream generation. The fish station off of gravel bars, points, rip-rap and pilings. They can be taken by drifting spring lizards or live tuffies by them or by tossing jigs or ripping medium-depth-running crankbaits.

Spawning action can be located along sloping gravel or rock shoreline, especially along 8-to-12-foot-deep "shelves." Plastic worms, grubs, jigs and crankbaits bounced through likely bedding cover can net an irate parent fish or two. Following the spawn the fish spread out along rock shoreline areas. During the May shad spawn, top-water action using Rapalas, Lunker Lures and Rebel Floater Minnows can be incredible. The July willowfly hatch is also a time for topflight topside fishing. Spinnerbaits and medium-depth-running crawdad-style crankbaits are also good May baits.

Early morning and late evening are always the best bronzeback fishing times, but beginning in June this becomes even truer. Top-water or shallow-depth-running plugs will be taken then, along with jigs and worms. Mid-June is the unofficial starting time for nighttime smallie fishing. Smallmouth bass are probably more at home feeding in darkness than under sunlight conditions. During hot weather, when the surface temperatures of many lakes can rise into the low 80s, the fish and many of their quarries retire to deeper, cooler zones. At night, though, the shallows and mid-range areas come back to life. Jigs are a favorite nighttime offering, followed by plastic worms, spring lizards and minnows.

Twelve-volt black lights like those used to illuminate fluorescent posters and fluorescent fishing line make night fishing easier. On an inky black night the illumination from the tubular violet lights makes an angler's line look like anchor rope, and the most deft pick-up can be seen in the moving white line across the black water and sky.

Largemouth Bass

Mr. Largemouth Bass is "ole numero uno" to an army of dedicated southern anglers. This member of the sunfish family *(Micropterus salmoides)* is found in great numbers and large sizes in virtually every Tennessee River Valley lake.

The world record largemouth hailed from the Peach State over 50 years ago, weighing a whopping 22 pounds, 4 ounces. North Carolina's record largemouth was caught from Santeetlah Lake in 1963. Just about every TVA lake has produced lake record bass in the 10-to-13-pound range.

The largemouth bass is a stoutly built, "broad shouldered" (and full-bellied) predator. Pound for pound, it is about as belligerent as an ole gator. "Ole Bucket Mouth" has a mouth only slightly smaller than its body girth. Largemouth bass have dark green to black backs, white bellies and green sides broken only by a broken single dark green to black lateral line.

The spotted, or Kentucky, bass is a look-alike relative that coexists in most TVA lakes with the larger-growing hawgs. The Kentucky bass *(Micropterus punctulatus)* was not acknowledged as a separate species until 1927. They rarely top the five-pound mark and can be distinguished from the largemouth by a small patch of teeth on the tongue and distinct dark spots along the lateral line.

The world-record Kentucky bass was caught from Lewis Smith Lake in 1978, and weighed a whopping 8 pounds, 15 ounces. Georgia's top spotted bass weighed 7 pounds, 12 ounces, and was caught in 1972 from Lake Nottely. The record-book Kentucky from North Carolina was a bantam-weight 14½-ounce specimen taken from Hiwassee Lake in 1980. Tennessee's number-one spotted bass was caught in 1976 from Chickamauga Lake; it tilted the scales at 5 pounds, 4 ounces. At times these fish are taken alongside the largemouth bass and at other times with smallies.

Potbellied largemouth bass abound throughout the TVA system. Broad, mainstream impoundments like Chickamauga, which produced this bass, offer outstanding fishing.

Black bass frequent tight structure and ambush their victims, rather than try to run them down. They lurk behind weeds, roots, rocks or in the shadows beneath lilypads or deadfalls, seizing victims that venture too close. While the largemouth bass is truly an opportunistic feeder, occasionally consuming such oddities as ducklings or snakes, its most common diet includes small sunfish and other gamefish fry, suckers and shad, frogs, mayflies, crayfish, worms and terrestrial insects.

Bigmouth bass spawn when water temperatures reach 65 to 72 degrees, and are most active when water temperatures range between 60 and 75 degrees. Like all sunfish, the largemouth is a nest-building, spring spawner. Bedding can occur almost anywhere, but back coves are commonly preferred. The males seek out areas 2 to 10 feet deep that have mud, sand, gravel or weedy bottoms. Each fans out a circular, bowl-shaped nest and then awaits a roe-laden female. Eggs are ejected into the nest and quickly fertilized by the male, who then assumes responsibility for protecting and rearing the offspring. Males aggressively guard their brooding area against intruders, such as bream. During this time actual feeding by bass is negligible, but strikes can be provoked by fishing bottom baits near nesting sites.

Following the spawn, bass migrate throughout the lake. Each lake has a different set of circumstances and seasonal variations, as any circuit-riding professional bass angler can tell you. Seasonal patterns are predictable, although fine tuning is the ultimate key to success.

In some lakes, cold winter weather sends the largemouth deep, while in others they concentrate in feeder creek embayments. Early spring sends bass into mudflats in some lakes, while in other lakes they move into headwater areas.

Late spring and early summer is a time of transition. Surface action can be torrid at this time, but bottom baits are also productive.

Hot weather sends bass deep in most Tennessee River Valley lakes, and with the long days many of them become nocturnal, deep-water feeders.

Even though the fish seek depths of up to 30 or 40 feet in some deep TVA lakes, structure is still the key to finding largemouth bass. Most lakes have submerged building foundations, abandoned railway tracks and roadbeds, brush and extended points, and are all worth ferreting out.

Black bass fishing rates among the most popular sports in the Tennessee River Valley.

Deep water is the most common holding zone until autumn's cooling winds "turn over" a lake's thermal layers. For a brief time the hawgs roam the shallows before cold weather makes the surface temperatures uncomfortable.

The vast majority of present-day bass fishing is done from boats. The so-called "bass boat" is a modern phenomenon which combines high-tech gadgetry with topflight engineering features and materials. Many are capable of speeds in excess of 70 miles per hour; contrary to the conventional wisdom, however, largemouth bass can be caught in great quantities without the services of a floating Cadillac.

Another old (or perhaps new) wive's tale involves live bait for bass. A wildlife officer tells of receiving upwards of two dozen calls each summer from novice fishermen asking if it is legal to use nightcrawlers for bass. Yes, Virginia, you can use nightcrawlers, and even worms trained in Kung Fu if such wigglers are offered for sale.

Prior to the arrival of the avalanche of plastic, wood, metal and foam baits offered for sale today, loads of hawgs were taken on freely available naturals, such as grasshoppers, spring lizards, bait fish, nightcrawlers, frogs, grubs and aquatic insect larvae such as the hellgrammite. Each has its own applications and prime time. All are proven bass takers.

The modern, well-equipped bass fisherman's tackle box holds an array of specialized artificial baits. Many knowledgeable bass anglers don't know all the bait applications or the techniques needed to catch fish with each.

Spinnerbaits. These evolved from the so-called "safety pin"–type, weedless baits. Construction often includes a stiff V-shaped wire frame sporting one or two metal blades and a jig head with either rubber or bucktail dressing. Yellow, white, black, green and combinations of these colors are the most popular colors.

Spinnerbaits are versatile lures used primarily between late winter and early summer, although they will catch bass year-round. A brisk retrieve keeps the bait shallow, which is desirable during the early spring. When allowed to sink, these baits can be fished deep or along the bottom. This is also a productive night-fishing offering.

Buzzbaits. This is one of the oldest lure concepts, and one currently enjoying a remarkable revival of popularity. Basically, buzzbaits are shallow- or top-water lures very similar in construction to a spinnerbait, particularly in their use of a wire frame. The wire frame commonly uses a U-shaped design. The top bracket holds a free-spinning baffle similar to that of a whirligig. This dual or triple blade churns or buzzes the water when the bait is retrieved. The bottom wire holds the hook, which is usually dressed in bucktail or rubber skirt.

Buzzbaits are most commonly used during the spring and at night. They are highly effective near vegetation, buck bushes, milfoil, cypress trees, and so forth, as well as rip-rap.

Crankbaits.   To many, crankbaits are merely plugs. They are constructed from wood, plastic or foam and are almost always topped off with one to three sets of treble hooks. Crankbaits are painted and shaped to mimic gamefish fry, shad, crawdads or other aquatic edibles, and most models come in a rainbow of colors.

Discounting color variations, much of the time their appearance is for the angler's sake, at least in our opinion. The crankbait's secret, as its name implies, is the bait's action when "cranked." Deep-diving baits with long bills or spoons can explore water up to 17 feet deep. Medium-depth-diving baits work in 6-to-8-foot depths, and shallow-running crankbaits work well in 1 to 5 feet of water. Top-water baits ride the surface. Admittedly, this is a very simple explanation of a tremendously diverse bait line which accounts for over a thousand different lures, all designed to do something special.

Jigs.   The Tennessee Jig is not a dance any more than the Virginia Reel is a piece of fishing equipment. All jigs have one thing in common: they all sport a leadhead around a single hook.

Thereafter, though, the sky is the limit. The leadhead can vary between 1 ounce and ⅛ ounce, with corresponding differences in hook sizes. Dressings include bucktail, rubber and plastic in all colors. Pork rinds are occasionally added to give these baits a natural feel. When added to a bucktail this combination is called a fly'n'rind, and when pork rind is spiked onto a rubber (or spider) jig, its proper title becomes "jig'n'pig." Jelly twistertails and beetles are also coupled with leadhead jigs. Like most popular bass baits, jigs are versatile enough to be used in different situations and work well with several techniques. They are regarded as year-round bottom baits, one exception being when twistertails are used.

Lift and drop retrievals are almost always productive for fly'n'rinds or jig'n'pigs, while slow swimming retrievals are recommended for bucktails and jelly twistertails. Jigs are also vertically jigged and flipped into and through dense cover.

Plastic Worms.   When Creme offered the first plastic or jelly worm back during the fifties, who could have guessed these stripes of pliable rubber would revolutionize bass fishing? If limited to only one bait, 9 out of 10 knowledgeable Tennessee River Valley bass fishermen would take the plastic worm. Shallow or deep, in grass or rocks, few baits can out-produce the worm. It is also worth noting that few baits require more patience or are more difficult to fish properly.

Plastic worms come in a spectrum of colors, shades, sizes and designs. The most popular are seven to nine inches long with augur-style (swimming) tails. Colors vary from lake to lake, and season to season, but because these baits are relatively inexpensive and compact, most bassers carry a selection which includes black (with glitter, orange firetail), blue (with glitter, blacktail), purple (grape, wine, with glitter), red (strawberry, with glitter) and pearl. Taste- and salt-impregnated worms are a popular new twist to these baits.

Seasonal applications and techniques vary considerably. During the spring worms are pulled through bedding areas. Strikes are subtle and difficult to distinguish from thumping a root or rock. Part of the secret to successful "worming" is knowing how to rig this bait. The three most popular riggings include Texas, Carolina and leadhead, but all have one thing in common: making sure the worm is hooked where it will hang straight with the line.

In late spring worms are fished faster, away from the bottom. Where grass is a key cover area, worms rigged to run weedless are swum over the growths. During hot weather when bass are deep, extra lead is added and the baits are slowly nudged along the bottom. Strikes can be so gentle that they don't register by feel. Accomplished wormers watch the line coming out of the water for telltale twitches.

Night worming is a specialized endeavor. Techniques are the same, but fluorescent line is used along with a tubular, 12-volt "black light" mounted to the boat's gunwale. The black light illuminates even fine fishing line, making it appear like baling twine against a dark night.

Spoons.   Once a vital component in every knowledgeable bass fisherman's tackle arsenal, the spoon has slipped in popularity in recent years. This is a shame because these are very productive baits under the right circumstances. Spoons come in a variety of sizes, shapes and finishes. Some are even weedless. Allowed to flutter down alongside suspended bass, these baits sometimes produce when all else fails.

Winter is one of the best times to use these heavy baits. When suspended bass are located and refuse everything thrown at them, try vertically jigging a spoon.

Spring point fishing using a light spoon and a fast return can be fun and productive. Where weeds hold shallow bass, a weedless spoon skipped atop the blooms is always worth a shot.

Crappie

What's the most popular gamefish found throughout the Tennessee River Valley lake system? If your answer is the largemouth bass, striper or rainbow trout, you're wrong. Try the much-berated crappie. This fish may not be a spectacular battler or for some even a challenge to catch, but when filleted and fried crispy brown, it becomes an instant superstar.

Best known in the Tennessee River Valley as the crappie, this fish is called more than 50 different names, ranging from bachelor perch, goggle-eye, and papermouth to speckle perch, calico and strawberry bass. It is a handsome fish, with a streamlined profile and a generally flat, or slablike, front. A three pounder may tape 12 inches long, yet be only 1½ inches wide, with a shape much like that of a platter. The crappie is generally dark green on its back, graduating to light green specks on its sides, and white on the belly.

The Tennessee River hosts two closely related crappie species, the white crappie *(Pomoxis annularis)* and the black crappie *(Pomoxis nigromaculatus);* like bream and largemouth bass, each is a sunfish in the Centrarchidae family. Both are widespread and abundant. In the TVA system the white crappie is usually more numerous than the black. Warmer, more turbid mainstream impoundments have greater percentages of the white crappie, while in rocky highland lakes the black is often the dominant species. It's also worth noting that lakes where the white species accounts for a significantly greater portion of the crappie fishery are usually noted for their good calico fishing.

It's easy to tell the two species apart. All crappie sport specks on their flanks. The black's specks appear to have been scattered at random with no distinguishable pattern. The white's specks, on the other hand, are arranged in distinctive vertical bars. The two fish can also be distinguished by the number of spines on their dorsal fins. The white's dorsal fins have five or six spines, while blacks have seven or eight dorsal spines.

The habitat requirements of these two fish also differ, but this variation is not very useful for distinguishing between the species. Whites are noted for their ability to prosper in the turbid water common to many large TVA reservoirs. They are most commonly found over muddy bottom areas. Blacks, which are sometimes called a river variety, are encountered most consistently over rocky areas. If this sounds like an easy way to key in on either fish, forget it, because in most TVA lakes both are available, and they are commonly caught together. Generally speaking, the variations between the white and black species do not affect the tactics or techniques used by anglers.

Crappie are slow-growing fish that seldom top four pounds in their four-year life span. The world record white crappie weighed 5 pounds, 3 ounces, and was caught in 1957 from Enid Dam, Mississippi. The record black tipped the scales at an even 6 pounds, and was taken from Westwego Canal in Louisiana in 1969. The state record crappie for Alabama was caught from Guntersville Lake in 1974, and weighed a respectable 4 pounds, 8 ounces.

Crappie are a gregarious fish that spend most of their lives in schools. Like other sunfish, this is a cover-oriented species. They are most at home near standing timber, brush piles, weed beds, stick-ups and stump beds, but they also frequent drop-offs, bars, rocky points and creek meanders. They survive by preying upon small fish, crawfish, mollusks and insects.

Crappie spawn during their second and third years. This occurs in shallow water, 3 to 10 feet deep, triggered by the rise of water temperatures into the sixties. Females commonly release 10,000 to 50,000 eggs, although clusters in excess of 150,000 have been documented. Small bowl-shaped nests are fanned out over a hard bottom to keep silt from contaminating or choking the eggs.

Most crappie fishing occurs during the spring, but this is truly an all-season fish. It's also a relaxing and generally simple chore to catch them. Only bream fishing requires less in the way of tackle and baits from the angler. Light tackle is a prerequisite to success. I use a 4½-foot Fenwick boron rod coupled with a graphite Ryobi reel. This rig weighs only a few ounces; when strung with 4- or 6-pound-test line, it is ideally suited for crappie fishing on most TVA waters.

These fish consistently prefer small offerings. Bait selection can be as simple as year-round producers like 1½-to-2½-inch tuffies or shiners or as elaborate as ⅟₃₂-to-⅛-ounce feather and hair dollflies and twistertail grubs, small shad-style crankbaits or ⅛-ounce spinners like those offered by Mepps. Electronic depth finders are an important aid for the crappie angler. These devices not only help locate calico schools but also permit fishermen to follow creek meanders and probe for saddle, brush, stump flats and drop-offs that commonly hold their quarry.

Winter crappie fishing is excellent on most TVA lakes. During this season these fish are suspended 10 to 25 feet deep and usually display a torpid disposition. On most lakes they can be found on the edge of drop-offs along submerged river or feeder stream courses. During cold weather, as always, finding the right cover is the key. They will strike baits, though, and when located during this time, they are more stationary than at other times. When good fishing is found at one location, it often holds there until a major weather front arrives and drives the fish out.

Fishing deep-water structure for these fish requires a deft touch. Light lines and stiff fishing rods are preferred by many valley crappie experts. If they're suspended deep, vertical jigging with a grub or live minnow is usually effective. When these fish are holding on or very near the bottom, try a steady, slow retrieve along the bottom.

During the winter months interesting things can happen to crappie

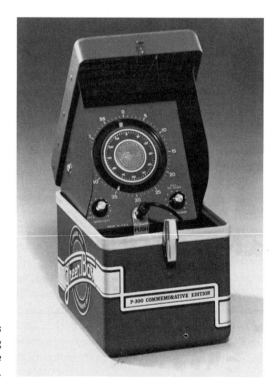

Electronic depth finders are useful for locating suspended crappie throughout the year.

fishing fortunes. It's not unusual for a week-long stretch of balmy, springlike weather to send the fish into feeding frenzies in 3-to-5-foot-deep shallows—even during January.

Crappie respond to warming spring temperatures by moving into backwater areas. In tributary lakes like Douglas this could be a cove with a red clay bottom, while in big Kentucky Lake it would be a side sluice infested with buck bush. What happens next depends upon the weather and water levels. Under ideal conditions, which would be several days of unbroken sunny weather and stable water levels, spawning can last for as short a period as one week to 10 days. This is highly unlikely, though, because April weather is seldom so cooperative. Broken spawning activity is to the crappie fan's advantage, however, for spoiled spawning attempts mean the troops must regroup and try again. This keeps the calicos in or near accessible shallow areas much longer than would be the case if the business of reproduction could be completed without any snags.

Prespawn crappie and those pushed out of spawning areas often retreat to 8-to-20-foot-deep creek meanders and ledges off of points. Fishermen who expect to find fish in the shallow areas where they were before a front passed or a dramatic lake level change occurred can expect disappointment.

Two outstanding ploys for taking prespawn or shifted crappie are spider rigging and trolling. Spider rigging is a novel approach which originated at Kentucky Lake several years ago. A 2 inch by 2 inch wooden frame for mounting four to eight rod holders is affixed to the boat's bow, along with an electronic depth finder and a trolling motor control. Telescoping 8-foot poles strung with 12-pound-test lines and rigged with two to four long-shank No. 4 gold hooks, which are attached to the primary line via a three-way swivel and a 12-inch leader, are mounted on the wooden frame. Each pole has three hooks baited with live minnows which are 10 to 12 inches apart. A ½-to-1-ounce sinker is attached to the end of the line. Each pole's hook rigging can be adjusted to the desired depth, thus enabling the boater to simultaneously probe several depths with his offering. Spider rigging was developed to permit crappie fishermen using electronic depth recorders to trace their boats along submerged creek channels. It's like having your own school of bait fish zeroing in on the quarry.

Trolling works well on lakes where creek channel retreats are less important than general mid-spawn scattering due to weather changes or prespawn staging. Many fishermen look down their nose at trolling, but many don't really understand it. Don was fortunate to study under one of Dixie's best crappie trollers, Arnold Kirk, who incidentally is his father.

Dad fishes Douglas Lake like a Baptist preacher crusades against

Crappie caught with a typical spider rigging setup.

the evils of Demon Rum. Since the late sixties, all told, he probably hasn't caught a good mess of fish casting. He's a dyed-in-the-wool troller. His secrets are simple, but to succeed his instructions should be adhered to closely.

First off, troll slowly. He uses an inexpensive electric trolling motor that would have trouble pushing the boat against a strong wind. He knows there are new "super generation" trolling motors, but you couldn't give him one because the one he's got ideally suits his slow-trolling techniques. When trolling slow, the flies or minnows bounce the bottom. That's the ideal, because when spring crappie aren't spawning in the shallows, they're on the bottom.

The second trick is to stay close to the shoreline. Most of the time when trolling with Pop you can almost leap from the boat to dry land. Under some circumstances he might move further out, but only rarely, and usually only as a last-ditch effort.

He never uses line heavier than six-pound test. Sure he hangs up frequently, but to avoid losing a tacklebox full of gear each spring, he opts for thin wire hooks that easily straighten out when pressure is applied. He also uses limber, medium-length spinning rods and open-face reels. The reels are not crucial, but a spaghettilike rod lets the bait bounce along on the bottom. Pop's standard offering is a tandem-rigged, ⅛-to-¹⁄₁₆-ounce homemade leadhead hair jig tipped with a 1-to-2-inch-

Crappie fishing is fun, relaxing, and enjoyed by most anglers.

long tuffie. The fly can be any color—as long as the first fly is yellow and the trailer is white.

How effective is his crappie trolling technique? Well, these days he only fishes one or two weeks each year because two to three thousand filleted crappie are all Mom will allow him to pack into her freezer. His trolling tactics are not only effective for prespawn slabsides but, modifed for greater depths, promise great success during hot and cold weather.

During the spawn, crappie fishing is great fun. In shallow lakes the most consistent action is found around flooded buck bushes, standing timber or weed beds. For this kind of fishing the old reliable cane pole is the best tackle. In lakes where natural cover is scant, locate a man-made fish attactor and you're in business. Minnows fished under bobbers or small jelly grubs worked deep are the best offerings for the spawning period. It's the season's easiest and most productive fishing.

Following the spawn crappie scatter and move into deeper water. Many anglers write these fish off then, but that's a mistake. If you can find where these fish spend their daylight hours, they can be caught. Also, summertime night fishing for these fish is good throughout the TVA system.

Kentucky Lake is one of the best summertime crappie hot spots in the United States. In hot weather the fish station around one of the abundant submerged, 10-to-20-foot-deep stump beds along the maze of old creek meanders. The trick to catching them is getting a minnow right in front of their eyes.

The best technique is "stump knocking." A telescoping pole rigged identically to the one described for spider rigging is used. Once a likely stump bed is located, let out enough line to touch the bottom. Using the terminal sinker, tap around for a stump. It takes a little practice, but once the skill of locating these cover items is mastered, the fun begins. When a stump is found, vertically jig the minnow rig around it for a minute or two. If no strike occurs, move to another stump. But rest assured, if a slabside is there, it will nab your bait.

Night fishing for crappie can be highly productive. Man-made brush piles are ideal for suspending a lantern over for crappie. The fish aren't attracted to the light like moths; nor are the bait fish, contrary to popular notion. It's plankton, or microscopic plants and animals, which are attracted to the light rays. These morsels in turn draw bait fish. When night fishing, vertically jig your flies or minnows beneath the light. Depth varies with water clarity.

Autumn calico fishing is a well-kept secret on most Tennessee River Valley lakes. In fact, it is not unusual for anglers to luck upon a brief period of fishing that's comparable to that of the spring spawn. Fall spawns are nature's way of insuring a few in each age class, for the spring crop might be wiped out by flood or some other disaster.

Walleye and Sauger

For centuries the Indians living along the Tennessee River referred to the native sauger *(Stizostedion canadense)* as the "mystery fish." This delicious fish was always abundant during the late winter and early spring months, but for the rest of the year it mysteriously disappeared. Oddly enough, for the average angler this label is as true today as it was then.

The walleye *(Stizostedion vitreum)* is also native to the Tennessee River drainage. These deep-water predators, along with their close kin the sauger, are widely distributed throughout the Tennessee River system, although they are only thought to coexist in fishable numbers in one TVA reservoir, Norris Lake.

Sauger and walleye are members of the perch family *(Percidae)*, which also encompasses the darters, including TVA's most famous fish, the snail darter. The Tennessee River Valley's only other gamefish in the perch family is the yellow perch *(Perca flavescens)*, which is found in several lakes and appears to be growing in numbers. They are similar in size to bream and are caught using the same techniques.

Walleye are long, tubular fish with large mouths full of sharp teeth. They are well adapted for living close to the bottom. Colors vary from a drab olive green to nearly silver. Large, foggy eyes are their single most distinctive physical characteristic. Ten-to-fifteen-pound marble-eyes, though uncommon in the TVA lake system, are occasionally taken. The world-record walleye, a 25-pound monster, was taken from old Hickory Lake, Tennessee, in 1960. North Carolina's state record walleye, a 13-pound, 4-ounce specimen, was taken from Santeetlah Lake in 1966.

There are five races or strains of walleye: the Great Lakes or Canadian, Missouri River, Cumberland River, Tennessee and White River (Arkansas). The last three are the largest growing and are sometimes called "yellow walleye." Only the White River walleye in Arkansas still commonly top the 15-pound mark. Dams on the Tennessee and Cumberland rivers are thought to have impeded the native walleye's spawning runs. The demise of the large-growing native walleye was also probably hastened by the widespread stocking of "silver or green" Great Lakes–strain walleye. The reason for the introduction of this non-native was that the northern strain readily reproduces in lake environments. Quality walleye fisheries exist in only a few TVA lakes, notably, Fontana, Santeetlah, Norris, Watauga and a few others.

Understanding the walleye's vision is a key to unraveling their behavior. Their eyes are extremely sensitive to light, and they are rarely caught in shallow water during bright daylight hours except during the height of the spawn, and even then this is uncommon. Typically the best walleye fishing is at dawn and dusk, during the twilight hours, on overcast days, or when suspended fish are located deep, usually over 30 feet down. The common denominator for red-hot walleye angling is low light.

Walleye spawn when water temperatures reach the 43-to-48-degree mark, which in the Tennessee River Valley is usually in February and

Many anglers regard walleyes as the best-tasting fish in the TVA system. They are most commonly found in tributary lakes.

March. These fish reproduce in either still or moving water. In some lakes, such as Santeetlah, they use both areas. In rivers spawning female walleye seek out areas with moderate to light current sporting a gravel, rock or sand bottom. In lakes they prefer rock outcroppings with crevices. Eggs are ejected into the water, and nearby males fertilize the free-drifting roe.

Following the river spawn, walleye migrate back downstream to their lake homes. These are cool-natured, schooling fish which spend the summer and autumn months following shad and alewife movements. They prefer 55-to-65-degree water and at this time they remain relatively deep during the daytime, between 25 to 50 feet, although twilight shoreline forays into much shallower water are common.

Sauger, which top out at around 7 pounds, have often been called the walleye's "little southern cousin," despite the fact that the world record rattlesnake fish, at 8 pounds, 12 ounces, was taken in the Great White North (North Dakota) in 1971. One Yankee writer called the sauger "an inferior fish" following a voluminous chapter on the walleye in his book, a "fishing encyclopedia" (of the Great White North).

Alabama's number-one sauger weighed 5 pounds, 2 ounces, and was caught at the Wilson Dam tailrace in 1972. Kentucky's record tipped the scales at 6 pounds, 1 ounce, and was caught from Kentucky Lake in 1972. Tennessee's top rattlesnake fish weighed 7 pounds, 6 ounces, and was taken from the Pickwick Landing Dam tailrace in 1973.

Sauger, as the early inhabitants of this land noted, are indeed a mystery fish. Once plentiful throughout the Tennessee River drainage, it is now found in high numbers only in a few lakes. The reasons for this are not well understood.

One theory is these fish are dependent upon sufficient riverine habitat for reproductive success. When Cherokee Lake on the Holston River was first impounded during World War II, it initially maintained a vibrant sauger fishery. A decade later, after a series of upstream dams on that river system were completed, the Holston's sauger fishery disappeared.

Nearby Douglas Lake, an impoundment of the French Broad River built at about the same time, however, has no significant upstream dams and until recently maintained a good sauger fishery. Since 1974 fishing success at Douglas Lake has plummeted and sauger stocking has begun. The apparent demise of the sauger fishery at Douglas is difficult to understand, especially since no research into the situation there has ever been carried out, according to Doug Peterson, Tennessee Wildlife Resources Agency (TWRA) fishery biologist. Water quality is one suspected culprit, as is competition with white bass during the sauger's spawning run.

Sauger are a popular winter and late spring quarry.

Ironically, lack of angler success does not always indicate low sauger populations. While doing river counts for sauger downstream from Pickwick Landing Dam in the 1970s, a group of TWRA fishery personnel were informed by local anglers and marina operators that spawning sauger had yet to ascend the river. Despite rock-bottom angling success, though, the biologist's survey samples revealed that the river held half a million sauger over a two-mile stretch.

Sauger occur in most TVA lakes and are particularly common in the mainstream impoundments. Physically, the sauger resembles the cylindrical walleye, although its flanks are brown, white and black in a splotchy, diamond pattern. The dorsal fin also sports distinctive specks. Spawning temperatures and areas are virtually identical to river-run walleye, and where the two coexist, they occasionally hybridize, producing a large-growing "hoss sauger."

In 1983 the TWRA and TVA stocked Cherokee Lake with hatchery-produced walleye-sauger hybrids. Local anglers call these fast-growing, aggressive crossbreeds "saugeyes." Other lakes may soon receive walleye-sauger hybrids. Walleye-sauger grow larger than the sauger but not as large as the walleye. The world record saugeye weighed 10 pounds, 6 ounces, and was caught from Lake Sakakawea, North Dakota, in 1975. Tennessee's record book saugeye was a natural cross that weighed 9 pounds, 15 ounces, and was caught in the Fort Loudoun Dam tailrace in 1983.

Like the walleye, the sauger returns downriver following the spring run, and it too appears to drop out of sight during hot weather. In truth they are always present, according to Wade Murphy of Morristown, Tennessee, who catches sauger at Douglas Lake throughout the summer months. His secret is to locate spring holes. Thermal considerations are one of the keys to summertime rattlesnake fish angling success.

Both perch species are considered premium tablefare, topping many fishermen's list of favorites. Fried golden brown, sauger or walleye fillets are a delicate treat few can resist. Were it not for their excellent taste, it is doubtful either would receive more than passing interest from fishermen, as once hooked, neither provides even a portion of the fight of a trout or bass.

Catching walleye or sauger can be ridiculously simple or as difficult as building a fast breeder reactor in your backyard. Success is largely dependent on your quarry's feeding and movement patterns and concentrations.

Feeding seems to occur en masse, with the early morning and evening hours almost always being the most reliable timeslots. When brisk feeding begins, virtually every square inch of water could produce a strike, particularly the last two inches before you lift your bait from the water. During the height of the spring mating run, casting ¼-ounce orange, white, green or yellow leadhead hair, feather or jelly twistertail grubs is the favorite ploy of experience perchers. Some use live minnows, and a few do quite well trolling nightcrawlers on special northern rigs. In such river settings these fish are considered to be structure oriented with downed bridge pilings, deadfalls, spillways, dams, river junctions, feeder creek entrances and shoals usually being hot spots. These are not the only places these fish hold, and even when holding at these areas, they can be incredibly close mouthed.

Most winter and spring fishing takes place either from the bank or very near it in a boat. Bankside anglers usually cast upstream to a 10 o'clock position, slowly bouncing their bait back in along the bottom. Some fishermen use bobbers to suspend their offerings.

Warmly clad winter sauger fishermen mob up on tailrace fish below major mainstream dams like Fort Loudoun or Pickwick Landing. These swift headwater reaches are the concentrating point for great numbers of sauger. Vertical jigging along lock walls, rip-rap and still water around turbine discharge boils works well. Drift fishing with several minnow-baited lines is effective, as is trolling. When river fishing from a boat, it is possible to locate schools in otherwise difficult-to-reach areas. Quartering across the current is productive, but when sitting atop a large school, such as at the tailrace at Pickwick, trolling is particularly effective. Many consider tailrace fishing the TVA system's best opportunity to catch sauger.

Sauger spawn in river environments during early spring.

Unless you are a seasonal walleye or sauger tracker, finding these fish in a lake during warm weather can be frustrating. Since both species are wanderlusters at heart, trolling is a way of either catching or simply locating this quarry. Occasionally in summer, lake walleye and sauger move in close to the shoreline or even surface feed. Twilight bass fishermen are usually the first ones to stumble upon shallow marble-eyes along the shoreline, as this is basically the same area they are working for black bass. Walleye routinely strike crankbaits such as Shad Raps, medium-depth-diving Rapalas, Bagley's Bee II, pig'n'jig combos, and small spinnerbaits. Under the stars even small surface plugs are sometimes relished.

A word of caution to those who have yet to catch their first walleye or sauger: take care landing and removing the hook. Both perch species sport a dandy set of needle-sharp choppers which can pierce the skin.

Pikes

The muskellunge and chain pickerel are the Tennessee River system's only native representatives of Esocidae, or the pike family. Two hundred years ago Ohio River–strain muskie were common to most of the river's system. Virtually all muskie caught in the Tennessee River Valley system today are stocked, and the state of North Carolina is working hard to reestablish reproducing river populations. Chain pickerel, on the other hand, were not terribly common here prior to the dam-building era. A third, non-native clan member, the northern pike, has been introduced at two TVA lakes: South Holston and Melton Hill. Only the latter now offers credible northern fishing. All these pike species are topflight predators with closely related diets, life-styles and spawning habits.

The muskie is the largest-growing pike family representative and its best-known member in the TVA system. The world record muskellunge *(Esox masquinongy)* weighed 69 pounds, 15 ounces, and was taken from the St. Lawrence River in 1957. Tennessee's state record muskie, which rocked the scales at 42 pounds, 8 ounces, was caught in 1983 from Norris Lake. Alabama's top muskie weighed 19 pounds, 8 ounces, and came from the Tennessee River in 1972. A 38 pounder from Blue Ridge Lake is Georgia's record fish. A 33-pound muskellunge–northern pike hybrid, or "tiger muskie," from Fontana Lake in 1984 is a North Carolina record.

Muskie are a peculiar fish, a relic from past eras. They are vicious predators which religiously utilize rock, wood or vegetation-shrouded structure. When lying in ambush, muskie like to hide in shadowy areas. Soft-ray forage fish, such as suckers, carp or shad, are their staples, although spiny-ray sunfish and even largemouth bass are sometimes preyed upon. "Old Briarmouth," as some call this toothed water wolf, zealously guards its domain. These fish are not above killing other fish just for the sake of killing or apparently to punish intrusions.

Muskellunge are cool-water fish. Spawning occurs in early May, usually in grassy, weedy or snag-rich areas. Their reproductive success is limited in Tennessee River Valley lakes. Established fisheries are the result of stocking efforts. Most valley states have stocked or occasionally still do stock these critters. Fontana, Norris, Cherokee, the Bear Creek lakes, Santeetlah, Blue Ridge, Melton Hill, Hiwassee, and Pickwick are the best bets for muskie action.

Anglers sometimes call the muskie the "fish of a thousand casts." They are never plentiful, even in prime muskie waters like northern Minnesota. Because there are no bonafide muskellunge lakes in the TVA system, staunch muskie anglers are scarce here. The muskie's moody, reticent nature makes the large-growing but unpredictable fish a prized catch, however.

A large percentage of muskie caught here are caught by mistake, as these fish occupy approximately the same habitat niche as black bass. Bass anglers probably catch more muskie than anyone else in the TVA system. When muskie are prowling the shallows, they will often strike large surface or medium-depth crankbaits, live shiners or spinnerbaits. Cast toward the bank and retrieved as though fishing for bass, these baits will usually do the trick.

Serious muskie fishermen, on the other hand, concentrate much of their effort on trolling. Large spoons, spinners and plugs in red, orange, green and white are proven offerings. Trollers often work on shoreline areas, sometimes using a steady, brisk speed called "power trolling."

There are a few tricks to this, though, according to Ray Jones of Oak Ridge, a well-known Norris Lake muskie angler. He likes trolling, but not your standard round and round approach. Jones believes muskie can be excited or taunted into attacking a bait. He attempts to isolate areas he feels hold muskie and then he concentrates his efforts there. If a strike is not recorded after a couple of passes, he moves his boat close to his quarry's lair and revs his motor. Sometimes he rides out from this area and charges it, turning the boat quickly at the bank. All of this creates a lot of "annoying" noise and clouds up the water. Jones then returns to standard trolling ploys. These tricks netted the Oak Ridge angler one former Tennessee record muskie.

February and March are traditionally the best muskie times, followed by November, December and January. Late spring and summer, though seldom touted as prime briarmouth months, usually provide fairly decent fishing.

Chain pickerel *(Esox niger)* are stunted first cousins of the northern pike. Like other pike, they prefer heavy cover and are vicious predators.

*Although not native to
the TVA system,
northern pike
transplanted to Melton
Hill Lake grow large.*

The world record chain pickerel weighed 9 pounds, 6 ounces, and was caught from Homerville, Georgia, in 1961. Kentucky's state record pickerel weighed 4 pounds, 4½ ounces, and was caught from Kentucky Lake in 1982. The Mississippi record "jack" was caught from Pickwick Lake in 1978 and weighed 5 pounds, 13½ ounces. Tennessee's record pickerel weighed 6 pounds, 9 ounces, and was lifted from Kentucky Lake in 1951.

Pickerel fishermen are few and far between, even where there's pretty good fishing for these toothed fish. Crappie and bass fishermen at Pickwick and Kentucky lakes are probably more familiar with these fish than other TVA anglers. The reason is simple: the techniques and lures used on the more desirable gamefish also attract the pickerel.

It's a shame the jack, as it's known in most locales, is not better tablefare; otherwise it would be the one attracting attention. Their bony skeletons make easy filleting almost impossible, and their flesh is somewhat strong—something like a white bass caught during hot weather. As a gamefish, they're aggressive and willing to strike an array of lures, plus they're an above-average fighter.

Early spring is the best time to catch chain pickerel. They respond robustly to warm spring temperatures and can be taken on live minnows, red and white spoons, small silver-hued crankbaits and spinnerbaits. The time of the best pickerel fishing roughly corresponds to the crappie spawn.

Northern pike *(Esox lucius)* were first introduced from northern states to the TVA system in the late sixties by Virginia fishery personnel. They stocked northerns in South Holston Lake, but this was a short-lived project that bore little fruit. In the late seventies the fish was transplanted to Melton Hill Lake. This lake's relatively constant surface level and frigid disposition as a result of upstream Norris Lake and its massive weed beds made it an ideal candidate for this cool-natured exotic.

The northern pike is similar in appearance to the muskie in size and shape. Muskie often (but not always) have a silverish hue and markings on their flanks, usually vertical bars. Northern pike, on the other hand, are usually greenish with yellowish specks or broken horizontal stripes on their flanks.

The world record northern pike weighed 55 pounds, 15 ounces, and was caught from Lipno Reservoir, Czechoslovakia, in 1979. (This is one of the rare fish native to both the Old and New worlds.) Tennessee's record northern weighed 20 pounds, 13 ounces, and was caught from Melton Hill Lake in 1986. Melton Hill is the only TVA lake where these fish presently exist. Interestingly, TVA is largely responsible for their presence there.

These cool-water fish are noted for their furious strike. I've caught northerns in excess of 20 pounds, however, and, personally, I was never impressed with the species.

Like other pike, they're ambush-style predators. Anglers can trigger the northern's urge to kill with bright, flashy artificials like spoons or rainbow-colored crankbaits. These should be worked parallel to weed beds or along creek meanders.

Catfish

The Tennessee River Valley just wouldn't be the same if it weren't for Jack Daniels sippin' whiskey and twilight hush puppy and catfish fries. Those unfamiliar with these southern gastronomic get-togethers have serious gaps in their understanding of Ole Dixie. The river valley boasts some of the nation's most bodacious angling opportunities for whisker fish. Outstanding year-round catches are possible from the mountains to the mouth of the Ohio River.

Catfish are a popular species, despite the fact that they don't always carry "sportfish" membership cards. Catfish specialists, though, are as true to their chosen object of pursuit as fly-flicking trouters or competition bass anglers are to theirs. Yet, like the crappie chasers, Mr. Whisker's fans are low key, if not almost invisible.

The Tennessee River system has no fewer than six major catfish species: channel, blue, flathead (or mud or yellow) and the yellow, brown and black bullheads. The latter three are small growing and generally considered insignificant by most lake fishermen. In most locations there is no limit on any catfish species.

The Tennessee record blue cat *(Ictalurus furcatus)* caught on hook and line rocked the scales at an even 68 pounds and was caught from the French Broad River in 1983. A 130 pounder was caught by commercial fishermen several years ago from Fort Loudoun Lake. Alabama's record blue cat was caught in 1980 below Guntersville Dam; it weighed 65 pounds. Kentucky's top hook and line blue cat, which was wrestled from the Tennessee River downstream from Kentucky Lake in 1970, rocked the scales at an even 100 pounds. By comparison, the present world record blue was caught from South Dakota's Missouri River in 1959 and weighed 97 pounds. Big blue cats are a common tailrace quarry.

Georgia's number-one flathead catfish *(Pylodictic olivaris)* came from Notterly Lake in 1969 and weighed 51 pounds, 15 ounces. A larger 57

31

Every TVA lake boasts excellent catfish. This 40-pound flathead catfish is by no means a rarity.

pounder from South Holston Lake in 1972 still holds the top spot in Virginia. The world record mud cat, as it is often called, weighed 91 pounds, 4 ounces, and was taken from Texas's Lake Lewisville in 1982.

Channel cats *(Ictalurus punctatus)*, though not as large growing as the blue or mud, are highly prized for their delicate flavor. Presently there are no state-record channel catfish taken by hook and line in the Tennessee Valley Authority system. The world record channel cat weighed a whopping 58 pounds and was caught from South Carolina's Santee-Cooper Lake in 1964. Channel catfish are the dominant "lake" cat in most Tennessee River Valley lakes. Ten to twenty pounders are not uncommon.

Tennessee's largest recorded brown bullhead *(I. nebulosus)*, or the fiddler, weighed 2 pounds, 14 ounces, and was caught in 1980 from Chickamauga Lake, which also provided the state's largest recorded yellow bullhead *(I. natalis):* a 4½ pounder. Black bullhead *(Ictalurus melas)* can also be found in the TVA system, although presently there are no state record fish. The world-record black bullhead weighed 8 pounds and was taken from New York's Lake Waccabuc back in 1951, while the largest recorded brown bullhead hit the scales at 5½ pounds, and was caught in 1975 from a Georgia pond. The title-holding yellow bullhead, which falls far below Tennessee's state record mark, weighing only 3 pounds, 12 ounces, was caught in 1983 from Arizona's Mormon Lake.

Catfish are large-growing fish devoid of scales. Their tough, leathery, slick skin and prominent whiskers, or "barbels," are their most prominent physical characteristics. Their weak, light-sensitive eyes are better suited to dingy water or twilight activity than daylight forays. Their nocturnal feeding and movements are aided by an incredibly well developed sense of smell. The head cavity contains a mass of odor-detecting sensors. The distinctive whiskers, as well as the skin itself, are also part of the catfish's complex olfactory system. Catfish spawn when water temperatures reach 80 degrees. They are "crevice spawners," meaning females seek out nesting sites in old pipes, cans, tires or caves.

Few fish have more "checkered" diets than the bottom-feeding Mr. Whiskers, although if the truth were known, many so-called gamefish also stoop to scavenging. Carrion is seldom snubbed by the catfish, nor is decaying corn (a favorite bait for illegal fish-trap baskets). Cats go after decaying shad as though it were a delicacy, but let a careless young bass or crayfish venture too near their lair and see if these supposedly docile fish let them pass.

Catfish are not considered difficult to catch, although understanding them is not as easy as one might think. Everyone knows Mr. Whiskers is most often caught at night, but in all Tennessee River Valley lakes these fish undertake seasonal migrations. Some of the best and biggest catfish catches are taken during the dead of winter, when these fish seek out deep, warm abodes. Few vie with these fish then, other than serious commercial fishermen whose livelihoods depend upon understanding their quarry's wintertime movements.

This is not to say most catfish fans are fair-weather fishermen. Rather, it is during the summer that these good-eatin' fish are most available in areas where they can be most easily taken by the average angler. In most lakes cold weather triggers a migration along the main river channel. Cats stay relatively deep then. While winter is still quite cold, their movements are generally toward the tailwaters or the dam, where the warmest habitat exists.

Catfish are extremely active in hot weather, spawning in coves and creek embayments where crevice cover is available. When the water reaches the 80-degree mark, usually in July and August, spawning activity peaks. Backwater areas, creek embayments and coves are frequented from then until late autumn.

There are more fun ways to catch catfish than there are to skin a 'possum (this scribe will forego further comparisons). Most catfish angling techniques are as relaxing as a noonday nap, but not all!

Whenever going after catfish, always use hooks large and, more important, stout enough to hold up to the punishment these hard-fighting fish can dish out. Standard 1/0 to 3/0 stainless steel hooks are fine for most lake-fishing situations. Whenever going after monster tailrace catfish, such as those below Pickwick or Chickamauga dams, 4/0 to 7/0 stainless steel hooks are in order. Line, too, should be heavy, at least 14-pound test in lakes, with 20-to-40-pound test being standard in tailraces. Sinkers weighing from ⅜ to ½ ounce are recommended for lake fishing, with sliding or pyramid sinkers. Tailrace fishing conditions are different and require larger sinkers and special riggings.

Traditional catfish baits are the kind of smelly organic items that even some of the biggest fans of this kind of fishing abhor spiking onto a hook. Cut shad, chicken liver, night crawlers, decaying shrimp, doughballs soaked in chicken blood and homemade stinkbaits are standard favorites, but hardly the only tidbits a lurking cat will take. Catfish, be they channel, blue or even flathead, will readily stalk an array of artificial lures.

Crappie fishermen are well aware of this fact. Trolling with dollflies or minnows over clay flats is very effective on channel catfish. The Bass Anglers Sportsman's Society (BASS) held a major tournament on Cherokee Lake in 1981. The largest fish brought to Ray Scott's scales was not a largemouth or smallmouth bass but a 15-pound flathead cat caught on a deep-running crankbait.

During the spring bottom-fishing baits such as cut shad or live minnows work best. Bait fishing on the bottom is effective year-round and on most lakes can be practiced day and night. Spring and summer are fantastic times to fish the tailraces downstream from the nine Tennessee River impoundments. Here, cut shad and chicken liver are the most productive baits.

When the turbines are active, excellent catches are possible by fishing the edges of boils. Despite strong currents, huge catfish crowd into these relatively small areas to feed upon shad cut up or injured by their pass through the generators. Two-to-four-ounce, pyramid-style weights are needed to counteract the swift water and hold the bait in the right spot. Some anglers position boats at the edge of the generator boils and fish downstream. If using this potentially dangerous approach, never anchor or tie the boat off on a stationary object. Sudden generation surges can swallow a boat in less than 20 seconds. Always leave the motor running and use its power to hold the boat against the current.

Floating baits from a boat along a tailrace current is another productive trick for nailing a big stringer of catfish. Keep the motor running and the boat pointed upstream to control the downstream drift. An electronic depth finder is very helpful in detecting old bridge pilings, drop-offs, rock piles and other structure likely to hold big catfish. When these are located, bottom bouncing is the favorite technique. Using heavy spinning or casting tackle, suspend a large 2-to-4-ounce sinker approximately one foot under a three-way swivel. Attach a second 12-to-18-inch line with a hook to the swivel. Tie the terminal line to the swivel's third eyelet. This rigging permits the probing of bottom cover while the bait moves above the bottom in the current.

Trotlines, a catfish specialty, can be used in either tailrace or lake settings. Modern trotlines use nylon line number 18 to 24 rather than cotton twine; up to 50 "drops" are legal. Barrel swivels are used to connect the drops to prevent twists in the line by large, rough catfish. Traditionally, trotlines are baited in the evening and checked for fish during the morning. Some fishermen bottom set trotlines using large rocks to weight their rigs down. Depths can be adjusted by using plastic jugs or bottles for floaters. Trotlines must have the owner's name and address attached and cannot be discarded while in use.

Limbline cat fishing is popular on many lakes. Drop lines identical

The authors' son, Jeff Kirk, with a stringer of eating-sized channel catfish.

to those used on trotlines are suspended from lakeside tree limbs. The bait is fished a few inches off the bottom where a shoreline-prowling cat can easily locate it. Once the fish is hooked, the limber tree limb can wear down even the most stubborn catfish's aggressive disposition.

During the summer and spring, jugging can be downright exciting at times. It provides loads of dependable fun when hot weather puts a damper on other pursuits. Jug fishing is similar to trotline fishing except the fisherman plays a much more active role. Plastic one-quart bleach bottles, gallon milk jugs and two-liter soft drink bottles are the most popular "jugs." A heavy, 20-to-30-pound line with a hook is attached to each bottle and suspended three to six feet below the jug. There are limits on the number of jugs allowed in most states. In Tennessee the limit is 50 jugs per angler. Shallow, sheltered coves are ideal, as strong open-water winds can quickly scatter a jug set. Bait and set out your jugs late in the evening, then settle back and watch. Before long one jug will begin to bob and move, then another and another. The sound of bobbing jugs will fill the night.

Bank sets are the most common summertime ploy. This is a simple operation which calls for casting a bait out and fishing silently on the bottom. Lawn chairs, lanterns and bonfires are the best paraphernalia for bank set fishing.

Fishing for Mr. Whiskers may not be the most glamorous form of angling or a line-wetting trick which will increase your bank account, but thousands of Southern anglers wouldn't trade one fried catfish fillet for all the rest of the gamefish.

Trout

The headwater lakes of the Tennessee River Valley are blessed with Dixie's finest lake fishing for trout. These lakes are found in the highlands of North Carolina, Virginia, Tennessee, and Georgia. A total of 16 impoundments hold these cold-water-dwelling fish, which include rainbow, brown, ohrid, lake and brook trout.

Lakes in the Tennessee River Valley system which regularly hold trout as a result of stocking are Calderwood, Chilhowee, Cheoah, Norris, Tellico, South Holston, Boone, Watauga and Wilbur in Tennessee; Blue Ridge and Chatuge in Georgia; and Fontana, Hiwassee, Apalachia, Nantahala and Thorpe in North Carolina. Trout are also periodically caught from Tims Ford, Douglas, Santeetlah, Fort Loudoun, Cherokee, Nottely, and Patrick Henry lakes.

When trout are found in a TVA lake, it is generally due to stocking efforts on the part of the host state. Some states stock certain species more than others, even when a lake is shared. For instance, Tennessee does not actively stock brookies in any lakes. Calderwood Lake atop the Tennessee–North Carolina line is annually stocked with specks by North Carolina fishery personnel, however.

Suffice it to say each trout species differs somewhat in habitat needs and behavior, but in the Tennessee River Valley's headwater lakes, all share a number of common factors. Very little natural reproduction occurs in these mountain lakes. Trout fisheries are maintained by stocking fingerlings and creel-size (9 to 12 inches) trout reared in hatcheries. This is termed a "put-grow-take" stocking effort, as compared to intensively stocked mountain streams where "put-and-take" releases keep many trouters content.

All of these highlands have trout fishing because cold water (not exceeding 68 degrees) is available year-round. During cold weather this requirement is met from top to bottom in these lakes. Hot weather is

The colorful brook trout is the Tennessee River Valley's only native cold-water game fish. However, it is found in only a few lakes.

not as accommodating. Surface temperatures on some so-called "cold-water lakes" surpass 80 degrees. A curious subsurface transformation occurs at such times, though. As surface temperatures rise, cooler water compresses deeper in gradually colder layers called thermoclines. Not uncommonly, these cold temperature bands in the 70-to-60-degree range have low levels of dissolved oxygen. Inflowing feeder creeks and tributary rivers, however, which are usually cooler than lake surface temperatures, sometimes provide a fresh supply of well-oxygenated water.

Growth rates in these cold-water lakes vary considerably. In some generally rich lakes it can be phenomenal, sometimes surpassing one inch per month. At other "pass through" lakes, which have limited holding capacities and low nutrient loads, growth rates are considerably lower.

Only the brook trout *(Salvelinus fontinalis)* is native to the Tennessee River Valley and the southeastern United States. The brookie is not a true trout, but a "char." Admittedly, it's the author's favorite fish (along with the smallmouth bass), which he has chased throughout all the southern states, the Rocky Mountains and uncharted portions of northern Canada.

Dixie's brook trout are holdovers from the last Ice Age. Only 75 years ago they were common in most cold-water streams from Virginia to just north of Atlanta, Georgia. Clear-cut timber harvesting, erosion, over-fishing and, most importantly, the introduction of non-native trout species hurt the brookie.

The world record for brookie is one of the oldest standing records, and one few expect to see topped. It was caught in 1916 from the Nipigon River in Ontario, Canada, and rocked the scales at 14 pounds, 8 ounces. North Carolina's state record brookie was a whopper. It weighed 7 pounds, 7 ounces, and was caught in 1980 from Raven Fork, a headwater tributary of Fontana located on the Qualla Reservation of the Eastern Band of Cherokee Indians. Tennessee's state record, a 3-pound, 14-ounce brook trout, was caught from the tailwaters of Apalachia Lake (Hiwassee River) in 1978. A 5-pound, 9-ounce brookie caught in 1980 from the Toccoa River (a tributary of Blue Ridge Lake) is the biggest speck on the pages of Georgia's record book.

Rainbow trout *(Salmo gairdneri)* were first brought to Tennessee, Georgia and North Carolina from California via Michigan for stocking in mountain streams in 1900. Sea-run rainbow trout, or steelheads, have also been stocked in a few TVA lakes in western North Carolina. Rainbow trout are the most popular lake-dwelling cold-water gamefish species in the TVA system. They are superior fighters, moderately easily caught when available in good numbers and excellent tablefare.

The North Carolina state record rainbow weighed 14 pounds, 1 ounce, and was caught from Glennville Reservoir (now called Thorpe Reservoir, an impoundment of the Tuckasegee River, a headwater tributary of Fontana Lake) in 1949. The world record landlocked rainbow trout weighed 26 pounds, 2 ounces, and was taken from Flaming Gorge, Utah, in 1979. The world record sea-run rainbow trout, which was caught at Bell Island, Alaska, in 1970, weighed 42 pounds, 2 ounces.

Brown trout *(Salmo trutta)* are found in limited numbers in most TVA cold-water lakes. These fish are from German and Scottish stock that is also thought to have found its way into the southern mountains around 1900. They have a reputation for unpredictability and loner behavior. They often achieve large size. After taking a brown trout, the angler can feel justly proud. The state record brown trout for North Carolina weighed 15 pounds, 7 ounces, and was caught from the Tuckasegee River (a headwater stream of Fontana Lake) on the Qualla Reservation of the Eastern Band of Cherokee Indians in 1982. The world record brown trout was taken in 1977, and weighed 33 pounds, 11 ounces. It was also caught from Flaming Gorge, Utah.

There are two very uncommon cold-water species plying some TVA mountain waters. Ohrid trout, a deep-dwelling close kin of the brown

Rainbow trout were introduced from the West in the early 1900s.

trout native to Lake Ohrid atop the Albanian-Yugoslavian border, were stocked experimentally in Watauga Lake during the early 1970s. This was one of the surprise results of the era of "detente" when the USFWS managed a deal with the Yugos to get these fish. Tennessee's state record ohrid was taken from Watauga Lake in 1986, and weighed 11 pounds, 13 ounces.

Lake trout *(Salvelinus namaycush)*, another lake-dwelling fish that is extremely common as far south as the Great Lakes, has been introduced into Norris Lake. Sometimes called Mackinaws, this near relative to the brookies is not a true trout, as are brown or 'bows, but rather a "char." It is a large-growing, very cold water fish that has never been planted further south than the TVA system. In these southern waters they commonly prowl 50-to-80-foot depths and, as one might expect, have very little competition in their ecological niche. The world record Mackinaw weighed 65 pounds, and was taken in 1970 from Great Bear Lake, Northwest Territory, Canada.

In most Tennessee River Valley states, trout lakes are open for year-round fishing, although there are exceptions and care should be taken to familiarize yourself with local regulations before fishing these waters.

In comparison to the legions that pursue Jack Frost season crappie, bass and stripers, cold-weather trout fishing is not highly practiced on most Tennessee River Valley lakes. Trout are scattered during winter, but are most often caught where their favorite forage fish—shad, alewives or suckers—are available. Crankbaits such as the Rapala Shad

An Eurasian native, the brown trout is found in only a few TVA lakes.

Rap or Bagley's Balsam Bee are typical deep-diving cold-season trout baits, along with minnows and spring lizards.

Tar Heel State anglers practice their own brand of winter trout fishing, notably for winter-run rainbow/steelhead trout below Nantahala Dam. Spinners worked through eddies and sweet corn or salmon eggs drifted with the current are lethal.

Early spring is usually considered the annual starting time to go out for these cart-wheeling gamesters. Spring trout are thoroughly scattered along the shoreline and at creek mouths. Early season depths vary between 5 and 15 feet, with 10 feet being the medium. Techniques vary considerably during this time. One popular ploy is point casting topwater crankbaits, such as 5-to-3-inch jointed Rebel minnows or Jitterbugs, or small single-blade spinners, such as the ¹⁄₁₆ ounce Mepps Aglia or Panther Martin Fly. Trolling shad-colored crankbaits is also productive at this time.

Summer tactics require anglers to plumb a little deeper on most lakes. During daylight hours trolling with downriggers using a variety of silver-colored crankbaits or small spinners at depths of 35 to 80 feet is common. At night anglers resort to using a variety of natural (and not so natural) baits, which include canned sweet corn, marshmallows, minnows, redworms and wasp larvae. Baits are simply tossed out and allowed to dangle at depths of 20 to 40 feet under the light from lanterns suspended over the water.

There are exceptions of course. Calderwood Lake is perhaps the coldest trout water, rivaled only by Cheoah, Wilbur and Chilhowee. A popular ploy on these super-frigid impoundments is to fly fish the debris lines. These begin in the wake of the upstream dam's boils during generation and move downstream along the lake's surface, resembling the rings in a bathtub. Trout patrol the lines singularly or in schools, snatching terrestrials and other floating tidbits. They are always on the move, usually sucking in food at 15-to-20-foot intervals. These are usually large trout in the 18-to-24-inch class. Using floating fly line and a long leader tipped with a black or brown nymph (No. 2 to No. 8), anglers watch the trashline for a "nosing" feeder. The trick is to place a fly where the trout is likely to make its next rise. The results can be breathtaking.

Autumn trouting on these lakes varies little from summer fishing. In fact, night fishing under the lights in October is tops on many lakes. Not until mid-to-late November do trout begin wandering out from truly deep water.

White Bass

"L ive fast, die young" aptly describes these gregarious, open-water predators. They're the "James Dean" fish of the Tennessee River Valley lakes. The white bass *(Morone chrysops)* is a member of the family Serranidae, which includes such true bass as the yellow and striped bass. This compact, spunky fighter may not tail dance across the water like a trout or a bigmouth bass, but pound for pound its hard-fighting, bottom-drilling determination makes the white a lightweight champ.

The white bass is abundant in virtually all Tennessee River Valley lakes. They are known by a variety of local nicknames, including whites, sand bass, silversides, and of course their best-known TVA-region tag, simply the "stripe." Many anglers, particularly those jaded by trout, black bass or other more glamorous gamefish, look down on the spunky stripe. Personally, I rate the white high as a fighter and believe they are fun to catch, although as tablefare I prefer several other fish before them.

We have watched well-known bass tournament anglers occasionally "stick" a stripe. Upon connecting with a strike, these "bluenoses of Angledom" almost always say, "I've got a nice little smallmouth bass," but then when the fish is boated and the sun reflects off of its silvery sides, they say no more! Any fish which has a fight which is confused, sight unseen, with a bronzeback deserves more respect than that given to the white bass.

The world record white bass weighed 5 pounds, 9 ounces, and was taken from the Colorado River in Texas. Alabama's top spot white (tie) weighed 4 pounds, 4 ounces, and was caught from the Tennessee River in 1978. Kentucky's record book stripe (tie) was taken from Kentucky Lake in 1943, and weighed an even 5 pounds. North Carolina's number-one white weighed 4 pounds, 15 ounces, and was caught from Fontana Lake in 1966.

Whites are native to the Tennessee River drainage, where they commonly reach the 3-to-4½-pound mark. Oddly, prior to the massive dam building projects of the 1930s and 1940s they were seldom caught or even seen by fishermen. Not until they were given access to open-water, reservoir-type habitat did they become a significant gamefish. This can be partially explained by the fact that this fish is one of the few land-locked members of the true bass family. For ages it has survived separated from salt water and one of its nearest brine relatives—the striped bass—much as the landlocked and Atlantic salmon exist apart from each other. Some fishery biologists contend that the two bass species were perhaps one and the same before the smaller white was isolated inland.

Whites are a handsome fish, sporting silvery flanks, bisected by sporadic brownish to black stripes from gill slit to tail. In appearance the white resembles its larger-growing cousin the striper, although the white is less streamlined and has a pronounced "humpback." Few whites survive past their fourth year; under optimum conditions they grow to around four pounds.

They are classified as open water forage fish which as adults forage

Always found in the Tennessee River Valley, the spunky white bass did not become a major game fish until it gained access to the TVA lake system.

primarily upon small gizzard and threadfin shad. Their diet also includes emerging nymphs, terrestrials and crustaceans. Throughout their lives these schooling fish roam impoundments and river stretches in large concentrations, ripping up shad schools. Their gregarious behavior is even more evident when nature beckons them to procreate and they ascend the lake's tributaries and headwater river during March and April to spawn.

White bass are quite prolific. A single female is capable of producing in excess of 100,000 eggs. Ideal water temperatures are approximately 50 to 56 degrees. Old-timers are fond of pointing to the pussy willow trees and noting that when the buds are the size of a squirrel's ear, the white bass run is under way. Redbud blooms are another Tennessee River Valley indicator of the beginning of the white bass's spawning run, according to longtime area anglers.

In the TVA spawning occurs in a riverine environment, although the actual act occurs in the calm backwater reaches of the river or stream. In northern "pothole" lakes these fish reproduce in the lake. River spawners find a variety of bottom strata from sand and gravel to rock or even grassy areas acceptable for the mating act. The female convulses the eggs to free float in the current, while attending males eject sperm and randomly fertilize the semibuoyant roe. The fertilized eggs travel downstream with the current for a couple of days before hatching.

Another lesser-known member of the Serranidae family, the yellow bass *(Morone mississippiensis),* also inhabits a portion of the Tennessee River drainage. The two fish are similar in appearance, life-style and habitat requirements, but the yellow bass is smaller growing, seldom over 1½ pounds, and has a goldish coloration. The world record yellow bass weighed 2 pounds, 4 ounces, and was caught from Lake Monroe, Indiana, in 1977. Tennessee's record book yellow bass weighed 12 ounces, and was taken from Watts Bar Lake in 1982. In the Tennessee Valley these fish are found primarily in mainstream impoundments, and even then are abundant in only a few areas. Even when plentiful, these fish are generally ignored by fishermen.

Fishing the white bass during the spring run is the most popular time to vie with these gamesters, although it should be noted this is a year-round gamefish. The lion's share of the spring silverside action occurs around moving water. Places where these fish stack up awaiting the urge to procreate include the base of dams, such as Fort Loudoun or Pickwick; headwater river confluences, such as where the French Broad and Nolichucky rivers meet at the headwaters of Douglas Lake; shoals and sandbars, like those found in the South Holston River; as well as deadfalls, deep pools and feeder stream entrance points.

Although underrated by many anglers, the white bass is a hard fighter.

Whites are primarily sight feeders, and they're lightning quick to seize a shiny lure. All-around favorite baits include 1/32-to-1/8-ounce doll-flies in white-red, green and yellow, 1/4-ounce spinners such as the Mepps Aglia and silvery crankbaits such as Storms Hot'n Tot or Rebel 1¾-inch Jointed Floater Minnow. Live minnows are occasionally used also.

When river fishing spinners, crankbaits or most other offerings, the trick is to cast upstream to a 10 o'clock position and quarter your bait back across the current at a fairly fast rate. Jigs are often fished in the same fashion, although one highly effective technique calls for placing a small floater 18 inches above the flies and slowly twitching the flies in the current and backwater eddies. Catches well in excess of 100 fish are common during this season.

Following the spawning whites return to the lake. Early summer white bass feeding is concentrated near the surface where newly hatched shad fry are available. This triggers the well-known break, or "jump," fishing for stripe. Hundreds, and sometimes even thousands, of hungry white bass erupt under surface-traveling shad schools. The attacks sometimes last only a few seconds, but can go on for up to fifteen minutes. It's virtually impossible to tell when or where surface action will occur. Small surface plugs are generally effective, but the best catches are made fishing below the top-water melee using small Roostertail-style spinners.

Night fishing for white bass is productive and well developed at most

During the spring, white bass run up most rivers in this region.

TVA lakes. Lanterns hung out over the water attract plankton, which in turn draw in the bait fish that attract hungry whites. Minnows or flies are jigged out of sight beneath the light. When these fish move in on lantern-lit areas the action can be torrid and non-stop. These two hot-weather ploys hold well into September.

During August these fish move toward the headwaters again for yet another, though half-hearted, spawning run. This run doesn't bring as many fish upstream, nor are they as aggressive during the fall. The action is reasonably dependable, however, and fun to fish. Cold weather finds the whites going deep like crappie and holding along the breaks of submerged river and creek meanders. If located, they can be caught using jigs, small crankbaits or minnows. One notable exception to this cold-weather behavior pattern occurs in the lakes or river areas where coal- or nuclear-fired steam plants discharge hot water. White are drawn to these areas like few other fish. In fact, wherever a hot water discharge canal can be found, it's a sure bet a mess of white bass can be taken.

As tablefare the white bass gets mixed reviews. Its biggest fans say the stripe is equal to any fish, particularly those caught during the winter or early spring when their pink flesh is firm and mild. Many note that the secret to preparing white bass is to remove the dark, fatty tissue from the sides of the fillets. The dark areas are where the strong, somewhat disagreeable flavor is concentrated.

Striped Bass

Striper! The name rings with raw energy and a never-say-die fighting spirit. These exciting lunkers are the stuff fishing dreams are made of—and for good reason. When stuck with a hook, these saltwater transfers become muscle-bound packages of TNT. Striper fever is more contagious than chicken pox and much longer lasting.

Striped bass are native to the Atlantic Ocean, but were transplanted into the Tennessee River Valley's hill country lakes as early as 1957. Tennessee is one of the nation's oldest "landlocked" striper states. When provided with suitable habitat and an abundant food supply, these bass achieve great size in freshwater impoundments. The world record landlocked striper rocked the scales at 60 pounds, 8 ounces, and was taken in 1988 from Melton Hill Lake in Tennessee. The world record saltwater striper was larger by almost 10 pounds. This Tennessee lake produced state-record stripers in 1986 and 1987, and a world record the following year. Still larger fish prowl its channels.

Upon seeing this fish for the first time many anglers are surprised how handsome it is. Stripers are bullet-shaped dynamos, sporting silver flanks, white bellies and dark brown to black backs. Its most distinctive feature, though, is a series of lateral stripes which extend unbroken (basically) from the gill plate to the tail. Its scales are heavier and coarser than those of most native Tennessee River fishes.

Striped bass *(Morone saxatilis)* are members of the true bass family Serranidae, whereas spotted, largemouth and smallmouth bass are actually sunfish. Nicknames include lineside and striper, while along southern coastal areas it is simply referred to as the rockfish. This is a relatively long-lived fish, capable of thriving 10 years or longer.

In their natural environment stripers are anadromous fish, much like the salmon. They spend their adult life in a brine environment, but early each spring run up rivers into fresh water to spawn. Females seek out backwater river bottom spawning areas that are washed free of silt by moderately strong currents. Roe is ejected in a free floating state to be fertilized by a nearby male. The striped bass's buoyant eggs may drift downstream in the current for several miles before hatching a few days later.

It was not until after the completion of South Carolina's Marion and Moultrie lakes during World War II that it was discovered the striper could survive for extended periods in a freshwater environment. When the dam gates at Santee-Cooper were closed, hundreds of thousands of stripers were trapped mating upstream. The gate closure cut off their exit to the Atlantic.

Professional fishery people were at first surprised to see that the imprisoned linesides not only survived their first season but also prospered in the Santee-Cooper Lake complex. When second-, third- and then fourth-year-class stripers from subsequent "in-house" spawns began showing up, however, surprise turned to amazement.

It didn't take long for word to get around that there was a big new brawler on the block. Tennessee and Kentucky were among the first to acquire samples of South Carolina's striper stock for stocking in their

Gerald Almy, angling editor for Sports Afield, *with a striped bass from Cherokee Lake. The high caliber of striped bass fishing in many of the TVA lakes has attracted national attention.*

lakes. In the more than half a dozen Tennessee River Valley lakes where these predators are now managed, 30 pounders are relatively common and 40 pounders are caught often enough to keep "stripermania" at an acute fever stage. In top-notch lineside factories such as Norris, there are 50 pounders. A few years ago a striper estimated to have weighed approximately 65 pounds was netted and released by Tennessee Wildlife Resources Agency fishery personnel.

Native to the Atlantic Ocean from New England southward and into the northern portion of the Gulf of Mexico, striped bass are voracious open-water predators. They're schooling fish which hunt open water (and occasionally shoreline and riverine areas) in packs for bait fish much the same as wolves. Once located, schools of forage fish are slashed away by open-mouthed rockfish. The slaughter is incredible during a lineside school's feeding frenzy.

The opportunity to establish a landlocked, trophy-class striped bass fishery is reason enough, but the real reasons for this fish's introduction into Tennessee River Valley lakes lie elsewhere.

Stripers feed primarily on open-water forage fish, which in this river system is the super-abundant gizzard shad, great protein-building links

Nationally noted angler Bill Dance with an "average-sized" striper. Photo by Tennessee Wildlife Resources Agency.

in the food chain connecting plankton and predators. Smaller fish feed on shad smallfry; the shad commonly grows to lengths of up to 12 inches, however. This is considerably larger than the much less abundant threadfin shad, which tops out at approximately 4 inches long.

The striper is an open-water nomad capable of daily consuming its body weight in forage fish. If the striper had foraging habits and appetites that put it in competition with the black bass, crappie or bream, odds are it would never have been introduced into the TVA system.

Few fish other than lunker black bass, walleye, and muskie can feed on 10-to-12-inch gizzard shad, and these predators are bottom- or shore-line-oriented feeders, while big shad commonly school in open water.

Gizzard shad have another facet which made the introduction of stri-pers attractive. A lake, be it Cherokee or Kentucky, can support only a specific poundage of fish per acre. This carrying capacity is largely determined by its nutrient load and dissolved oxygen (DO) level. Tennessee River Valley fisheries are dominated by rough and forage fish, with the combined gamefish population usually constituting only a 10 to 25 percent share.

During late summer when they are most abundant, gizzard shad can make up over half of a fishery's tonnage. Fishery biologists are constantly seeking ways to convert "x" pounds of forage fish into "x" pounds of gamefish. When this cannot be accomplished with native fish species, exotics are sometimes sought out.

The introduction of stripers into the Tennessee River Valley lakes was in part an effort to convert a percentage of shad or other forage fish into gamefish. Judging from the rockfish's popularity, it must be agreed the lineside project is something of a success.

The Tennessee River Valley lakes presently under rockfish man-agement programs are Cherokee, Boone, Norris, Tims Ford, Watts Bar, Kentucky and Guntersville. With the exception of Norris, all have heavy shad loads.

There is no significant striped bass reproduction in any Tennessee River Valley lake. The Eagle Bend Hatchery, a $2 million facility located in Clinton, is where the Tennessee Wildlife Resources Agency annually rears millions of striped bass fry.

Also found in the TVA system is the striped bass–white bass hybrid. These fish are closely related, and under natural circumstances some-times cross and produce hybrid offspring. They were first introduced into the TVA system in the 1960s. In the Tennessee River Valley all seven states stock hatchery-reared whiterocks (but not necessarily in their TVA waters). These are often simply called "hybrids" because this was the first crossbred fish introduced into the valley, and that name was applied and stuck.

Whiterocks display predominantly white bass parent features until they top the 4-pound mark, after which they act more like striped bass and often travel in their company where the two coexist, as in Cherokee Lake. Some states, notably Alabama, presently concentrate more on the hybrid than the pure striper, because the crossbreed is more adaptable to warmer impoundments.

Whiterocks can achieve 20 pounds, and they are extremely agressive and quite willing to strike artificial lures. The world record striped bass–white bass weighed 20 pounds, 12 ounces, and was caught from the Savannah River, Georgia, in 1982. Tennessee's record hybrid weighed 18 pounds, 1 ounce, and was taken from Boone Lake in 1985.

The mature whiterock's life-style is closely akin to that of the striper. Fishing techniques for the two are essentially the same, although the hybrid is found in water with structure such as stick-ups, stump beds and creek meanders more often than its larger-growing parent.

Catching rockfish is remarkably easy once the biological basics are comprehended. Of course, there are a number of minor equipment modifications and technique adjustments anglers must make when delving into "stripermania," but nothing the average fisherman cannot easily master. Striper fishing has been termed "souped-up" bream fishing, but in this writer's opinion, that's an oversimplification.

For serious, all-season rockfish chasing, a good depth finder is a must.

When packing for stripers, think big. Note the 12-gauge shell, placed to show perspective.

A temperature-oxygen calibration unit is also helpful, particularly during hot weather. Downriggers are still not as popular in the Tennessee River Valley as they will be in coming seasons, when more anglers discover how they permit one to pinpoint-troll deep holding stripers.

Other than this, standard fishing tackle will do the job. I once wrote a newspaper article about a 12-year-old boy who landed a 19-pound rockfish while bream fishing at Cherokee Lake with a Zebco 33. That's a feat in itself, but the kicker was that his reel was strung with four-year-old, 12-pound-test fishing line.

That experience notwithstanding, most serious striper addicts use tackle that is somewhat heavier than that the average panfish angler uses on these lakes. Personally, I prefer a hefty rod and reel combo when striper fishing, and use a Shakespeare Sigma 050 coupled with a 7½-foot Shakespeare Ugly Stik. The Zebco Quantum XLS 6-foot, medium-action spinning rod with a GMD 70 Reel is another stout, responsive outfit with plenty of power. Strung with 12-to-15-pound-test line, it will land rocks up to 30 pounds with little difficulty. The Zebco Quantum twosome is very light considering its heavyweight construction.

Terminal tackle needs outside those commonly used for black bass or crappie fishing include spoons as large as 3 ounces, large surface baits such as the Cordell Redfin, and ½-to-2-ounce jigs. Red, white, yellow, green and silver are the top colors for catching landlocked striper.

Live bait is considered the most lethal offering for taking these finned water pigs. Commercially offered tuffies and shiners are usually not available in sufficient size (four to seven inches long), however. Bait fishing for striper means using native gizzard shad or bluegill. Where it's legal, use bluegill caught by hook and line as bait for rockfish. Spiked through the back, "free lined," these hardy little fish are excellent striper baits.

The best live bait for Tennessee River Valley stripers, though, is the gizzard shad. These are rarely available for sale, but can be gathered most of the year from a lake with a circular throw net or from a dam tailrace with a large dip net. Gizzard shad are a year-round bait, suitable for many ploys which can be modified for different depths. Trolled slowly over a striper school, or even still fished, a lively shad is the perfect way to attract a lineside's attention.

Rockfish are constantly moving in search of productive feeding areas, but there are other considerations in Tennessee River Valley waters. Rule number 1 is, always bear in mind you are seeking to catch an open-water fish with thermal requirements akin to those of a trout. These fish are seldom found in water over the 72-to-75-degree mark.

Places to look for rockfish during the spring include backwater and shoal areas in headwater rivers, as well as upper lake cove mouths and

The TVA system was the first to stock X-striped white bass hybrids. These hardy, fast-growing, and hard-fighting game fish are welcome additions to many lakes.

over submerged islands. During this season the fish are rarely deeper than 5 to 10 feet. During early spring the best fishing is often found in river settings, particularly below dams. Live or cut shad free drifted in the current is a favorite trick, although heavy Daredevle spoons also work well. Even small, silver-finished deep-diving crankbaits are good then.

Usually by mid-May stripers migrate back into the main lakes. Using a good electronic bottom-reading device, check the main river channel, deep points and cove mouths. At this time surface fishing using big shad baits like the Cordell Redfin can be outstanding off of red clay points.

Late summer always sends these fish deep, away from soaring surface temperatures. Depths of 80 feet are not uncommon in well-oxygenated lakes, while in other impoundments the fish seek out creek embayments where cool inflow water creates "thermal refuges." This is a time of limited migration. Trolling with downriggers and deep jigging bait over suspended fish are both good for prime hot-weather action.

Autumn finds the big linesides on the move again, gradually working their way back toward the headwaters during the winter months. Depths vary greatly at this time, from shallow to as deep as 20 feet.

Bream

The bream is just about every angler's first fish. These bantam-weight battlers have all the qualifications of a perfect gamefish. They are plentiful, easily caught on a variety of baits, put up a terrific fight when hooked, and as tablefare eclipse nearly all other freshwater fish.

Bream, or brim, are members of the sunfish family which in the Tennessee River Valley includes the ever popular bluegill *(Lepomis machrochirus)*, redear or shellcracker *(Lepomis microlophus)*, green *(Lepomis cyanellus)*, longear *(Lepomis megalotis)*, redbreast or robin *(Lepomis auritos)*, and warmouth or stumpknocker *(Lepomis gulosis)*, as well as the vaunted black bass clan. Bream are highly prolific, structure-oriented fish well suited to living along rock, gravel, clay, grass or wooded shoreline. Their primary foods include crustaceans, terrestrial and aquatic insects, and newly hatched fish.

The bluegill, the sunfish family's most abundant species, can be found in all Tennessee River system lakes. Hand-sized bluegill are what most bream fishermen dream about, but larger specimens are occasionally taken. The world record bluegill, a mammoth 4-pound, 12-ounce fish, came from Alabama's Ketona Lake in 1950.

The 'gill is a beautifully marked fish displaying a wide range of colors from a metallic green to deep violet. The bluish-black mark that extends back from the gill plate gives the bluegill its name. Vertical bars are usually evident on the compact, flat, round fish. Most sport a bright yellow breast, which fades when the bluegill is caught.

The redear, or shellcracker, is prominent in several mainstream impoundments, notably Chickamauga and Guntersville. These fast-growing fish are lighter colored than bluegill and sport a distinctive red-edged "ear" along the gill plate. The shellcracker prefers water deeper than most brim, and it is a well-known forager of snails. The

Fishing for bluegill on a flyrod during willow fly hatches is great fun.

world record shellcracker weighed 4 pounds, 8 ounces, and was taken from Chase City, Virginia, in 1970.

Green, longear and redbreast bream are not common in most TVA lakes, although they are usually present. These are usually considered stream-dwelling fish and form only a minor or locally important portion of bream fishing in the TVA lake system. Notable exceptions to this are the highland lakes of western North Carolina, which hold fair numbers of nice redbreast bream.

The warmouth is an unusual story. These highly aggressive fish may very well be the most overlooked gamefish in the Tennessee River Valley. The stumpknocker is a stunning fish. Its ornate mouth is painted in turquoise, while its flanks are olive and its belly is a bright gold. In appearance the warmouth looks more like a scaled down, customized smallmouth bass, but rest assured, this rascal is all bream.

One reason the warmouth is only seldom sought out is that few understand its exacting habitat needs or realize its abundance. Several years ago while fly fishing for largemouth bass at Indian Boundary (a small lake located on the headwaters of Tellico Lake), Joann and I noticed we were getting more strikes along deadfalls and exposed stumps from warmouth than bass. We switched to smaller flies and concentrated our efforts along wood structure. We soon had a fine stringer of ½-to-1-pound stumpknockers. Few fish are more closely tied to a particular bit of structure, such as wood, than the spunky warmouth.

The world record warmouth weighed 2 pounds, 7 ounces, and was caught from Florida's Yellow River in 1985. Tennessee's top spot goggle-eye weighed 1 pound, 12 ounces, and was taken from the Nolichucky River immediately upstream from Douglas Lake in 1984.

Bream can be caught year-round, as any Minnesota ice fisherman will quickly attest, but "down South" these good-eating fish are usually considered a fair-weather quarry. Little bluegill fishing is done prior to April, as most brim are still deep and scattered.

This changes abruptly as water temperatures approach the 60-degree mark and rising water (in some lakes) allows these fish to occupy shallower cover. Spawning begins when water temperatures approach 70 to 75 degrees, which can occur as early as April or as late as July. Brim are gregarious fish and usually spawn in colonies of up to several hundred square feet. Nesting usually takes place in three to seven feet of water in back-cove, bowl-shaped areas with sand, clay or gravel bottoms. Circular nests are fanned out by the male. The female lays her eggs in the nest of her choosing, and the male fertilizes the roe. Thereafter, the male bream assumes the sole parenting duties.

A noteworthy exception to this spawning pattern is the redear sunfish. These fish commonly nest in three-to-six-foot depths in creeks and rivers where there is a sandy bottom.

Fishing for bream during the nesting period is extremely popular and is almost always dynamite fun. Feeding rarely occurs during the spawning and fry-rearing (protecting) process, but the male aggressively guards the household and will strike lures or bait dabbled in or near the nest. Fishermen spike grubs, millworms or redworms on a small hook and fish these baits below a bobber. Another method growing in popularity in the TVA system is to use ultralight tackle and line coupled with small $\frac{1}{32}$-ounce leadheads with green, smoke or yellow jelly beetles. These are cast across a bedding area, and with the rod tip held tight, slowly inched back across the bottom. A one-pound shellcracker or bluegill on light tackle and two-pound-test line is great sport.

Fly fishermen can achieve the same results knotting on wet flies or nymphs and using sinking fly line. The trick is to allow the line to sink and then "twitch" the fly back.

Following the spawn bream remain easily available along stump beds, black willows, bluffs, creek embayments and shaded areas. Previously noted baits are still lethal offerings. In many lakes large, "bull" bluegill are fond of hiding in 7-to-15-foot water along bluffs. A favorite method for taking these cliff dwellers is using redworms deep without a sinker or very small crankbaits such as a Rebel Wee Ree or Wee Crawdad.

On mainstream impoundments July is the most productive bream

Some mainstream impoundments sport outstanding redbreast sunfish angling.

The gear needed to catch sunfish is very simple.

fishing period. This is the time of the willowfly, or mayfly, hatch. For several weeks large burrowing ephemeridae emerge nightly. During the newly emerged, or dun, stage, the winged adults ride atop the water while their wings dry; they then fly in great numbers to lakeside willow trees for a day or two until the nuptial flight over water. At this time good bream fishing is only a matter of locating a hatch or a fly-laden willow bush. These can be spotted at considerable distance by their dark coloration. Fly rodders can have a field day when bream are surface feeding on duns or falling flies. Bait fishermen also do well fishing shallow under bobbers with crickets for bait.

One of the bream's nicest attributes is its easy availability during hot weather. Bass may be 25 feet deep or catfish feeding only at night, but the dependable sunfish is always within even a child's casting range. Add to this the fact that these fish are superb tablefare.

Our two favorite cooking methods start with filleting the small flank strips. Fried crispy and brown in peanut oil, they are better than crappie. When they are boiled five minutes in seasoned water and then cooled on ice, you can't distinguish them from crab!

PART TWO

Mainstream Impoundments

Kentucky Lake

SIZE: extremely large

ACCESSIBILITY: excellent to very good

LOCATION: Tennessee (Hardin, Humphreys, Houston, Stewart, Wayne, Perry, Benton, Henry, and Decatur counties) and Kentucky (Livingston, Lyon, Marshall, Trigg, and Calloway counties)

PRESSURE: moderate

PRIMARY GAMEFISH: crappie, bluegill, largemouth bass, catfish, sauger

SECONDARY GAMEFISH: white, smallmouth and striped bass, chain pickerel, redear sunfish

BEST MONTHS: April, May, June, September, October, March

BEST BAITS: live minnows, jigs, plastic worms, spinnerbaits, crankbaits

BEST BET: crappie fishing with live minnows during April

Kentucky Lake is the first of a series of man-made lakes extending in a chain from Kentucky upstream into six other southern states. The total drainage covers an incredible 40,200 square miles and reaches over 6,600 feet above sea level, the highest elevations east of the Rocky Mountains. Kentucky Lake, which has often been referred to as an inland sea, is one of the world's largest impoundments and offers a recreational and fishery resource really deserving of its own book. It's a well-developed tourist Mecca, and rates as the best known of the man-made TVA lakes.

Kentucky Dam is located 22 miles upstream from the mouth of the Tennessee River at the Ohio River. Construction on this structure began in mid-1938, and was completed over six years later at a cost of 118.5 million dollars. The dam is a staggering 8,422 feet wide and 206 feet high and houses five hydroelectric turbines with a combined generating capacity of 175,000 kilowatts. A lock system permits river traffic.

Kentucky Lake is even more impressive. At full pool it covers 160,000 surface acres and extends 184.3 miles to its starting point at Pickwick Landing Dam. Its 2,380 miles of shoreline surpass that of some coastal states. For its size, this is a relatively shallow lake, though deeper in its lower end and along the river channel. At full pool Kentucky Lake stands at 359 feet above sea level, and at minimum pool it stands at 354 feet above sea level.

The Barkley Canal, which is located on the eastern shoreline slightly less than three miles upstream from the dam, connects Kentucky Lake and Lake Barkley. This mileage-saving channel connects the Cumberland and Tennessee river systems, as well as giving the inland port of Nashville a shortcut to the Gulf of Mexico via the Tennessee-Tombigbee Waterway.

Kentucky Lake is located in two states: Tennessee and Kentucky. In Tennessee it borders Hardin, Decatur, Wayne, Perry, Benton, Humphreys, Houston, Henry, and Stewart counties. In Kentucky the lake bounds Livingston, Lyon, Marshall, Trigg and Calloway counties. The nearest major towns in Tennessee are Paris, Camden, Waverly, Clarksville, Dover, Nashville, Parsons, Decaturville, Clifton and Savannah. The nearest major towns in Kentucky are Calvert City, Cadiz, Benton, Murray, Paducah and Gilbertsville.

Access to the lake is good, although bridges across this wide impoundment are few. East-to-west access routes in Tennessee include US 64, which crosses at Savannah (river mile 190); TN 114, which crosses via the Clifton Ferry at Clifton (river mile 158); TN 20-100, which spans the lake at Perryville (river mile 135); I-40, which crosses at the Tennessee National Migratory Wildlife Refuge (river mile 116); and US 79 at Paris Landing State Park (river mile 66). In Kentucky these are US 68, which bisects the lake at Kenlake State Resort Park (river mile 42), and US 62 and 641, which cross the Tennessee River atop Kentucky Dam.

From south to north, Kentucky Lake's western shoreline in Tennessee is accessed by TN 22, TN 69, TN 114, US 79 and TN 119; in Kentucky, western access routes are KY 121, KY 94, KY 444, KY 280, KY 732, KY 1346, KY 80, US 68, KY 962, KY 408, KY 1422, KY 963, KY 693 and KY 58. From south to north, the eastern shoreline in Tennessee is accessed by TN 128, TN 69, TN 114, TN 20-100, TN 13 and TN 147; in Kentucky, the access roadways are KY 453 (The Trace), KY 722 and US 62-641.

Kentucky Lake's recreational offerings are virtually boundless, and few public areas in the United States can match TVA's unique "Land

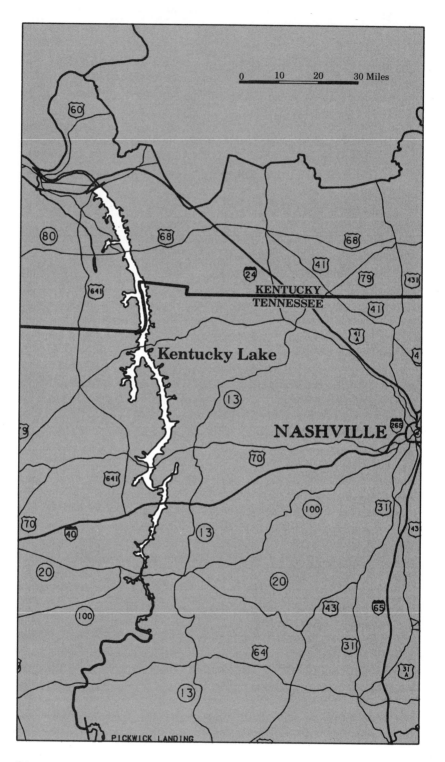

64

Between the Lakes" (LBL). This 170,000-acre federally owned tract is a national experimental recreation area showcase. It straddles the Tennessee and Kentucky state lines between Kentucky Lake and Lake Barkley, which was a project of the Corps of Engineers. Prior to the arrival of TVA, the narrow band of land between these two great rivers was the center of a thriving moonshine business. Now tourist dollars have replaced those dollars that were once brought in by corn squeezin's.

LBL's impressive outdoor recreational offerings include three highly developed family campgrounds—Hillman Ferry, Rushing Creek and Piney—plus several group camping areas. The 40-mile-long tract, steeped in Civil War history, is laced with foot trails. You won't find any commercial establishments here, but there is the Home Place 1850. Here, TVA has preserved a number of nineteenth-century farm structures that serve as a model of rural life in 1850. Daily re-creations of such folk activities as soap-making, gardening, cider-milling or blacksmithing are featured.

Nearby is a herd of bison, transplanted from western herds. The last eastern woodland bison in the Tennessee River Valley were wiped out in the late 1840s.

LBL is a hunter's delight. Its rolling hills harbor white-tailed and fallow deer, raccoon, wild turkey, bobwhite, cotton rabbits, red and grey fox, coyote, and grey and fox squirrel. Hunting is permitted on an annual fee basis under each state's general game laws. Fall hunting for white-tailed deer and spring wild turkey is among the best in the Tennessee River Valley.

The lower reaches of Kentucky Lake are regarded as some of the best waterfowl hunting for several hundred miles around. Several nearby waterfowl refuges keep birds close to this body of water throughout the winter, as ice-overs are uncommon. Big Sandy River, a Tennessee River tributary, and the Obion River, which flows westward to the Mississippi, serve as a duck highway between Kentucky Lake and the Mississippi River–Reelfoot Lake area. In fact, the Indians used to portage their canoes between these two points.

Waterfowl hunting around Kentucky Lake is at its best when the Mississippi River runs high and its surrounding bottomlands are flooded. This pushes webfoot species like Canada geese, mergansers, mallards, ringnecks and many others down the Big Sandy. This area has many commercial duck guides who maintain season-long blind and decoy set-ups.

Public access to the lake is the best in the Tennessee River Valley. There are at least 80 public boat-launch ramps and almost as many (73 at this writing) commercial boat docks and marinas.

The public camping opportunities around this lake are almost limitless, but the campgrounds at the lake's four state parks and the three LBL sites are the best available at Kentucky Lake. These parks are outstanding, showcase examples of each state's park program. In Tennessee these are Paris Landing State Park, near Paris in Henry County, and Nathan Bedford Forrest State Park, in Benton and Humphreys counties near Camden. In Kentucky these are Kentucky Dam Village State Resort Park, near Gilbertsville in Marshall County, and Kenlake State Resort Park in Marshall and Calloway counties. The Friday night buffet at the park restaurant at Kenlake is outstanding.

Additional public camping in Kentucky is also available at Grand Rivers Municipal Park, near Grand Rivers in Livingston County, and two TVA recreation areas, Barge Island in Marshall County and Pacer Point in Calloway County. TVA-maintained facilities in Tennessee include Big Eagle Recreation Area in Henry County, Beech Bend Recreation Area in Decatur County, and the Pickwick Landing Dam Reserve in Hardin County.

Other public-use areas around Kentucky Lake in Kentucky include

Catching spawning crappie from buck bush tangles at Kentucky Lake is easy. This lake's crappie fishery rates among the best in the United States.

the Kentucky Dam Reservation in Marshall and Livingston counties and Land Between the Lakes in Lyon and Trigg counties. In Tennessee these areas include Big Sandy Municipal Park near Big Sandy and Eva Park near Eva in Benton County, Ladyfinger Bluff (a TVA Small Wild Area with a 2.5-mile trail) and TVA's Packett Point Public Use Area in Perry County, Clifton City Park and Clifton Boat Harbor near Clifton in Wayne County and the Shiloh National Military Park in Hardin County. This last site commemorates one of the bloodiest confrontations between Federal and Confederate armies during the War of Northern Aggression.

The Tennessee National Migratory Wildlife Refuge, found along Kentucky Lake, is a scattered holding in Henry, Benton, Humphreys and Decatur counties. One major tract is located at the mouth of the Big Sandy River embayment; this section is referred to locally as the Big Sandy Refuge. The largest portion of the refuge encompasses both sides of the lake from the mouth of the Birdsong Creek embayment to the Decatur County line, approximately 17 miles upstream. A small holding is also found upstream from this area along the Cub Creek embayment and the nearby western edge of the main channel in Decatur County.

The game departments of Kentucky and Tennessee maintain wildlife management areas (WMAs) along the lake in addition to LBL. In Kentucky these are located at the headwaters of the Jonathan Creek and Bear Creek embayments and along the main lake channel near Shawnee Bay Resort in Marshall County, and the Snipe Creek, Wildcat Creek and headwaters of the Blood River embayment areas in Calloway County.

In Tennessee these include the Big Sandy WMA (and Gin Creek unit) along the Big Sandy River embayment and the West Sandy, or Springville Bottoms, WMA along the West Sandy Creek embayment in Henry and Benton counties, the Harmon Creek WMA along the western edge of the main channel near the mouth of the Harmon Creek embayment, and the Camden WMA in Benton County near the US 70 crossing at TVA's Johnsonville Steam Plant.

TVA's Johnsonville Steam Plant is also deserving of mention as a public access area. As at other thermal-type electricity-producing facilities around the TVA lake system, during cold weather the hot-water discharge area attracts loads of various gamefish and warmly clad anglers. It's located on the eastern banks of the lake in Humphreys County, just over three miles east of Camden.

Despite the fact that this is the most highly developed lake in the TVA system, it is also quite a lovely lake. Heavily timbered ridges and well-manicured farms line the vast majority of its entire length. It's one of the few TVA lakes where tupelo and cypress trees grow alongside the lake.

To accurately describe the character of a man-made body of water of the size of Kentucky Lake isn't an easy undertaking. This 184-mile-long impoundment is really more like three lakes. The first 87 miles from Pickwick Landing Dam downstream to the Benton County line is very much riverine in nature. Here the lake is narrow, often flowing between high bluffs, like those near the mouth of Lick Creek in Perry County. Along this distance, Kentucky Lake averages slightly less than a quarter mile in width.

From the southern boundary of Benton County downstream to the mouth of the Big Sandy River, the lake widens to over a mile and a half across. Here you find wide shallow reaches and long winding feeder stream embayments. Beyond the mouth of the Big Sandy, the lake sprawls out even wider, to average one and a half to two miles in width. This part is almost like an inland sea, and wave swells of over five feet high are not uncommon.

Kentucky Lake's bottom is composed of sand, clay, gravel, bedrock and mudflats. The Tennessee River channel is the lake's most pronounced fishing structure. Its importance is greatest in the lake's first 80 miles, and particularly at its headwaters. Virtually all of the lake's main channel side coves and minor feeder streams have significant stump bed flats. Stump beds can also be found along the main channel downstream from the mouth of the Duck River.

Also, from the mouth of the Duck River upstream to Perryville the lake is lined with long, fingerlike sloughs. There is no significant milfoil infestation at Kentucky (at least not at this writing); however, the lake's shallowest back-cove areas are covered in low-growing button willow trees. This scrub, which most local fishermen refer to as a "buck bush," is one of the few temperate-climate trees that can withstand regular periods of flooding of as long as 90 days and still prosper. The bushes are very important fish-concentrating cover, particularly during the early spring when they are newly flooded. Crappie and other popular gamefish seek out the submerged limbs and root systems for nesting sites.

Kentucky Lake's feeder stream system dwarfs that of any other TVA impoundment. Its major feeder rivers are the Blood, Big Sandy, Duck, Buffalo and Beech rivers.

Fishing Information

Kentucky Lake is one of the finest fisheries in the South. Black bass, crappie, sunfish, white bass, sauger and catfish are available in great numbers and good sizes. Threadfin and gizzard shad are the primary forage fish, followed by chubs and sunfish. Kentucky's state record white bass, a five pounder, was caught from this lake in 1943, while the top blue catfish, a staggering 100-pound leviathan, was caught below Kentucky Dam in 1970.

Tennessee's oldest number-one white bass, a 4-pound, 10-ounce specimen, was caught in Kentucky Lake's headwaters, as was a 7-pound, 6-ounce state record sauger in 1973. The Pickwick Landing Dam tailwaters have also produced state-record northern carpsuckers, spotted gar, and longnose gar (talk about ugly fish!). The state's biggest-ever chain pickerel, a 6-pound, 9-ounce beauty, was taken from Kentucky Lake in 1951.

Each spring Kentucky Lake becomes the focal point for anglers from across the Southeast and Midwest. There's a reason for this, although not a particularly large one—at least not one which ever weighs over four pounds. The reason is the lake's famous white and black crappie fishery. The blooming of the lakeside dogwoods is the signal that these gregarious fish have moved into Kentucky Lake's creek embayments, sloughs and back coves to spawn.

Actually, winter fishing for crappie is quite good and growing in popularity at this impoundment. Winter slabsides are usually 10 to 25 feet deep and found along the channels of major feeder streams, like Cypress Creek or the Buffalo River. Locate a good stump bed where these fish can be marked on an electronic graph, and you're in business. Tightline fishing with minnows or small twistertail grubs is the best winter ploy, although crappie are often taken in considerably shallower water by trollers working in the vicinity of the hot water discharge channel at TVA's Johnsonville Steam Plant. Relatively shallow wintertime calicoes are also taken in the swift water of the lake's first few miles below Pickwick Landing Dam.

During early March, Kentucky Lake's slabsides begin to respond to lengthening daylight and the urge to procreate. At this time stump beds along the main channel or backwater areas are ideal places to look for prespawn crappie action. Tightlining over this structure is still effective, but so is trolling. A local technique known as "spider rigging" is also practiced now and during the spawn. (This is discussed at length in the chapter that is devoted to crappie.)

When the rising spring lake level refloods the buck bush–crowded back coves, it's a safe bet that the lake's lovesick crappie won't tarry long before moving in on this cover. When conditions are right, fishing the buck bushes is about the simplest and most productive angling any fisherman could ever hope for. Most local crappie specialists take a very simplistic approach, preferring to use only a long cane or telescoping fiberglass pole, line, cork bobber and long-shanked gold hook and a small, lively minnow for bait. They probe thoroughly around a single, submerged buck bush and then move on to another and so forth throughout the day.

Following the April through mid-May spawning period, the crappie move out of the buck bush hollows into deeper water. They're still schooled, and can be found in 10-to-18-foot-deep water. Submerged stump beds are a preferred area to look for these fish, and during hot weather a local technique known as "stump knocking" is the most productive approach. (Stump knocking is also discussed in the chapter on crappie.) This mode of fishing holds well into cool weather in early November.

Largemouth bass have been a Kentucky Lake staple since the lake was formed. Dozens of bass tournaments are held here, one virtually every weekend of the year, and it often takes a twenty-pound catch to win. Cold-weather bass anglers do well here if they concentrate their efforts in the headwaters of any one of the dozens of feeder flows.

The water entering the lake from these tributary creeks and branches is usually slightly warmer than the lake's surface layers. Bait fish concentrate in and along the submerged creek meanders, and these in turn attract predators—like the largemouth bass. By using minnows, plastic worms or fly and rind combos and fishing slowly at 10-to-20-foot depths along creek channel drop-offs or adjacent stump beds, it's possible to find fast action. This ploy is productive from December into March, although there is also riverine-style green bass fishing downstream from Pickwick Landing Dam and some shallow-water bassin' in the vicinity of the Johnsonville Steam Plant's hot water discharge canal area.

Warming trends and sunny days serve to coax the green bass into shallower water. Kentucky Lake's mudflats, backwater sloughs and shallow dewatering areas (at Camden, Big Sandy and West Sandy Creek) are ideal for bass fishermen fond of working shallow-running crankbaits or spinnerbaits. Later, when the lake's buck bush coves are flooded, these hawgs move in there to forage on baitfish and later to nest. Small yellow or white spinnerbaits are one of the top offerings from spring through early summer.

During the very early morning and late evening hours in late May top-water bass fishing action in the lake's backwater cove and slough areas is good. Mayflies begin to hatch in June, signaling the advent of good fly fishing for bass. Most of the best hot-weather hawg hunting success, however, comes either by deep-water worm fishing along 15-to-30-foot drops or night fishing the same structure with plastic worms in slightly shallower water.

The Barkley Canal area is another prime hot-weather bassin' spot. Slight water-level changes in either lake create a current between these two bodies of water, and the rip-rap along the mile-and-three-quarters-long, 400-foot-wide canal attracts loads of bait fish. The result can be fantastic jig and crankbait fishing for both largemouth and smallmouth.

During the autumn largemouth move back into major feeder waters like the Big Sandy, Blood and Duck rivers and Jonathan Creek. Medium-to deep-running crankbaits, jigs and live baits are the top cooling-season producers. The excellent quality of the largemouth bass fishing in September and October at this lake is a well-kept secret.

Until recently smallmouth bass were not listed among Kentucky Lake's sport angling offerings. Granted, the Pickwick tailwaters have always been rated among the world's finest brown bass fishing holes, but this fishery extended only a few short miles downstream from the dam. Since the late seventies, however, for reasons not easy to explain, there's been an influx of smallies throughout the lake. Today bronzeback catches are relatively common everywhere, and some very nice fish are being taken.

Changes in Kentucky Lake itself are thought to be the reason behind this. Smallmouth bass were native to this reach of the Tennessee River prior to the creation of Kentucky Lake. When the rich riverside bottom land was flooded, however, they disappeared from most of the new lake. One theory for their absence was that the new lake lacked the rocky points and gravel beds preferred by these fish.

Ironically, this theory also helps to explain the reappearance of the smallmouth. As Kentucky Lake has "aged," points and spurs have gradually lost their earthen cover, exposing the underlying bedrock and creating smallmouth bass habitat.

At Kentucky Lake, smallie fishing is relatively undeveloped, except in the headwaters, where the technique of drift fishing with the current using live baits, jigs, crankbaits or spinners is practiced year-round. In the lake's lower half, point fishing is the primary approach. Point setting with multiple sets of live minnows has proven effective in cold weather, while during the summer a few adventurous fishermen have discovered that night jigging deep off of points is a productive tactic.

Bluegill are the major bream species found at Kentucky Lake, followed, in a distant second, by the redear sunfish. Bream become available to anglers in large numbers around the middle of April. Heavy catches of big "bull-gills" are made during the May and June nesting cycle, when they seek out shallow, relatively clean-bottomed coves. Crickets and redworms are highly effective then, but they're also year-round bream producers.

When Kentucky Lake's fabled willowfly emergences begin in June, excellent sunfish stringers are easy to come by, according to Tennessee Wildlife Resources Agency information officer Ged Petit. Every summer Petit and his wife, Shirley, catch loads of bluegill by fly fishing the lake's western edge, where these aquatic insects flock to lakeside willows following their emergence, or "dun stage." Early July is the peak of the willowfly hatch, and this is the best time to fish, at least until you're literally "worn out."

During extremely hot weather, the lake's bluegill go deep and can be unexpectedly difficult to catch. Then the bluffs along the main channel are the ideal place to prospect for these panfish. Find a shaded cliff and, without using a bobber, cast out a hook baited with a cricket or redworm. Very slowly retrieve the bait, while allowing it to sink to 10-to-15-foot depths. Strikes usually accompany each cast.

Kentucky Lake's sauger fishery rates among the country's finest, although it's estimated that less than 20 percent of this fishery is utilized annually by sport fishermen. Most of the sauger are caught in cold weather either below Pickwick and Kentucky dam or at the hot water discharge canal at the Johnsonville Steam Plant. Jigging the edge of fast water with flies or minnows is a productive tailwater ploy, as is trolling, which also works well at the steam plant. In addition to these, several major feeder systems, such as the Duck, Blood and Big Sandy rivers, traditionally offer good cold-weather sauger fishing. Limits are often taken by those willing to brave the coldest February evenings.

Sauger are concentrated in headwaters between December and early April, although fair numbers remain in these river settings throughout the year. Following the advent of warmer weather, they scatter throughout the lake, but commonly concentrate 15 to 40 feet deep off of deep, rocky main river channel points. Hot-weather trolling can be good, and an increasing number of fishermen are discovering this challenging, richly rewarding deep-water trick.

White bass are another cold-weather gamefish. These fish follow much the same winter movement and feeding patterns as the sauger; however, they usually prefer flashier and faster-moving baits and stay in headwater areas about a month longer than the sauger. Once the white bass spawn is completed in mid-spring, they scatter throughout the lake in large feeding gangs. Following the gizzard shad hatch in May, white bass ply open water, ripping the surface-swimming schools of immature shad. This feeding behavior, which anglers refer to as "jump" or "break" action, is exciting to fish with small spinners, crankbaits or top-water or shallow-running lures.

For years the Tennessee Wildlife Resources Agency has tried to establish a quality striped bass fishery at Kentucky Lake, with only mixed success. This stocking was undertaken in an attempt to take advantage of the lake's estimated 13 million pounds of gizzard shad to produce a harvestable gamefish. What has happened to the almost one million rockfish placed there over a period of several years is something of a mystery, although, as one biologist confided to me, these stockings were apparently only "a drop in the bucket" in a lake of this magnitude.

A modest rockfish fishery has emerged below Pickwick Landing Dam, where specimens over thirty pounds are often taken. Drift fishing using shad for bait is the most common local striper approach, and when the upstream current is strong and these fish have moved in to feed, angling for linesides can be quite brisk.

The superlative quality of the whiskered fish offerings of Kentucky Lake and its tailwaters is difficult to overstate. Where else have you heard of 100-pound catfish having been caught? All species—white, blue, channel, flathead and bullhead catfish—are found here in great numbers and size. It's one of the few man-made lakes where catfish make up over half of the total annual catch of commercial fishermen.

Where catfish are concerned, the lake's headwaters and tailwater areas offer such outstanding and essentially different fishing from the rest of the lake that they deserve special notation. Tailwater fishing is a year-round endeavor that can be astonishingly productive when the right fishing conditions come together. All species of catfish inhabit these swift-water reaches, and for good reason. The upstream dams provide an unending smorgasbord of chopped up and injured shad. The pickings are easy, and the catfish grow fat and sassy gorging on these morsels.

Hook and line anglers fishing these tailwaters do best when they can locate a reliable underwater crevice or hole that's consistently utilized by these fish. Once found, such a spot will yield up amazing bounties of whiskered fish. Success is also possible by drift fishing bait from a boat or the riverside.

Catfish chasing is a year-round endeavor for many lake anglers. In cold weather, fish move about the lake bottom in great numbers. Trotlines baited with chicken liver or cut shad and strung near the mouth of a feeder stream are usually productive. The Johnsonville Steam Plant area, the Barkley Canal and Camden are excellent winter catfish spots.

Channel cats move into shallow water at about the same time that crappie and bluegill seek out these abodes. They can be taken there on hook and line, but between then and October, jug fishing (see catfish chapter) is not only productive but also more fun than watching a monkey do tricks on a hundred yards of grapevine.

Excellent catfish spawning action catches are made at night during July and August. The fish nest and mate throughout the lake, but they can be consistently caught around bridges or rip-rap, which provide crevice-ridden structure that is ideal for their spawning requirements.

Chain pickerel are also found in Kentucky Lake, although this is not a very important fishery. Most catches are made unintentionally during the spring by crappie or bass fishermen working weedy lakeside cover. Pickerel, an aggressive, predatory fish, are most active in warming water and during the winter months.

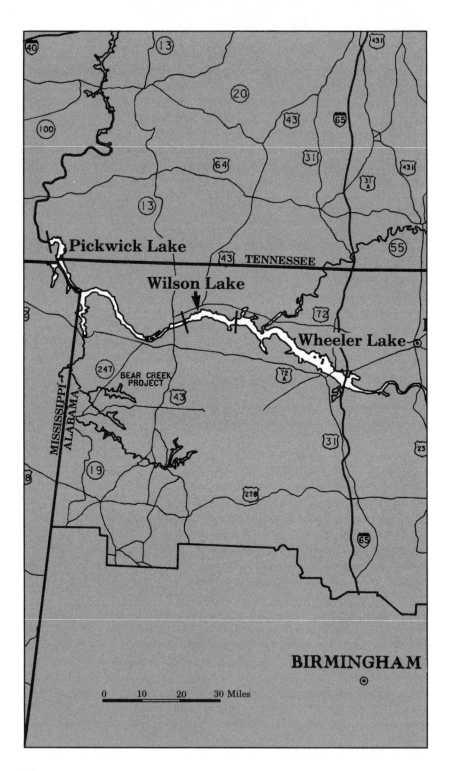

Pickwick Lake

SIZE: medium

ACCESSIBILITY: excellent to very good

LOCATION: Tennessee (Hardin County); Mississippi (Tishomingo County); and Alabama (Lauderdale and Colbert counties)

PRESSURE: moderate to heavy

PRIMARY GAMEFISH: crappie, bluegill, largemouth and smallmouth bass, catfish, sauger

SECONDARY GAMEFISH: white bass, redear sunfish

BEST MONTHS: April, May, June, October, March

BEST BAITS: live minnows, crickets, hair jigs, plastic worms, spinnerbaits, deep-running shad-style crankbaits

BEST BET: smallmouth bass in winter and spring, largemouth bass year-round

On one cold February evening in Nashville a few years ago, Don asked Bill Dance what was his favorite bass fishing lake. The question wasn't his preferred TVA lake, but what was his all-time favorite honeyhole for catching bass. Everybody who watches the tube knows Dance fishes all over North America, but not everyone knows that his favorite bass-fishing lake is none other than Pickwick Lake.

Why? Well, according to Dance, this lake offers high-quality angling for every black bass family member and in a wide variety of fishing situations, plus it has high-octane fishing for several other gamefish species. 'Nuff said.

Pickwick Landing Lake, as it's technically known, is the second of nine TVA mainstream impoundments of the Tennessee River. Construction on the dam began in 1934, and was completed in 1938 at a cost of $210 million, making it the most expensive waterway project ever undertaken by this federal agency.

The dam is located approximately 206 miles upstream from the Tennessee River's mouth at the Ohio River. At full pool the lake covers 43,100 surface acres, extends almost 53 miles to Wilson Dam and has nearly 500 miles of shoreline. The lake's full pool elevation is 414 feet above sea level, while its minimum pool elevation is 408 feet.

The controversial Tennessee-Tombigbee Waterway project provided a barge-navigable canal between this lake, via the Yellow Creek embayment, and the Tombigbee River, which empties into the Gulf of Mexico. TVA's Bear Creek project impoundments are located upstream from Pickwick Lake's Bear Creek embayment. These small bodies of water are discussed at the end of this chapter.

Pickwick Landing Dam is located in Tennessee, but most of the impoundment is found in Alabama, with a small part of the lake also extending into Mississippi. It's the only TVA lake which borders three states. Pickwick Lake borders Hardin County in Tennessee, Lauderdale and Colbert counties in Alabama, and Tishomingo County in Mississippi. The nearest major towns include Savannah and Corinth in Tennessee; Florence, Muscle Shoals, Tuscumbia and Sheffield in Alabama; and Iuka in Mississippi.

Like most of TVA's mainstream lakes, Pickwick is blessed with ample access, although its main channel is crossed only once, by the scenic Natchez Trace Parkway which crosses the lake at river mile 236.5. TN 128 crosses Pickwick Landing Dam, while TN 57 accesses the lake's southern shoreline until this route crosses into Mississippi, where it becomes MS 25. US 72 provides additional access to the southern shoreline area from Tuscumbia to the Bear Creek embayment area.

Pickwick Lake has an enormous number of public access and recreational areas. There are 17 public boat-launch ramps and 8 commercial boat docks along this lake. Public camping is permitted at the Pickwick Dam Reservation and Pickwick Landing State Park in Hardin County, Tennessee; the Goat Island Recreation Area and J. P. Coleman State Park in Tishomingo County, Mississippi; Colbert County Park and Buzzard Roost Park in Colbert County and McFarland Bottoms Park in Lauderdale County, Alabama.

Additional public access areas include the Burton Branch State Recreation Area in Hardin County, Tennessee, and the Cooper Falls Small Wild Area and a state recreation area which is located at the mouth of Mill Creek in the upper reaches of the Bear Creek embayment in Mississippi.

In Alabama these public areas include Brush Creek Park (near Wright), Waterloo City Park, the Second Creek Recreation Area, Florence Municipal Park and the Old First Quarter Small Wild Area at TVA's National Fertilizer Development Center.

The lake's north shore in Alabama from near Waterloo to the state line is devoted to the Lauderdale County WMA, and upstream near Florence there is another wildlife area which extends 11 miles along the lake's northern edge (which also includes Sevenmile Island and the Colliers Slough area). TVA's Colbert Steam Plant is located near the mouth of the Cane Creek in Alabama, while there is an additional generating site located on the Yellow Creek embayment in Mississippi.

Pickwick is a very scenic, bottomland lake. It encompasses more different fishing situations and habitats than any other TVA impoundment. The original riverbed covered 9,580 acres and cut its way through rolling farm country between high bluffs, wide flood plains and choppy hills. The lake averages almost one mile in width. Its submerged cover includes sandbars, rocky points, constantly moving and sometimes swift headwaters, wide and deep feeder creek embayments, gravel bottoms, sunken islands, stump-ridden shallows and backwater areas and mudflats.

Some man-made fish attractors have been placed around the lake. Deep-water attractors are located along the main channel and Bear and Yellow creek embayments. Shallow brush piles are thick along the Mississippi portion of the lake, particularly the eastern edge of Bear Creek downstream from the mouth of Mill Creek, the Indian Creek embayment, and the Yellow Creek embayment from its mouth to the Yellow Creek Inland Port site.

Fishing Information

Pickwick Lake is one of the country's premier smallmouth bass fisheries. It's also a dandy for a number of other species including sauger, largemouth bass, crappie, bream and catfish. The lake is rich in nutrients and has relatively good water quality. Threadfin and the larger-growing gizzard shad are the primary forage fish, followed by suckers, chubs and sunfish.

Alabama's state record paddlefish, or spoonbill catfish, a 52-pound, 12-ounce whopper, was caught here in the headwaters in 1982. The state's record book sauger, a nice 5-pound, 2-ounce beauty, was caught there 10 years earlier. Mississippi's top smallie, a 7-pound, 5-ounce specimen, was lifted from Pickwick Lake in 1976, while a 9-pound, 10-ounce walleye caught there in 1985 is also a state record catch. A 5-pound, 13½-ounce chain pickerel caught from Pickwick in 1978 is the third Mississippi state record gamefish from this lake.

Smallmouth bass are this writer's favorite fish (at least when I'm unable to fish for trout in the Great Smoky Mountains National Park). These fish get big in Pickwick Lake, and if you're looking for a trophy to hang on a den wall, there are no better or more productive waters in the nation. Brown bass fishing at this lake is a year-round sport, and good catches are made virtually every weekend.

Pickwick Lake is known for its record-class black bass fishing, but its crappie fishery is also outstanding.

Cold-weather fishing for Pickwick's smallies is usually quite good in the lake's headwaters below Wilson Dam. Headwater fishing is not affected as much by seasonal weather changes as are other areas in the lake. The temperature of the water entering the lake is relatively stable and usually warmer than the lake's downstream portions.

Drifting with the current while working live baits like threadfin shad or spring lizards is a traditional, year-round lunker-slaying method, although during hot weather drift fishing is doubly effective during the twilight hours. Other anglers know that when water enters Pickwick Lake at Florence, smallmouth bass stack up on points and the tips of islands along the main stream all the way downstream to Kogers Island. These fish are taken by "point setters," who bottom fish big minnows or slowly work plastic grubs and worms down through the cover. The bluffs and cliffs along the Sevenmile Island area are extremely productive for spotted, largemouth and smallmouth bass fishing. Crankbaits worked up the steep channel drop-offs also work well most times of the year.

During the spring and summer months these headwater ploys remain effective, but by then it's also easier to catch brown in other parts of the lake. Beginning in late March these fish move into large backwater areas like Bear and Yellow creeks, where they concentrate on stump beds and 8-to-10-foot-deep gravel shelves. At this time jigs and spinnerbaits worked slowly along this structure are deadly. During the spring the stump-filled coves and sharp points around Waterloo are trophy smallmouth bass areas that most newcomers have a tough time learning about.

Largemouth bass don't usually play second fiddle to any other finned critter, but that's not the case at Pickwick. Granted these fish grow big here, sometimes topping 10 pounds, but this lake's reputation was built on its fantastic bronzeback fishery. Winter largemouth bass fishing also rates excellent in the headwaters, although on days when the mercury drops below the 35-degree mark, catches usually aren't impressive. During mild weather, though, good fishing is available there.

The Colliers Slough area is an excellent winter and spring hawg-hunting spot, as are the Second, Bear and Yellow creek embayments. The stump bed flats in Bear Creek's Buck Branch and around Mill Creek Dock are usually worthy of investigation. During cold weather largemouth bass also concentrate in the Cane Creek embayment and immediately downstream from its mouth. They're there to feed on shad which are attracted by the Colbert Steam Plant's hot water discharges.

Pickwick Lake's largemouth bass usually begin spawning in April, and at this time the man-made brush piles at Indian and Yellow creeks are red-hot hawg spots, as are the stump bed flats along the main channel downstream from Waterloo. Summertime night bass action at Pickwick is well above average. When water is being pulled from the lake, the sunken islands and stump beds on the lake's southern edge near Pickwick Landing State Park can stack up an astonishing number of green bass. When water enters the lake at its other end, on the other hand, these fish position off of points, at creek mouths and around bridge pilings and island points as far downstream as the Natchez Trace Bridge.

Sauger fishing is super at Pickwick Lake. Beginning in late November these fish are caught in good numbers in the lake's headwaters immediately downstream from Wilson Dam. Cold-weather sauger fishing holds well into March. Orange, white, yellow or green quarter-ounce jigs tipped with live minnows or plastic twistertail jigs are the favorite local offerings. Jigged in the fast flow of the tailwaters or trolled between the head of Sevenmile Island upstream to the tailrace, these baits produce tons of good-eating sauger. Tailwater sauger catches may peak during the winter, but periodic stringers are taken here year-round.

Catfish grow big in just about any size waters, but they seem to do better in great lakes such as Pickwick. Abundant forage and plenty of

Big stripers fin below Pickwick Dam. Catch them with live shad.

elbow (fin?) room combine to make this lake a premier location for whiskered fish. All species common to the Tennessee River system—blue, channel, flathead and bullhead catfish—are found here in good numbers. Commercial fishermen rate Pickwick's big channel catfish among the valley's best fisheries.

Tailwater catches are good year-round, although only a hardy few pursue these fish with hook and line during cold weather. The Colbert Steam Plant also concentrates whiskered fish during cold weather. Most tailwater-area catches are made during mild weather using stinkbaits, chicken liver, cut and live shad and nightcrawlers. The lake's backwater areas are also productive for still fishing, trotlines and jug fishing.

Crappie fishing at Pickwick Lake is not highly touted, but it's a solid fishery that keeps most area slabside specialists happy and close to home. Winter fishing in the Waterloo area, where stump beds often accompany drop-offs, or at the deep-water man-made fish attractors located at Dry and Bear creeks can be outstanding, as well as at the Colliers Slough area. Deep water (10 to 20 feet) trolling and tightline fishing with minnows or grubs over stumps and drop-offs are good in these areas.

Spring spawning action is first class in the Yellow and Bear creek embayments, as well as in many other backwater areas where stump beds or other similar shallow cover can be located. Summer fishing for slabsides rates above average for the TVA system if you fish at night and work over 8-to-15-foot-deep stumps and man-made brush piles.

White bass inhabit Pickwick Lake and provide good to excellent year-round fishing opportunities. This a reliable cold-weather gamefish if you concentrate your efforts at Pickwick's headwater and steam plant areas. During the winter, stripe, as most 'Bama casters call the white bass, make daily feeding runs from the upstream tip of Sevenmile Island to the dam and up the narrow Cane Creek embayment. When they move into a river stretch, they're often so thick that it's difficult to catch anything except stripes for a brief time. Trollers can do particularly well at these times.

Summer catches in the lake's headwaters (and other areas of the lake) are good when these fish surface feed on newly hatched, immature shad. Good night catches are made by anglers who suspend lanterns off of points.

Pickwick Lake also sports a very good bream fishery. Bluegill and redear sunfish are the lake's staples; they are caught most often during warm weather. Nesting-time catches of each are made in virtually all backwater areas. During hot weather big stringers can be caught during the willowfly hatch and later with live crickets fished 6 to 12 feet deep along the lake's bluffs.

TVA's Bear Creek Lakes

During the mid-1970s TVA constructed four non-power-producing dams on the headwaters of Bear Creek, a tributary of Pickwick Lake, for flood control. These lakes are Little Bear Lake, a 1,560-acre impoundment finished in 1975; Cedar Creek Lake, a 4,200-acre impoundment finished in 1979; Upper Bear Lake, a 1,850-acre impoundment completed in 1978; and Big Bear Lake, a 670-acre impoundment finished in 1969.

These have been managed for a variety of species including crappie; muskie; spotted, largemouth and smallmouth bass; walleye; sunfish and catfish. Fishing pressure is generally light on these small but beautiful lakes. Each of the Bear Creek project impoundments have at least one public boat launch, and all have campgrounds, but at this writing there are very few to no marinas here. A nominal daily user fee is assessed for each person entering the Bear Creek watershed.

Wilson Lake

SIZE: relatively small and compact
ACCESSIBILITY: excellent
LOCATION: Alabama (Lauderdale, Colbert, and Lawrence counties)
PRESSURE: moderate to heavy
PRIMARY GAMEFISH: bluegill, smallmouth bass, catfish, sauger
SECONDARY GAMEFISH: white and hybrid (whiterock) bass,
    largemouth bass, crappie, redear sunfish
BEST MONTHS: March, April, May, October
BEST BAITS: live minnows, spring lizards, jigs, crankbaits
BEST BET: smallmouth bass fishing with live minnows below Wheeler
    Dam

Wilson Lake is the oldest major impoundment in the TVA system. Construction was begun by the Army Corps of Engineers during World War I, when vast amounts of electricity were needed at a giant nearby nitrate plant. It was not completed until 1924, however, and the last hydroelectric generation unit did not go on line until almost forty years later, in 1962.

Wilson Dam has the incredible generating capacity of 629,840 kilowatts, the largest in the TVA system and more than almost any other dam in the world. In fact, its generating capacity is more than that of all of the TVA-system tributary dams combined, save Fontana Dam.

Wilson Dam is located on the Tennessee River some 260 miles upstream from its mouth at the Ohio River. The dam is a concrete structure which stands 137 feet high and is a whopping 4,541 feet across. It's equipped with a lock that permits watercraft and barges to move freely up and down the river. The impoundment's elevation is slightly over 507 feet above sea level, and at minimum pool is 504.5 feet above sea level. At full pool the lake covers 15,500 surface acres and extends up-

Wilson Dam, on the Tennessee River at Muscle Shoals, Alabama, was built by the Corps of Engineers between 1918 and 1924. The TVA acquired Wilson Dam when the agency was created in 1933. Today the dam's 21 units generate 629,840 kilowatts. TVA photo.

stream from the dam for a distance of 15.5 miles, with 154 miles of shoreline. Prior to the building of Wheeler Dam in 1936, Wilson Lake extended further upstream and covered more surface acres.

This is a well-developed lake with many homes and private moorings along its edge. It is located in Lauderdale, Colbert and Lawrence counties. The closest major towns are Florence in Lauderdale County, and Sheffield, Muscle Shoals and Tuscumbia in Colbert County. Major access routes to Wilson Lake include US 72 and 43 and AL 2 and 101 along the northern shoreline, and AL 184 and 101 along its southern edge.

The lake also features plenty of commercial and public access and recreation areas. There are seven commercial docks and four public boat-launch areas. Public camping is permitted at Joe Wheeler State Park in Lawrence and Lauderdale counties and Point Park at Florence in Lauderdale County. Day use is permitted at the Lock Six day-use area in Lauderdale County.

Since Wilson Lake is relatively wide, it is not significantly affected by upstream generation releases or winter drawdowns. It's a structure-rich body of water which still sports loads of old, submerged stump beds, as well as several significant feeder stream embayments, steep shoreline, rocky points, bluffs and riverine style and tailwater fishing. Most of the lake bottom is bedrock covered with sand and mud, while the shoreline is shale and clay. Deep-water fish attractors have been placed in the vicinity of the mouth of Town Creek. Weed infestation is not significant.

Fishing Information

Wilson Lake is a food-rich lake which supports a first-class, diverse fishery. This is a year-round fishing lake with a good reputation for keeping fishermen happy. Smallmouth and largemouth bass, whiterock hybrids, catfish and more are found here in quality and quantity.

Alabama's state record smallmouth bass, a 10½ pounder, was taken in 1950 from the headwaters of Wilson Lake below Wheeler Dam. This fish was the world record holder for five years, and according to local legend, had the fisherman, Owen Smith, gotten the fish to official weight scales, he might still have a claim to catching the world's number-one smallmouth bass. It took Smith over 48 hours to get his catch weighed, which, according to some, could have exceeded 12 pounds at the time it was caught.

Brown bass fishing is a year-round endeavor on this lake. In fact, some of the best bass are taken during the worst winter and early spring weather. Trophy-class smallies are a staple in the lake's headwater reaches, but they're quite common throughout the lake. Five-to-seven pounders are relatively easy to take, and some local anglers don't start counting them until they reach eight pounds.

Live baits such as shad, spring lizards and nightcrawlers rate as the top smallmouth bass assassins at the headwaters of Wilson Lake. Regardless of season, when these baits are free drifted with the current along rip-rap, boils or other areas that show signs of breaks in the current, they are productive. Hardware casters do well in these tailwaters using brown, black and purple jigs tipped with pork rind, medium-depth-running crankbaits and spoons. Winter fishing is also good along the lake's shoreline.

During the spring, nesting smallies are often located in steep-banked major feeder creek embayments, such as McKernan and Shoal creeks. Spinnerbaits or medium-depth-running plugs are most effective at this time. During the summer months smallie fishing remains good, although except at the lake's headwaters, it becomes a nighttime affair. Jigs and live bait are the top hot-weather brown bass offerings.

Largemouth bass fishing rates a solid good at Wilson Lake. These fish are abundant throughout the lake, although they don't attract as much attention as the smallies in Wilson or the largemouth fisheries in Pickwick and Guntersville lakes. Winter hawg hunters do well to concentrate their efforts at the mouth of Town Creek, as well as working the backwater reaches of McKernan Creek. Small live minnows, as well as plastic worms and fly and rind combos, are deadly cold-weather offerings.

Spring is spawning time for these fish, and the grassy shallows in the rear of Town Creek and the upper reaches of Blue Water and Shoal creeks are favorite nesting locations. Later during May these fish can be caught on top-water plugs. Private docks, houseboats, overhanging trees and shrubbery and other similar structure are all worth casting beside, especially when the willowflies hatch.

Following the arrival of hot weather these fish are most easily caught during the very late evening or early morning hours and at night. Upstream from the mouth of Town Creek the best fishing is when water is entering the lake, while downstream from Shoal Creek the best catches are made when water is being pulled through Wilson Dam.

The winter sauger fishery that is found below Wheeler Dam rates among the country's finest. Limits of these good eating fish are common, and the colder the weather, the better the fishing. Beginning in December and lasting until March, these fish instinctively move upstream, where they ultimately stack up against the dam. Here anglers jigging or trolling live minnows, hair flies or grubs do well. At this tailwater area, sauger aren't just a cold-weather quarry; they're caught here throughout the year.

The white bass and hybrid white bass–striped bass are other common tailwater dwellers that get everyone's attention when they crash a bait. Whites are common throughout the TVA system. The non-native hybrid has been stocked at Wilson by the state of Alabama since the 1970s, when it was determined that the striped bass being planted there were no longer considered desirable in this lake. Both fish grow fast in the lake's headwaters, where they feast upon the chopped and injured shad coming through the turbines at Wheeler Dam.

Despite the fact that these hybrids have been stocked as far south as Florida, where they're called the "sunshine bass," they are remarkably cold natured and during the winter remain as active as any Wilson Lake gamefish. Like the white bass, or stripe, they feed voraciously year-round in the vicinity of the fast-moving current of the tailwaters, where they're caught in reasonably good numbers on threadfin shad or spoons.

There are exceptions to this. During hot weather these fish often move throughout the lake with smaller white bass. They surface feed on topside finning shad, in what is known as "jumps." At this time small top-water plugs or subsurface-running spinners are an angler's best bet. Additionally, during the cold weather and late spring these fish sometimes suspend over deep-water cover. TVA has installed a number of such structures at the mouth of Town Creek, and these are marked by buoys. Vertical jigging jigs or bait or still fishing bait works well there on these whiterock hybrids.

Wilson Lake crappie fishery gets three stars. Winter fishing is relatively good along deep creek meanders and drop-offs along the old river channel. These fish stay 18 to 30 feet deep during cold weather, but by mid-March begin moving into shallower back-cove areas. During spring spawning time the fishing is best in the creek embayments and coves along the main river channel. Minnows fished 2 to 4 feet deep under a floater are the most popular local offering.

Bluegill and redear sunfish are the lake's two best-known panfish, although neither receives the attention given to bream fishing at other nearby TVA lakes. These fish become available to fishermen in early April, when they concentrate in the lake's feeder streams and backwater coves. Nesting occurs in early May, and at this time both species are caught in great numbers in Town, Shoal and Blue Water creeks. In July when the lake's giant mayfly hatches begin, these bream can be taken in large numbers on popping bugs or live crickets.

Wilson Lake, particularly its extreme headwaters, is a fine catfish fishing hole. All species common to the Tennessee River are found here. A close look at a topographical map of the tailwaters downstream from Wheeler Dam reveals that upon leaving Wheeler Lake, the water immediately passes over a bedrock shoal area. This shoal area is riddled with crevices, openings, holes and other cover that is ideal for sheltering a whiskered fish from the fast overhead current while also giving it an opportunity to see and quickly snatch morsels that periodically pass overhead.

Knowing where these areas are is the secret to big catches of these fish. Electronic depth-reading devices are helpful in this endeavor. Bottom fishing with stink baits is productive there, as is drift fishing with the current while baits are suspended off of the bottom. Trotline fishing is common further downstream, and during the spring and summer months jug fishing for catfish is popular in coves and feeder stream embayments.

Wheeler Lake

SIZE: large

ACCESSIBILITY: very good

LOCATION: Alabama (Lauderdale, Limestone, Morgan, Lawrence,
Madison, and Marshall counties)

PRESSURE: moderate to heavy

PRIMARY GAMEFISH: crappie, bluegill, largemouth and smallmouth
bass, catfish, sauger

SECONDARY GAMEFISH: white and whiterock hybrid bass, redear
sunfish

BEST MONTHS: January, February, April, May, June, July, March

BEST BAITS: live minnows, crickets, twistertail jigs, purple and motor
oil–colored plastic worms, deep-running crankbaits

BEST BET: winter sauger fishing with jigs below Guntersville Dam

Wheeler Lake is the second largest of the northern Alabama TVA impoundments. It offers exceptional fishing for a variety of popular gamefish, including largemouth and smallmouth bass, crappie, brim, white
bass, sauger and catfish. Like other TVA mainstream impoundments,
it has a rich nutrient base and moderately good water quality, and is
regarded as a healthy, diverse fishery. Alabama's largest-ever catfish,
a 78.5-pound blue catfish, was caught from the Tennessee River in 1985.

Wheeler Dam was built between 1933 and 1936 and was one of the
first TVA projects. Construction here began seven weeks after the agency's "flagship" project was begun at Norris Dam. The dam stands 74
feet high, is 6,342 feet long, and contains nearly 1.2 million cubic yards
of concrete. It is equipped with a modern lock system which permits
barge traffic to move freely along the fully navigable Tennessee River.
The entire project carried a $88.7 million price tag.

At full pool Wheeler Lake covers 67,100 surface acres and extends over 74 miles with 1,036 miles of shoreline. Prior to the lake's creation, the portion of the Tennessee River now impounded to form the reservoir covered 17,600 acres. Full pool elevation is 507.5 feet above sea level, while the maximum draw down is to 504.5 feet above sea level, although the lake's drop rarely exceeds more than a couple of feet.

Wheeler Lake is located in Lauderdale, Limestone, Morgan, Lawrence, Madison, and Marshall counties. The closest major towns are Florence in Lauderdale County, Decatur in Morgan County, Athens in Limestone County, and Huntsville in Madison County.

Access to the northwestern shoreline is by US 72, which runs from the dam upstream to the Elk River embayment, crossing near Oliver, and then going on to the city of Athens. From Athens US 31 goes south to the lake and crosses it at the Wheeler National Wildlife Refuge to arrive at the city of Decatur (near river mile 305). Interstate 65 also passes by Athens before heading south and crossing the lake near river mile 310. Also south out of Athens, US 431 roughly follows the lake and has a number of paved county roads which lend additional access.

The lake's southern shoreline is accessed near its headwaters by US 231 and AL 36 and 67 downstream to Decatur. Beyond Decatur US 72 Alt. (AL 20) follows the lake to its junction with AL 101, which proceeds northward to cross Wheeler Dam.

This well-developed lake has plenty of public access and recreational facilities. Nine commercial boat docks and two dozen public boat-launch ramps ring Wheeler Lake. Public camping is permitted at Joe Wheeler State Park, TVA's Wheeler Dam Reservation, and TVA-maintained recreation areas at Mallard Creek and Round Island. Other public-use areas include Limestone Park in Limestone County, Point Mallard Park in Morgan County, the Decatur Day Use Park and Municipal Boat Harbor in Limestone County and Huntsville-Madison Park in Madison County.

There are several major wildlife refuges along this lake. These include the Wheeler National Wildlife Refuge in Limestone, Madison and Morgan counties, the Mallard Creek WMA, the Fox Creek WMA and the Harris Sweetwater Dewatering Project. Good waterfowl hunting is available here during the winter months.

Other points of interest along this lake includes TVA's controversial Browns Ferry Nuclear Plant in Limestone County and the federal government's nearby Redstone Arsenal. Browns Ferry is one of the oldest southern atomic-powered stations, while the Redstone Arsenal holds, well, enough explosives and other goodies for the state of Alabama to win the Second War of Northern Aggression single-handed!

Wheeler is more like the mixture of many lakes. Portions of it pass through modern river town ports and by busy factories. Other river areas

Whiterock, or X-striped white bass hybrids, are relative newcomers to Wheeler Lake, although they already have a faithful following.

are flanked by rich hardwood forests and marsh areas more typical in appearance of Louisiana. Its headwaters are narrow, riverinelike, while downstream from Decatur Wheeler Lake spreads out to an average width of over a mile for a distance of over 30 miles.

This relatively shallow lake contains virtually every sort of cover an angler might care to imagine, including rocky points, steep drops, cliffs and bluffs, deep submerged creek meanders, gravel bars, cool feeder streams, stump beds, bayou-type sluices and steep bluffs. The bottom is mud, sand, rock, limestone and gravel. Milfoil infestation at Wheeler is negligible.

Major feeder streams include the Elk, Paint Rock and Flint rivers.

Fishing Information

Like all of the northern Alabama TVA lakes, Wheeler has a healthy, diverse fishery. Threadfin and gizzard shad are the primary forage fish, and largemouth, spotted and smallmouth bass, sunfish, crappie, hybrid whiterocks, catfish, sauger and white bass are the major sport fisheries.

Sauger fishing is first-rate at Wheeler Lake. Winter fishing is generally the most productive, but very good catches can also be made in summer. During cold weather these fish concentrate in the headwaters between Guntersville Dam and the mouth of the Flint River. Trollers working such offerings as quarter-ounce orange or green jigs tipped with a tuffie or small minnow-type crankbaits do very well. Other anglers have success moving up close to the dam or areas near the rip-rap and vertically jigging similar baits. This type of fishing holds relatively steady from late November until the end of March.

From late spring through early autumn sauger scatter throughout Wheeler Lake, although tailwater action below Guntersville Dam remains relatively steady (if somewhat diminished from its wintertime height). In recent years, a growing number of fishermen have discovered that these fish are also a first-class hot-weather quarry, when they station at 15-to-30-foot depths off of rocky mainstream points from the dam upstream to the Mallard Point area. Once located, they can be taken throughout the day by trolling.

At Wheeler Lake largemouth bass must share billing with the spunky smallie. Smallmouth bass were common in the Tennessee River before these dams were built, according to TVA regional fishery specialist David Sample.

"Shoals dominated the old river system which extended from Decatur to the Muscle Shoals area. These shoals often extended one-half to three-quarters of a mile wide. You can actually see the old shoal areas below Wilson Dam. Since these rocky reaches were flooded they have continued to approximately where the smallmouth bass fisheries have been the strongest," notes Sample.

Wheeler's smallmouth population doesn't completely dominate this lake, but they are prevalent in some areas. These include the Elk River embayment, the lake's headwaters downstream to the mouth of the Flint River, the Second Creek, and of course the lake's well-known tailwater area.

Smallie action is very good during cold weather, when they feed on adult threadfin shad which are in relatively shallow 3-to-8-foot-deep water. Big, live minnows, Shad Rap crankbaits or spinnerbaits worked off of points and along creek meander drop-offs and rock piles are lethal. Tailwater-style fishing in the lake's headwaters is best during water releases at Guntersville Dam.

Spring smallie action concentrates in the upper reaches of feeder creeks. Spinnerbaits worked by floating debris along the shoreline or pig'n'jig combos flipped in stump beds are deadly. During hot weather these fish become nocturnal. Night fishing with jigs, plastic worms and live spring lizards along the areas mentioned above can be very good from June until mid-October.

Largemouth bass grow fast, feeding on the abundant supply of threadfin. Winter fishing is best during mild weather, when forage fish are shallow. The meanders of feeder creek embayments such as Spring Creek or the shallow flats located along the lake's northern edge from the mouth of Round Island Creek upstream to past Decatur are excellent prospecting spots during cold weather.

The spring spawning time provides some of the season's best fishing action. Stump flats and the maze of backwater coves, where 2-to-6-foot-deep, clean-bottomed areas are common, are ideal for casting spinner-baits or still fishing big, live shiners. Shortly after spawning, these fish disperse along the lake's shoreline. Excellent top-water action can be found in stump beds, buck bush coves and where overhanging greenery provides cover for the bass.

Summer bass fishing is slower on Wheeler than at grass-laden Guntersville, but not if you're a night fisherman. The headwaters between Ditto Landing and Mallard Point are excellent deep-water worming and crankbait locations when water is entering from upstream. The rip-rap near Wheeler Dam is an overlooked hawg-holding spot in hot weather, as are the piling at the two bridges crossing the lake near Decatur and the many private and public docks encircling the lake.

Wheeler Lake enjoys an excellent reputation as a crappie fishery, although it doesn't receive as much angling pressure as nearby Guntersville Lake. Live minnows may not be the only way to catch these fish here, but if a local poll were taken, you might think that was the case. Fished under a float, minnows are the number-one crappie offering, followed by small jigs and grubs.

Winter crappie anglers can do well if they're equipped with an electric depth finder which enables them to locate 15-to-30-foot-deep stump beds or steep drop-offs along the primary feeder creeks or even the main river channel. Crappie remain schooled and relatively active throughout the winter, but as always, they must be found to be caught. A good electronic depth finder–marker makes this possible.

Beginning in early March crappie move out of deep water. Pre-spawning and spawning action concentrates in shallow, cover-rich back-water areas, such as Indian and Flint creeks. Dabbling minnows around stumps or other structure is the standard ploy, and catches are usually very good. This sort of fishing can last into June. Following the advent of hot weather, Wheeler's slabsides move out deep into areas very similar to those used during cold weather. Wintertime fishing tricks work well at this time, as does fishing live minnows 4 to 8 feet deep under a suspended lantern.

Bluegill and shellcracker fishing don't get a great deal of attention at this lake, but it can be awesome. Fishing the spring spawning beds is first class in those areas which were previously noted for crappie. Later during July, when mayfly hatches blossom along the lake's edges,

Wheeler Lake is known for its lunker smallmouth bass, but largemouth bass are also plentiful here.

superb fly rod action with popping bugs can net a heavy stringer on almost any summer evening.

Commercial fishermen rate Wheeler Lake's catfish population among the best in the Tennessee River Valley. Channel catfish are the most abundant, followed by huge-growing blue cats and flathead catfish. Winter catfish action is very good throughout the lake. Heavy trotline catches are made in the vicinity of the US 31-72 bridge and upstream to the Lily Pond area, as well as from the Guntersville Dam tailwaters downstream for a distance of about three miles. Cut bait and chicken liver are the preferred catfish baits.

Spring action is good in most feeder stream areas, as well as along the main river channel and of course in the lake's extreme headwaters, which provide excellent year-round whiskered fish action. Summer action rates high at Wheeler, and always draws crowds at the mouth of feeder creeks and at rocky points. The best fishing, aside from the tailwater angling, is found along the shoreline from Harris Station downstream to the dam.

White bass are abundant throughout the lake. During cold weather they slowly move toward the lake's headwaters, where they concentrate in its upper three miles from February through March. Large catches of these hard-fighting fish are caught by float fishing with the current and casting small crankbaits, spinners or white and red twistertail jigs. Summer action moves to the main body of the lake, where jump, or surface, fishing can occur anywhere on any given summer evening.

Wheeler has a tremendous shad forage base. To make some use of these smellie fish, the state stocks hybrid white bass–striped bass at an annual rate of about ten per surface acre. These grow fast in this lake, often topping 10 pounds. Hybrids, as most local anglers refer to these fish, are caught most often in the company of the more common native white bass. Tactics, techniques and baits used for whites work well on these fish, and considerations of season and movement are very similar.

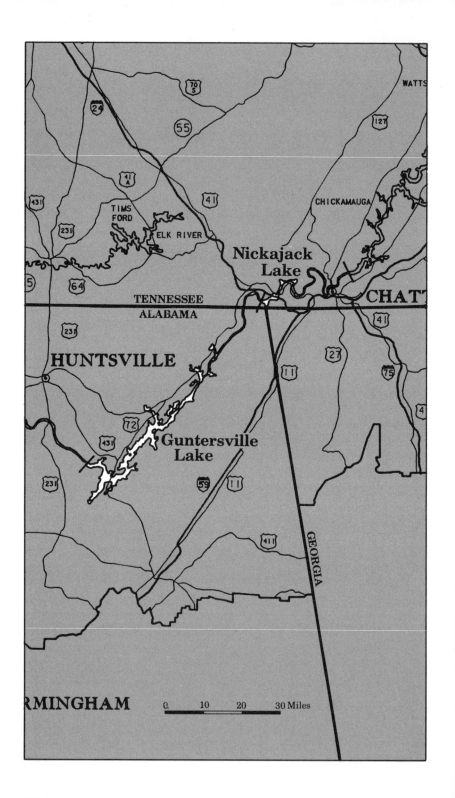

94

Guntersville Lake

SIZE: large

ACCESSIBILITY: very good

LOCATION: Alabama (Marshall and Jackson counties) and Tennessee (Marion County)

PRESSURE: relatively heavy

PRIMARY GAMEFISH: bluegill, redear sunfish, largemouth bass, crappie, catfish

SECONDARY GAMEFISH: white hybrid (whiterock) bass, sauger

BEST MONTHS: March, April, May, June, July, October

BEST BAITS: live minnows, jigs, twistertail grubs, buzzbaits, spinnerbaits

BEST BET: redear fishing with crickets over their nests in May, and fly fishing for bream during the July willowfly hatch

Guntersville Lake, one of four major mainstream impoundments on the portion of the Tennessee River that flows through Alabama, is often rated among the Tennessee River Valley's top three fisheries. Largemouth bass, crappie, shellcrackers and catfish not only are abundant but also grow large here.

When the TVA Act became law, harnessing the Tennessee River for flood control, hydroelectric power production and navigation was the first order of business. The completion of the Guntersville Dam project was among the most important of the nine mainstream steps. It was initiated in late 1935 and completed in January 1939 at a cost of slightly over $54 million.

The dam stands 349 feet high and measures 3,979 feet across. Like all mainstream dams, Guntersville has a lock system that is open to all craft. It is the southernmost dam in the TVA system. At full pool the lake reaches 595 feet above sea level, while at minimum pool its elevation is 593 feet. At full pool it covers 67,900 surface acres and extends

*Many anglers rate Guntersville as the most scenic TVA lake. TVA
photo.*

over 75 miles, with 949 miles of shoreline. It is the second largest reservoir in the TVA system.

Chattanooga, Huntsville, Gadsden, Fort Payne and Scottsboro are
the nearest towns. In Alabama, the lake bisects Marshall and Jackson
counties. In Tennessee, Marion County borders this impoundment. AL
69, 40, 35 and 117, US 431 and TN 156 access the lake's southern shoreline areas. US 72 and 431 and AL 117, 35 and 79 are the major access
routes along the lake's northern edge.

Guntersville is one of the most heavily developed recreational lakes
in the TVA system. Much of the lake's shoreline is publicly owned, which
makes access and water-related sports easy for everyone. Public camping
is available at TVA-maintained Honeycomb Creek and Siebold recreation areas, Donahoo (Langston) and Vaughn's (Guntersville) recreation
areas, Marshall and Jackson county parks, Scottsboro and Stevenson
municipal parks, Goose Pond Colony (Scottsboro), and Lake Guntersville
(Little Mountain) and Buck's Pocket state parks.

Other public-use areas include the Guntersville Dam Reservation,
Langston City Park, Guntersville Municipal Park and the Lindsey-
Honeycomb Creek Small Wilderness Area. Seventeen commercial mar-
inas and 41 public boat launches are found around Guntersville Lake.

The state of Alabama maintains Wildlife Management Areas along the lake's southern shoreline between Raccoon and Long Island creeks and on the north side from the Mud Creek embayment upstream to near Crow Creek Island. State-controlled waterfowl refuges are located along the North Sauty and Crow Creek embayments. The Blowing Wind Cave National Wildlife Refuge is located along the North Sauty Creek embayment. Each winter the areas adjacent to and between these areas provide excellent waterfowl hunting.

This is a typical Tennessee River mainstream impoundment, which is best termed as a mix between riverine and lake type habitat. The original riverbed covered 12,065 acres, surrounded by rich bottomland and rolling hills. The lake's depth varies considerably, from nearly 100 feet along the old Tennessee River channel to 4 to 5 feet or less in several coves and backwater areas. Guntersville averages almost a mile across in its lower half, but only a few hundred feet across above the mouth of Mud Creek.

Guntersville is rich in structure and cover. The bottom is composed of mud, sand, gravel and rock. Prior to the initial flooding, all standing timber was removed, but numerous stump-bed "forests" still canvas the lake's coves, creek embayments, and shallows along the main channel, along with loads of old building foundations.

The lake has a tremendous Eurasian milfoil infestation—a problem if one is a high-speed pleasure boater or assigned to the TVA "Aquatic Weed Control Corps," but a godsend for fishermen.

TVA operates two coal-fired and one nuclear-powered electricity-producing facilities at Guntersville Lake. The coal-fired Murphy Hill Generating Plant is found in Marshall County, while the Widows Creek Steam Plant is located near Bridgeport. The Bellefonte Nuclear Plant is located near Scottsboro. These facilities are worth noting by Guntersville fishermen, because their hot-water discharges can have profound effects on gamefish movements, particularly during the cold-weather months.

Fishing Information

Guntersville's reputation as an outstanding fishing spot is well deserved. Alabama's record blue catfish (it weighed 65 pounds, and was caught in 1982), buffalo (it weighed 50 pounds, and was caught in 1982), yellow perch (it weighed 1 pound, 11 ounces, and was caught in 1983), and crappie (it weighed 4 pounds, 8 ounces, and was caught in 1974) were all taken here. The popular largemouth bass is generally regarded as this lake's most noteworthy sport fishery, however.

Few lakes anywhere produce better bass fishing than this old TVA impoundment. There are several reasons for this. One is the great abundance of cover, such as stump beds and milfoil. Another is the large forage base of small, shoreline-oriented fish, like perch or bream. Excellent fertility aids the baitfish's growth, and the milfoil concentrates them near the grass. The fact that this lake has very stable water levels helps ensure maximum annual spawning success. A final reason is that this is a very large lake that isn't fished to death. The bass here have time to grow up and become lunkers.

Cold-weather bassin' on Guntersville is perhaps the finest in the TVA system. The mouths of feeder creeks are the traditional icy-weather bigmouth hangouts, although fishing is astonishingly brisk along the discharge canal areas and downstream below the lake's coal and nuclear plants when these operations are generating electricity.

At Guntersville, milfoil is year-round bass-holding cover, even though it "browns out" and trims back during cold weather. Places where milfoil borders a feeder creek are always worth a cast or two with a 6-inch plastic worm or ¼-ounce spinnerbait. Worked deep alongside grass or creek drop-offs, these baits are lethal during the winter. Prime locations for winter largemouth bass action include Browns Creek, the Town Creek–Bellefonte Island area, Short and Crow creeks, and the river downstream from the Widows Creek Steam Plant.

Spring bigmouth action gets underway in March, but April is regarded as the number-one month for shoulder-wrenching action. Bedding activity draws the hawgs in close to the shoreline. The trick then is to work spinnerbaits or big minnows in alongside the lake bank. These bass nest in depths of three to seven feet, but because the nests are protected by a maze of snags and obstacles, such as grass, stump beds and pier pilings, heavy line in the 12-to-20-pound-test class is recommended. Spawning activity is concentrated between the Browns Creek and Raccoon Creek embayments. Buzzbaits and weedless spoons are ideal for this time of the year.

Following the spawn the bass disperse along the shoreline, where breaks in the milfoil offer good vantage points for ambushes. This is an excellent time for even first-time visitors to this lake to catch hawgs, and lots of them. Job number one is locating your quarry. There's a lot of milfoil on Guntersville Lake following the spring bloom. The trick is to find a weed bed that borders the drop along a creek meander or where there's an abrupt shift in bottom contour. Many times this is precisely the structure that an ole bucketmouth finds most appealing.

Plastic worms rigged to run weedless are cast alongside the weeds and bounced back. The results can be awesome. Excellent hot-weather fishing along the grass is available in the Siebold, North and South Sauty, and Roseberry creek embayments and at the mouth of Browns Creek.

Autumn bassin' is exceptionally good at Guntersville, particularly from late October through mid-November. The advent of cool weather brings these fish closer to the surface, as well as nearer to the main river channel. Buzzbaits and crankbaits are standard fall-season bass offerings. Work buzzbaits right over the grass and rip crankbaits along the edge of weed beds.

Spotted and smallmouth bass are also found in Guntersville Lake. Spot fishing is quite good in the lake's upper reaches from the Nickajack tailwaters downstream to Scottsboro. They follow seasonal patterns similar to those of the lake's largemouth bass. Smallies, which can be found throughout the lake, are not fished for as they are at Wheeler, nor are they considered a significant fishery. On the other hand, small-mouth bass numbers and catch reports appear to be on the increase.

Guntersville enjoys a reputation as an outstanding bream fishery. Most sunfish species are represented here, but bluegill and redear sunfish are dominant. Beginning in April and through late May the bluegill bed in backwater coves, feeder creek embayments and shallow, clean-bottomed areas along the mainstream. These fish are large, often reaching the one-pound mark, and at this time heavy stringers are the rule.

Later in July, when the willowflies hatch, these fish can be caught in great numbers all up and down the lake. Fly rodding with popping bugs is the favorite method, but live crickets or red worms fished a foot deep under a bobber are also effective.

For shellcracker fans Guntersville is the best-known, most heavily utilized redear sunfish lake in the TVA system. These fish spawn at about the same time that the bluegill nest. Redear prefer to spawn in back of the sandy creek embayments, such as Big Spring, South Sauty, Jones and Town creeks. Bottom-fished crickets or red wigglers are lethal spring through fall offerings. Following the spawn these fish are taken in good numbers during the willowfly hatches and then later on bait fished three to six feet deep along the shoreline.

Crappie are plentiful and large at Guntersville. Slabside anglers love this lake because it is rich in easily found stump beds, old bridge pilings, private docks, and other crappie-attracting cover. These fish are caught year-round here.

Winter catches are made in the major embayments and along the main river channel, where these fish are taken on minnows, jigs and grubs off of the edge of 12-to-30-foot-deep creek meanders and channel edges.

Spring crappie action arrives early at Guntersville Lake. Excellent prespawn action can be counted on to occur by early March, and nesting usually takes place by early April, lasting until the end of that month. Large stump beds like those at Roseberry, Town, Siebold and Big Spring creeks or along the south shoreline of the main river channel between Romans Light and Chisenhall Cemetery provide fast-paced crappie action at 3-to-6-foot depths. Cane pole fishing using live minnows along these areas and newly flooded bushes is the favorite local technique.

Following the spawn these fish scatter, but they still offer good fishing. Locating deep stump beds or old building foundations along the main river channel or a big tributary can lead to good hot-weather action with jigs or minnows. Nighttime fishing under a suspended lantern is effective in the vicinity of the dam and other areas.

Winter sauger action at Guntersville is not as highly touted as it is at Wheeler and Pickwick lakes, but it can be red hot when everything comes together. Most of the sauger caught here weigh two pounds or less, but larger fish up to four pounds are sometimes taken. In early December these fish concentrate below Nickajack Dam in the lake's headwaters, as well as in the Guntersville Dam tailrace. Good catches are made from right against the dam to up to ten miles downstream. Minnows or hair flies jigged along rip-rap, bridge pilings, the edge of eddies and other swift areas is the favorite ploy, although trolling slowly against the current often produces when all else fails.

This sort of angling prevails through March, usually topping out between mid-January and late February. Following upstream spawning, these fish scatter throughout the lake. In the warm-weather months they occupy 12-to-25-foot depths. Catches during this time are likely to be sporadic. Until recently these fish were ignored during hot weather, but the advent of modern electronic depth-finding equipment has made them more available on an on-going basis to trollers.

Catfish grow fat and sassy in this food-rich lake. All species are represented here, although channel, flathead and blue catfish are the most sought after family members. During the winter months these fish move about the lake in relatively large but generally incoherent schools. The main channel holds the greatest concentrations of whiskered fish, and the general movement is toward the headwaters. Cold weather is ideal for making good trotline catches between Raccoon Creek and the upper end of Long Island. Naturally, the dam tailwaters and the discharge canals of the power plants are also good. In fact these areas are year-round catfish hot spots. Shad, cut shad and chicken hearts are favorite winter catfish baits.

Channel and flathead catfish move into the shallow flats at about the same time as crappie. Jug fishing is an effective way to stock up on these fish when they're feeding in shallow backwater areas. Stinkbaits and shad are great spring and early summer baits. Spawning occurs in July and August. Cats generally choose backwater areas for reproduction, but the rocky crevices provided by the rip-rap around the back side of the dam and around virtually every highway bridge piling are hot spots for twilight action.

White bass are common to Guntersville Lake, but because this lake offers better fishing for higher quality fish, stripe are overlooked by most anglers. Winter action concentrates in the headwaters and at the lake's three thermal plants, where good catches are reported on small crankbaits, spinners and minnows. Later in April these fish begin moving downstream back into the lake, where they school up and feed on shad in open water and large coves.

Yellow perch is a non-native species which entered the lake via downstream migration from TVA's mountain lakes in northern Georgia. Most perch catches weigh under a half pound, but larger fish have become more common in recent years. Most yellow perch are caught in 10-to-20-foot-deep water off rocky points during cold weather. Crappie jigging techniques are the best bets for prospective perch chasers.

Pickerel also occur here in small numbers. Most often, they are taken by bass or crappie fishermen while fishing in the headwaters of grass-choked feeder streams. Striped bass were once stocked in this lake by the state of Alabama, but this program was abandoned when it was determined that hot weather often fatally stressed these fish. A few stripers are caught here still, however, as well as white bass–striped bass hybrids which are stocked rather intensively at downstream Wheeler and Wilson lakes.

Nickajack Lake

SIZE: medium
ACCESSIBILITY: excellent
LOCATION: Tennessee (Hamilton and Marion counties)
PRESSURE: moderate to heavy
PRIMARY GAMEFISH: crappie, bluegill, largemouth and smallmouth
   bass, catfish
SECONDARY GAMEFISH: white bass, sauger
BEST MONTHS: April, May, June, July, October
BEST BAITS: live minnows, crickets, hair jigs, deep-diving crankbaits,
   spinnerbaits, buzzbaits
BEST BET: night bass fishing with buzzbaits in June, and tailwater
   catfish below Chickamauga Dam in August

Nickajack Lake begins in the heart of Chattanooga, Tennessee. Early
settlers passing downstream to the Ohio and onward to New Orleans
made this site a commercial center of the early western frontier. One
thing which made Chattanooga a popular stopping spot was the treach-
erous water downstream. Here the river knifed between towering ridges,
such as Little Cedar, Lookout and Raccoon mountains and Walden Ridge.
Dangerous river stretches and obstacles starting at Lookout Shoals along
Moccasin Bend and continuing to the Narrow "Pan" accounted for 15
miles of potentially hazardous navigation. Today the "Pot," "Pan,"
"Skillet," "Suck Shoals," "The Suck," "Tumbling" and "Lookout" shoals
are all beneath the surface of Nickajack Lake.

   Chattanooga was the gateway to Atlanta, the heart of the Confed-
eracy. Three major Civil War battles—Lookout Mountain, Missionary
Ridge and Chickamauga—were fought nearby. Today this modern city
of 180,000 features Civil War museums and national military parks, as

The Nickajack tailwaters are an outstanding, year-round, catfish hot spot.

well as natural attractions such as Ruby Falls and Rock City atop Lookout Mountain.

During the autumn Chattanooga's Annual Fall Color Cruise takes visitors down Nickajack Lake through the famous "Grand Canyon of Tennessee," which is located between Lookout and Little Cedar mountains. Along this unique 30-mile river route the lakeside terrain is so steep that human encroachment has hardly disturbed its natural beauty. It rates as one of the most varied hardwood forests in the United States, and when the autumn foliage is in full splendor, the fall colors lick the lake like flames.

Nickajack Dam stands 81 feet high and is 3,767 feet across. Built for navigation, power production, flood control and water storage, the dam was started in 1964 and finished in 1967, at a cost of $71 million. It replaced the old Hale's Bar Dam, which was six miles upstream. At full pool Nickajack stands at 635 feet above sea level, and it covers 10,370 surface acres. There is a maximum three-foot late autumn drawdown. The lake begins at Chickamauga Dam and extends 46 miles downstream with 192 miles of shoreline.

Chattanooga and its sprawling suburbs are the nearest towns. The headwaters are located in Hamilton County, while downstream from "The Suck" the lake is in Marion County. US 41 (64 and 72) accesses much of the lake from where it crosses at the old Hale's Bar Dam site along the lake's southern edge to the highway's starting point. TN 27 crosses near river mile 464 and US 127 travels alongside (or close to) portions of the upper reaches of the northern shoreline.

There are four commercial docks and ten public boat-launch ramps. Camping is available at the Nickajack Dam Reservation and Running Water Recreation Area. Day-use areas include the Maple View Recreation Area, Marion County Park, Ross's Landing and the various components of the Chickamauga and Chattanooga National Military Park. Maclellan Island, located near the Walnut Street Bridge in Chattanooga, is the home of the Audubon Society Wildlife Refuge. Prentice Cooper State Forest (and WMA) fronts Nickajack on the north from Middle Creek 19 miles to the Bennett Lake area.

Nickajack Cave near the Maple View Recreation Area is a huge underground tunnel of considerable historical and natural importance. During the summer it is the maternity cave for one of the region's gray bat colonies, and on summer evenings over 100,000 members of this endangered species leave the cave on nocturnal forays. It's a sight well worth viewing, but one which must be seen at a distance to protect these creatures.

Nickajack is more like two lakes than one. From Chickamauga Dam downstream to Mullins Cove, a distance of 35 miles, it is a typical, narrow-river-type impoundment, characterized by eddies, steep river channel drop-offs and scant cover aside from bluffs, points and rocks. Below Mullins Cove shallow weed-choked coves, deep water and abundant structure in the form of brush piles, rock piles and treetops are common. The bottom strata are rock, gravel, sand, and clay.

Fishing Information

Nickajack is best known as a first-class crappie-producing lake. Each year tons of white crappie are caught here. This is a fertile lake, rich in the threadfin shad that slabsides feed on. Winter crappie fishing can be incredible here. Locate a creek mouth, slough or other depressed area in 15-to-25-foot-deep water near the main river channel and you're probably in business. The southern shoreline near the dam or Brendalene Slough between I-24 and US 41 are custom-made cold-weather starting points. These areas offer good catches of big 1½-to-2-pound crappie well into April, when spawning patterns change this quarry's movement habits.

Bedding action always draws a crowd at Nickajack. The locations noted above are always productive, but so are Rankin and Mullins coves and the Bennett Lake area. Just about anywhere brush can be marked, good fishing is available in 2-to-6-foot-deep water. Minnows are the year-round favorite here, followed by grubs and feather jigs in green, white, yellow and blue.

Postspawn action gets better marks here than on most Volunteer State lakes. At this time crappie concentrate in the lake's lower reaches downstream from the gorge area. Key areas again include Rankin and Mullins coves and Bennett Lake, as well as Hale's Bar. The common denominator is an abundance of milfoil, which holds large amounts of crappie food. Anglers should concentrate their efforts along edges and pockets in these weeds. Still later, good slabside catches can be made around the old Hale's Bar Dam area and the numerous mid-lake rock piles. Deep trolling 18 to 20 feet is effective, as is bottom bouncing minnows with the sinker beneath a dual bait rig.

Largemouth and smallmouth bass populate Nickajack. Largemouth are the most popular species, although it could easily be argued that the smallies are the most rewarding. Bigmouth bass are abundant in this medium-size reservoir, and they grow large feeding on the threadfin shad. Hawgs in the six-to-seven-pound class are not uncommon.

Winter and spring are synonomous with pig'n'jig fishing on this lake. A rubber-legged quarter-ounce jig tipped with a chunk of soft pork is the equivalent of a ticket to a prize fight. During late winter and early spring the green bass are 10 to 18 feet deep (or deeper) in rock cover. Concentrate your efforts downstream from Mullins Cove. When the right combination of cover and water depths is found, stick with it. Slowly work it, back and forth, up and down, side to side, and if that doesn't work, then slow down more and do it again.

Mid-April finds the bigmouths moving back into coves into much shallower water. Spinnerbaits are ideal at this time, as are jigs flipped around brush and treetops. Postspawn action rates high in the time preceding the milfoil bloom. Fishing along the edges of weed beds produces good catches of big fish well into June. Willowfly hatches dominate early summer bass-fishing activity. Fly rodders using big flies during the late afternoon and evening hours can have a ball. Night fishing along rip-rap, over rock piles and along sloping points and weed beds rates high during the summer. Worms are first-class producers, but the reliable pig'n'jig combo is tops. Probed slowly along fish-holding structure in 10-to-20-foot depths, this venerable bait is murder on Nickajack's crackerjack bass. Good late-autumn largemouth bass fishing, in splendid surroundings, is a local tradition. Crankbaits or spinnerbaits pulled and ripped alongside weed beds work well following the arrival of cool weather. Point fishing with live bait is also productive.

Nickajack is not a household word among avid smallmouth bass anglers. Much of the lake doesn't offer quality smallie opportunities, but

Nickajack Lake has an underrated crappie fishery that is better than most anglers acknowledge.

some areas do. Good-to-excellent year-round bronzeback fishing is available downstream from Chickamauga Dam to the far side of Moccasin Bend. Turbine activity is conducive to good catches. Live minnows or spring lizards, jigs, beetle spins and deep-running shad crankbaits are tried-and-true local favorites. Dock and bridge pilings, rock piles, points and other areas that break the current are always worth a couple of casts.

From mid-June to December good smallie fishing can be found on sloping points downstream from Moccasin Bend to the end of the "canyon." During the hot-weather months fish at night using live bait or jigs. Smallmouth bass holding depths vary with the moon phases and generation; they can be anywhere between 3 and 20 feet. Between late October and Christmas daytime fishing using 1-to-2-inch grey, green or black grubs in the same areas is often productive.

Nickajack's headwaters and tailwaters are catfish factories. Big blue and flathead catfish prowl the turbulent boils there. Fish in excess of

40 pounds are not unusual for these two cousins, while channel cats up to 10 to 15 pounds are abundant. Catfish also inhabit other areas of the lake.

Although there is some winter catfish angling, the prime season begins in April and ends after the first frost. When fishing a riverine area, use a depth finder and try to locate holes in fast water. Big whiskered fish will lay in a depression where they can wax fat on injured shad. Trotline and jug fishing are popular and productive in the Bennett Lake, Mullins Cove and old Hale's Bar Dam areas, as well as near the dam. The rule of thumb is the hotter and darker it is, the better action there will be at Nickajack.

Like most of the mid-range mainstream impoundments, this lake is a prime producer of bluegill and shellcrackers.

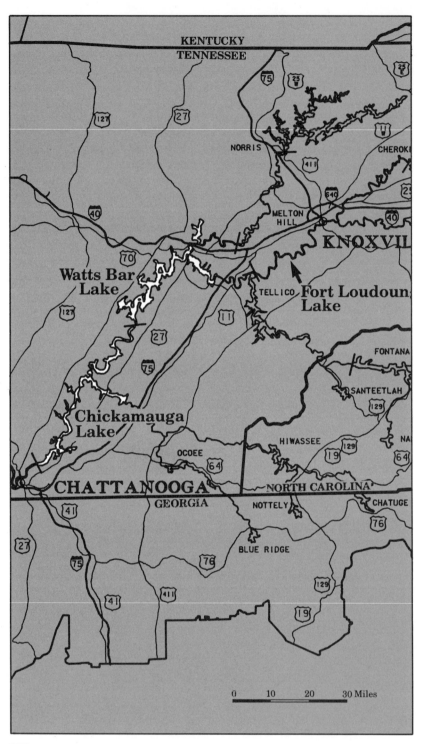

Chickamauga Lake

SIZE: large
ACCESSIBILITY: good
LOCATION: Tennessee (Hamilton, Rhea, and Meigs counties)
PRESSURE: moderate
PRIMARY GAMEFISH: bluegill, largemouth bass, crappie, catfish
SECONDARY GAMEFISH: white bass, sauger, striped bass, redear
    sunfish, smallmouth bass
BEST MONTHS: March, April, May, June, October
BEST BAITS: live minnows, jigs, popping bugs, crickets, grubs,
    buzzbaits, spinnerbaits
BEST BET: largemouth bass fishing with crankbait and spinnerbait
    over the grass beds in March

Chickamauga Lake is the seventh of nine Tennessee River impoundments under the domain of the Tennessee Valley Authority. It is a large,
diverse lake which, despite its age, offers excellent fishing for largemouth
and smallmouth bass, catfish, shellcrackers, white bass and crappie.

Chickamauga Dam is located in the heart of Chattanooga. Construction on the dam began in 1936 and was completed in 1940. It stands
129 feet high, and it's the fourth widest concrete structure in the TVA
system, topping 5,800 feet across. The lake extends 59 miles from end
to end and is navigable for barge traffic along its entire length. Its elevation at the top of the dam is 685 feet above sea level, and at minimum
pool it drops to 675 feet. At full pool, Chickamauga Lake covers 35,000
surface acres, with over 800 miles of shoreline and a maximum width
of 1.7 miles.

Hamilton County borders Chickamauga's southern end, while Rhea
County bounds its upper area to the west and Meigs County to the east.

Chickamauga Dam is the focal point of much serious fishing in the Chattanooga area. TVA photo.

Chattanooga, Soddy-Daisy and Dayton are the nearest towns. TN 58 traces along the lake's eastern edge, while US 27 follows along the western shoreline. I-75 crosses the Hiwassee River embayment at river mile 15. White Oak Mountain and McMinn Ridge rise to the lake's east, while Walden Ridge provides the scenery to the west. Many rate Chickamauga the most scenic mainstream lake in Tennessee.

A valley lake, Chickamauga is flanked by a mixture of timbered ridges and rolling farmland. It is a large, winding, generally scenic lake with sufficient open water to attract a small but growing flotilla of sailboats.

Two state parks that offer camping flank the lake: Harrison Bay and Booker T. Washington, both in Hamilton County. Harrison Bay State Park rates among the state's most highly developed public recreational facilities. Its full-service marina offers boat rentals and other angling and pleasure boating amenities. Its restaurant offers excellent dining for those enjoying the swimming pool or lake-front beach. Booker T. Washington State Park also offers a swimming beach and camping.

Beaches are also located at the Chickamauga Dam Reservation and Chester Frost County Park in Hamilton County. There are also two city parks on Chickamauga Lake: Soddy Municipal Park near Soddy-Daisy and Dayton Municipal Park in Rhea County. TVA maintains seven recreation areas around the lake. These are Agency Creek and Armstrong Ferry in Meigs County and Grasshopper Creek, Skull Island, Sale Creek, Chickamauga Dam Reservation and Possum Creek in Hamilton County. All except the dam area offer camping. There are fifteen commercial boat docks and over two dozen public boat-launch ramps around the lake.

The Tennessee Wildlife Resources Agency administers seven "wildlife management areas," or WMAs, at Chickamauga Lake. These are generally small and are managed primarily for waterfowl and small game, although deer hunting is permitted. They are located at the mouth of the Soddy Creek embayment, the headwaters of the Sale Creek embayment, the mouth of the Blythe Creek embayment, between Richland Creek and upstream toward Gillespie Bend, the Cotton Port WMA, which is located near the mouth of the Crawford Branch embayment, the Washington Ferry WMA on the outside of Hunter Bend, the Bush Creek WMA near Watts Bar Nuclear Plant, and the Goodfield WMA along the Goodfield Creek embayment.

The Hiwassee River embayment hosts its own massive concentration of WMAs, as well as the Blythe Ferry Goose Management Area. WMAs are located in the headwaters of the South Mouse Creek embayment, along the headwaters of Candies Creek, the Ledford Island area and the Rogers, Sugar and Agency creek embayments. The Hiwassee Wildlife Refuge is located between Gunstocker Creek and Hiwassee Island.

This is an incredibly diverse lake; it includes a little bit of everything from big lake environs to riverine settings. There are bluffs and rock points, the latter becoming more common as soil erodes from the surrounding hillsides, particularly upstream from the Hiwassee River arm. Under the surface, the foundations of old houses, barns and other buildings are common along this once-peopled area. Oh, many of these are still inhabited, but by catfish and bass!

Before Chickamauga Lake flooded the surrounding countryside, this area was known as prime bottomland farm country. Therein lies the key to understanding the lake's bottom contour and present-day structure. Like a typical river farm, which has long flat fields extending to the river's edge, broken only by ditch lines and winding creeks, so lies Chickamauga Lake's bottom. Where once fertile fields produced grain and tobacco, expansive mudflats and grassbeds are now found.

All standing timber was stripped from the lake area prior to flooding. Stump beds over 15 feet deep are still relatively common, since they only rarely have contact with the air. Eurasian milfoil has become an important factor in fishing success at Chickamauga. Shallow flats which remain flooded year-round are ideal habitat for this adaptable aquatic weed. Its presence has added a new, sometimes exciting and at other times troublesome dimension to fishing here.

Fishing Information

First and foremost, Chickamauga is a largemouth bass lake. It is rated as one of the top bass lakes in the Southeast, a prime reason the 1986 BASS Masters Classic was held here. The lake has a rich forage base, which in turn supports a heavy population of lunker-class hawgs, although in this balanced lake all three major black bass species are well represented. Tennessee's record 5 pound, 4 ounce Kentucky, or spotted, bass was caught here in 1976.

Bassin's a year-round sport at Chickamauga, and always rating good to great. Winter bass hunters must dress warmly and fish slow and deep, but the rewards are sometimes the season's biggest hawgs and smalljaws. Weed beds, creek meanders and old building foundations are preferred holding zones for largemouth bass during cold weather. The lower portion of the Hiwassee River embayment, the Savannah Bay area and the Possum and Sale creek embayments are well-known wintertime largemouth lairs.

The discharge canal area of the Sequoyah Nuclear Plant when warm-water releases are underway or have recently occurred is another area which produces excellent winter bass angling. Spinnerbaits or shallow-to-medium-depth-running crankbaits worked along grass or shoreline are lethal. Should the Watts Bar nuclear facility ever get approval to operate, similar fishing should exist there.

Largemouth bass remain shallow and generally accessible as long as the weather holds sunny and mild, but the passing of a cold front often sends the fish to deeper water. This sort of back and forth movement continues well into April when a solid shallow-water pattern emerges. At this time try fishing feeder creek headwater areas with a little color. And whatever you do, do it s-l-o-w-l-y.

Prior to the spawn Chickamauga's largemouth bass concentrate along rip-rap, old railroad and highway beds, the edges of grass beds, man-made fish attractors and 4-to-10-foot-deep stump beds. Fishermen use a wide gamut of baits, lures and techniques to undo hawgs at this time, but plastic worms in purple, blue and black are usually deadly. When these fish are active, worms can be swum gingerly through the water. When this quarry is sluggish or being stubborn, a methodical, very slow lift and drop retrieval works.

One of the best, but least-known local tricks for taking prespawn and bedding bass starts with motoring as far as possible into a dense weed bed, then poling your way on. The object of all of this trouble is the sometimes difficult to find washtub-size openings in the milfoil. Big bass lurk in these "skylight" ambush spots. The trick is to cast a big live minnow, spinner or buzzbait into the hole. Some fishermen toss only jigs or pig'n'jig combos. Jigs, with or without pork rind dressings, are without question one of the finest baits ever used here. It's not always easy to maneuver a ¼-ounce jig through thick milfoil, but the payoff can be a hawg in the 8-to-9-pound class.

During bedding time, few ploys out-produce flipping brown-brown or black-black pig'n'jigs. Chickamauga Lake has a good reputation as a good late spring top-water lake. Surface lures like Skipjacks, Jitterbugs and Rebel Floater Minnows are all good choices. Topside action stays good well into June and later with the advent of the willowfly hatch.

As at most East Tennessee lakes, at Chickamauga a large portion of the serious summer bassin' occurs at night. Plastic worms, jigs and deep-running crankbaits in chartreuse, purple, black, and sometimes blue are effective. Prime hot-weather night fishing is available along the old Tennessee River channel. Excellent late summer and early autumn largemouth action remains in or around the milfoil beds, although backwater areas such as Savannah Bay in the Wolftever Creek embayment, Dallas Bay and the Soddy Creek and Possum Creek embayments are always consistent medium-depth bass producers.

The lake turns over fast in late October, and fish get shallow very fast. Fishing spinnerbaits along the edges of points and weed beds often produces outstanding results well into December.

Smallmouth bass fishing does not get a great deal of attention in a lake known best for its weed bed fishing for bucketmouth bass. Still, these fish can be found throughout Chickamauga Lake, with the best fishing being upstream from the Hiwassee River embayment. The lake's Kentucky bass often share habitat zones with their smallie cousins, although the spots move among largemouth bass too.

Long-lining big minnows deep along rocky points is the number-one trick for winter smallmouth bass fun. Bronzebacks congregate here to ambush passing baitfish, as well as to forage for crawfish. Brown-blue or black-blue rubber-legged jigs tipped with pork rind are a favorite cold-weather offering.

During late March and early April super yet overlooked smallie fishing explodes upstream from Dayton in the heads of the scores of "fingers" leading off of the main river channel. Big prespawn smallies station under trash in the backsides of these mini-backwater areas. Flippin' jigs is fine, but bouncing a spinnerbait off of the bank into the water, then working it slowly through the debris is even better.

Early May is mating time for the brown bass, and sloping rock or gravel points 5 to 15 feet deep are reasonable bets to provide action.

Mid to late May is the time for exciting top-water smalljaw fishing. Bagley's Bang-O-Lure, Rebel Floater Minnow and other similar surface baits are deadly when fished off rocky, main channel points. When the willowflies make their massive July emergence fly rodders also have their "surface surprise" days here with smallmouth bass. Popping bugs or large, No. 6 to No. 10 mayfly imitations are amazingly effective for coaxing a brawling bronzeback to the top.

Most hot-weather bronzeback action occurs at night. Point fishing upstream from the Hiwassee River is excellent using plastic worms, deep-running crankbaits and jigs. One exception to the summertime night fishing "rule" is the tailrace stretch downstream from Watts Bar Dam. Upstream electricity generation provides hot brown bass fishing along gravel shoreline areas and around old pilings. Jigs and live bait are good bets for this action.

The bluegill is one of Chickamauga Lake's stars, and it's always a crowd pleaser. This bream species, along with the spunky shellcracker, gives this impoundment a one-two combination when it comes to panfish. Bluegill and bluegill fishermen seem to emerge at the same time on this lake, usually just when the dogwood trees flower. Super live-bait fishing using crickets or redworms is available in almost any cove or hollow.

Chickamauga Lake holds one of the Volunteer State's best redear sunfish, or shellcracker, fisheries. These large-growing bream often approach the one-pound mark. They differ from bluegill in habitat preference and are more likely to be found along sandy bottoms where snails are available. Shellcrackers are most concentrated and available to anglers during the June and July spawning period. They school spawn throughout the lake in sandy backwater areas in four-to-eight-foot-deep water, although the Hiwassee River embayment between the Blythe Ferry Goose Management Area and Agency Creek is considered the best shellcracker bed fishing area.

During mid-July, Chickamauga Lake's sunfish come alive with the advent of the willowfly hatch. This period of aquatic insect abundance usually lasts two weeks, but foul weather can extend it. Bream relish these easy-to-seize, protein-rich morsels. A fly rod and popping bug are the only tickets you need when the evening curtain rises on this event. The west shoreline and northerly points of islands are the traditional spots for the best willowfly fishing. Late summer finds the bluegill scattered. Prime areas include edges and "holes" in milfoil beds and five to eight feet deep along main river channel bluffs and cliffs.

Chickamauga rates as one of eastern Tennessee's better whiskered fish fishing holes. All major species are well represented, and catches not only run big but also go high in sheer numbers. Winter catfishing is excellent, although unless you stay with it, it's not easy to keep track of the cat's wanderings around the main channel. Trotline fishermen do well to string across the mouths of coves and feeder stream embayments in hopes of waylaying a passing school.

Beginning in late March these fish become more common in back coves and embayments. Here and along bluff areas are the best catfishing until mid-June. At this time Mr. Whiskers seeks out shallow back-cove areas, although it's generally futile to vie with him until late in the evening or at night. Cut bait, chicken liver and blood baits are the best offers.

There is excellent year-round fishing in Chickamauga's headwaters. The boils below the turbines at Watts Bar Dam attract tons of big flathead, blue and channel catfish. Still fishing with the aid of heavy sinkers or drift fishing with the current are the recommended tactics for this area.

Watts Bar Lake

SIZE: large

ACCESSIBILITY: very good to good

LOCATION: Tennessee (Loudon, Roane, Rhea, and Meigs counties)

PRESSURE: moderate to light

PRIMARY GAMEFISH: crappie, bluegill, largemouth and smallmouth bass, catfish

SECONDARY GAMEFISH: white bass, sauger

BEST MONTHS: February, April, May, June, October

BEST BAITS: live minnows, crickets, hair jigs, deep-diving crankbaits, spinnerbaits

BEST BET: tightline jigging along the old river channel with live minnows for crappie in February, or casting jigs for sauger at the lake's headwaters below Loudoun Dam that same month

The Tennessee River Valley's lakes are the most diverse in the United States. Everything from gin-clear smallmouth lakes to cypress-lined, bayou-style bigmouth lakes can be found here. Which of the valley's more than three dozen lakes offers the best bass fishing? Well, what do you want? Smallmouth or bigmouth, or maybe spunky Kentucky bass? Name ya poison, or perhaps you might prefer a smorgasbord fishing hole where you can get it all!

Assuming most folks prefer a lively existence spiced with variety, the top choice is logical: Watts Bar Lake. Black bass galore, plus trophy stripers and hybrids, crappie, sauger and giant catfish. It's all here at the "Bar."

Watts Bar is the largest TVA impoundment in East Tennessee. Built to aid navigation and flood control and to generate power it cost $35 million in 1942. The dam stands 112 feet high and is 2,960 feet across. At full pool the lake level is 745 feet above sea level and covers 39,000

116

Downrigging for striped bass at Watts Bar Lake is growing in popularity.

surface acres. It extends 96 miles and boasts 771 miles of shoreline. Drawdown usually occurs in late fall when the lake level is lowered 7 to 10 feet to a minimum pool of 735 feet above sea level.

Watts Bar is located near Spring City, Rockwood, Kingston and Loudoun, in central eastern Tennessee. Its headwaters are bounded by Loudon County, its central portion by Roane County, and its southern shoreline by Rhea and Meigs counties. US 27 follows Watts Bar's western edge; TN 58 traces its eastern shoreline to Kingston. I-40 crosses at Kingston, and I-75 crosses at the lake's headwaters at river mile 585.

There are 18 commercial boat docks and over 60 public boat-launch ramps on this lake. Public camping is permitted at the Watts Bar Dam Reservation and TVA's Fooshee Pass, Hornsby Hollow and Riley Creek recreation areas. Day-use areas include Meigs and Roane county parks and Spring City, Rockwood Community and Southwest Point parks. There are several Tennessee Wildlife Resources Agency WMAs around the lake including Duck Island in the Piney River embayment, portions of Half Moon and Thief Neck islands, the Paint Rock and Long Island areas in the main stream between river miles 570 and 576 and at TVA's

Kingston Steam Plant at the junction of the Emory and Clinch rivers.

Along the river channel the shoreline is moderately steep, yet interspersed with cliffs and bluffs as well as gently sloping banks. The channel area's shoreline is primarily a mixture of rock and clay, ranging from predominantly large, boulder-type cover, to a mix of medium-size rock and clay, to clean clay, gravel and slate banks. A large percentage of shoreline extends along backwater coves, hollows and feeder streams. Prior to the creation of this large TVA reservoir, most of the property adjacent to the river was prime bottomland agricultural acreage. Much of old creek and river bottom areas are shallow flats. There is abundant cover here in the form of stump beds, dead falls, log jams, humps, weeds, brush and brush piles, treetops and logs.

Watts Bar Lake is one of only a handful of Tennessee River Valley impoundments where the aquatic weeds, particularly milfoil, are a significant cover factor in fishing technique. This hardy, fast-growing, colonizing plant is thought to have entered Watts Bar from Chickamauga Lake with help from heavy upstream barge traffic. Milfoil is a non-native exotic from Asia that flourishes here, making almost impenetrable growths. At milfoil's summertime height, it often chokes off entire coves to boaters who find the weed impossible to keep out of their propellers. While many folks curse milfoil as a bane, it also has its positive side. For fish like the black bass, it provides sorely needed cover. Bass are seldom found where they do not have some sort of structure to provide concealment from their enemies and prey.

Fishing Information

Where to start isn't a problem, because bass fishing is the current craze here. The lake holds sizable populations of all three bass species. Each group is plentiful and represented in well-distributed age classes. Smallies get big here, but the bigmouth is king. This is also one of Tennessee's better spotted bass fisheries.

The "Bar" is one of the best early season bassin' holes anywhere. Excellent hawg hunting is available in the headwaters of many of the feeder streams in the lake's last 30 miles and in the vicinity of the Kingston Steam Plant. Bass, often big ones, concentrate in creek meanders along drop-offs and stumps, particularly in Cane Creek (this area is locally referred to as "Blue Springs"). At the steam plant bass (and a number of other gamefish species) are attracted to the hot-water discharge area, where comfortable temperatures and food are plentiful. During late winter and early spring, spinnerbaits and plastic worms worked "dead slow" are effective.

April is without question Watts Bar's hottest green bass fishing time. Super shallow-water spinnerbait fishing can be found in the headwaters of a number of creek embayments. Cane and Whites creeks and the Piney River area are excellent at this time, especially when the water is clear.

During hot weather largemouth bass fishing is excellent in the lake's lower reaches off points and deep humps in the main channel and creeks in 10 to 15 feet of water. Jig and pork combos and plastic worms in brown, red and purple are excellent choices. There is a prolific willowfly hatch here in July. At this time, the best bigmouth fishing is around islands where stumps line the edge of deep water or where lakeside bushes grow along deep water. Autumn hawg-hunting season opens in late September and runs until early December. Crankbaits worked off points in major embayments are good, as are dark colored worms.

Watts Bar Lake has a well-deserved reputation as a bronzeback lunker hole. Big smallmouth bass are not unusual here. Late winter and early spring offer two-prong, high-low fishing. Deep feeder creek embayments near the dam, such as Piney River and Lowe Branch, are always good places to point set with live minnows or to jig green or black twistertail grubs. The next honeyhole is all the way up the lake to the steam plant, where super fishing in shallow water off sloping bars is available for jig and spinner fishermen.

Late spring spawning action concentrates the brown bass in tributaries upstream from Cotton Port to the Emory River. The sloping points in the headwaters of the Emory and Clinch rivers are always worth looking at (also try the Poplar Creek embayment in the Clinch River arm), as are the inlets, small islands and embayment areas around the Paint Rock WMA. Flippin' is a bonafide trick if the fish aren't over eight feet deep, while live crawfish or brown-purple jigs tipped brown with Uncle Josh 101 pork rind are good bets for deeper tightline fishing.

June is a prime time for day and night smalljaw bass fishing here. Fly hatches during July make top-water fishing great around rocky points near mud or sand flats. Some fishermen use 4-inch-long, $\frac{1}{8}$-to-$\frac{1}{4}$-ounce, icicle-colored grub and jig combos, swimming them through rocky 3-to-8-foot-deep water. Medium-depth crankbaits, like Model A Bombers, are also effective.

The best night fishing is when water is being drawn through Watts Bar Dam. At such times big bass station on main channel points to ambush forage fish. Jigs, grubs, worms and live bait are all effective. Autumn bassin' for brownies hits high gear in mid-October when the lake's timbered shoreline comes alive with blazes of red, yellow, purple, orange and gold. It's still a river channel game, but the fish are shallower, in 3 to 10 feet of water. Some fishermen stick to night fishing, while others do well during the daytime, with the added bonus of soaking in the warm fall sunshine.

Watts Bar Lake is presently enjoying enormous popularity as a star-studded crappie-fishing spot. Slabsides here grow large, and schools of three pounders are not uncommon. Catches run high, sometimes topping 300 calicos per day. Most of the time the lake's crappie are shallow enough that they can be caught by anyone. This has not always been the case, though. Watts Bar Lake's crappie are what fishery personnel call "cyclic," meaning their population ebbs and flows over long periods of time. There were times when these fish were far more scarce than they are at this writing, and it could happen again, although fishery management receives more attention now than even a decade ago.

Winter fishing for crappie at Watts Bar has a large cult following of warmly clad anglers. Beginning in December good catches are made along drop-offs in the old river channel between Thief Neck Island and the I-75 bridge, as well as in a number of major feeder streams. Then the slabs are 10 to 35 feet deep, and typical offerings include small $\frac{1}{16}$-to-$\frac{1}{8}$-ounce grubs, hair jigs and minnow rigs tightline fished. The days when the wind is not blowing you off of the ledge lines are the best.

Spring spawning action often begins in early April and can last well into May. Stump beds, brush and treetops are the primary slabside spawning areas. Fishing minnows 2 to 6 feet deep under bobbers is the most popular approach, followed by jigging grubs and trolling around coves and over points. Nighttime fishing for summer crappie with minnows under lantern lights is popular and productive on Watts Bar. Good fishing is available up and down the lake off points, in creek channels and over sunken brush.

During the winter and very early spring sauger is great fishing in the lake's headwaters below Fort Loudoun Dam, in the tailwaters below Watts Bar Dam and downstream from the discharge area at the steam plant. Sauger like to locate behind rocks, humps and pilings adjacent to the swift runs below these structure. Live minnows or hair flies cast out in the current and worked deep are best for taking these good eating fish. In late March the sauger move back downstream. Although the fish are plentiful, few at Watts Bar work the points and underwater structure preferred by sauger during the summer and fall.

White bass are another of Watts Bar's late winter–early spring headwater celebrities. Between January and late March, where sauger congregate, so do the stripe. Their preferred habitats are almost identical. Small spinners, jigs and live bait worked into pools and around bottom structure are deadly.

Good hot-weather stripe action is available throughout the lake when the fish surface feed, or "break." Small spinners or top-water baits are effective at this time.

Watts Bar is an excellent catfish hot spot. Year-round catches of

channel, flathead and blue catfish are made in the headwaters immediately downstream from Fort Loudoun Dam. Main channel trotline
fishing is effective from November through April. Trollers do well on
channel cats working over mudflats in April. Night fishing back coves
with bottom sets or jugs is productive throughout the hot-weather
months.

Bluegill are the most abundant sunfish in Watts Bar Lake. They
also achieve good size in this nutrient-rich impoundment. From April
through late May catches are most easily made by dabbling redworms
or crickets two to four feet beneath a bobber in quiet backwater areas.
Main channel bluffs and the mouths of feeder creeks provide the best
hot-weather 'gill catches. One notable exception occurs during the July
willowfly hatch, which concentrates these fish near shoreline greenery.

Fort Loudoun Lake

SIZE: medium

ACCESSIBILITY: excellent

LOCATION: Tennessee (Loudon, Blount, and Knox counties)

PRESSURE: heavy to moderate

PRIMARY GAMEFISH: bluegill, smallmouth and largemouth bass, crappie, catfish

SECONDARY GAMEFISH: white bass, sauger, striped bass, rainbow trout

BEST MONTHS: March, April, May, June, October

BEST BAITS: live minnows, jigs, smoke-colored grubs, deep-diving crankbaits, spinnerbaits, plastic worms

BEST BET: smallmouth bass fishing with crankbaits or plastic worms off of rocky main channel point in October

A portion of the headwaters of Fort Loudoun Lake ripple in the shadow of Knoxville and the University of Tennessee's Neyland Stadium, home of the Volunteer football team and the "Holy Place" for pilgrims of the "Orange Blood" sect. During the autumn when the Vols play at home the "Tennessee Navy" arrives by water to cheer the local boys on to victory. UT and Washington State University are the only college stadiums with "port facilities." The "Orange Armada," as it is also called, can number over 100 craft ranging from runabouts to 75-foot-long cruisers.

The lake was named in honor of a pre-Revolutionary War British outpost manned by South Carolina provincial troops to check French encroachment in the Tennessee River Valley. Built in 1756, it was named in honor of the colonial leader, the Earl of Loudoun. Four years after construction it was besieged by the Cherokee and forced to surrender. The terms granted by Oconostota and other Cherokee chiefs included safe passage back to South Carolina. Three days later, however, the garrison was ambushed near the junction of Cane Creek on the Tellico River; most of the troops were killed.

Fort Loudoun Lake impounds the Tennessee River which begins in the lake at the confluence of the French Broad and Holston rivers. The dam is a concrete structure that stands 122 feet high and is 4,190 feet across. A lock system permits access downstream to Watts Bar Lake. Dam construction began in 1940 and ended in 1943 at a cost of $41 million.

At full pool the level stands at an elevation of 815 feet above sea level and covers 14,600 acres. It snakes along riverlike for 61 miles with a total of 360 miles of shoreline. Fort Loudoun, a mainstream impoundment, has an annual autumn drawdown that is far less dramatic than that of most upstream tributary lakes. It averages only 6 to 8 feet (minimum pool level is 807 feet above sea level) and usually occurs in November.

Knox County borders the lake's northern shoreline to river mile 610. The southern shoreline to river mile 607 is located in Blount County, and Loudon County bounds the lower reaches and Fort Loudoun Dam. Knoxville and Lenoir City are the nearest towns. US 11E (and 70) parallels the lake's northern course, while TN 73 accesses much of the southern shoreline areas. TN 95 crosses the dam and accesses a small part of the western banks.

There are 10 commercial boat docks and 20 public boat-launch ramps. Camping is permitted at the Yarberry Peninsula Recreation Area, and Concord Park. Lakeside day-use areas include the Fort Loudoun Dam Reservation, Poland Creek Recreation Area and the Carl Cowan, Farragut, Lenoir City, Louisville Point, I.C. King, Blount County and Sequoyah parks.

Despite passing through Knoxville, most of the lake is free of urban shackles, although lakeside dwellings occupy much of the shoreline. Recent water quality improvements have allowed a noteworthy upswing in the fishery. Part of the credit goes to tougher water quality laws, but the creation of Tellico Lake and subsequent channeling of its flow into Fort Loudoun hiked the latter's water quality. Although the Tellico Dam project was a curse to the Little "T," its positive effect on Fort Loudoun has been acknowledged.

Typical of most Tennessee River impoundments, Fort Loudoun winds like a serpent through foothill surroundings. Almost every bend carries a name dating back to the era when barge traffic on the river was the region's lifeblood. It is a moderately shallow lake characterized by a pronounced river channel flanked by high bluffs, meandering creek embayments and shallow coves.

Fort Loudoun Lake, near the top of the "stairs" of the TVA system. TVA photo.

The lake bottom is composed of rock, gravel, sand and clay. There are numerous flats, as well as many steep rocky points and bends. There are few stick-ups, but at full pool hardy black willow trees are sometimes submerged. Stump beds can still be located, and grass has yet to become a significant factor.

Fishing Information

There is no question that Fort Loudoun rates among Tennessee's finest bronzeback fisheries. Smallmouth bass in the one-to-three-pound class are abundant, and five to six pounders are common. Abundant rocky point habitat and a good forage base combine to make this a smalljaw hot spot with a bright future.

Cold-weather bassing for this species gets better than average marks. Crawfish, a primary forage food, are remarkably abundant here during the biting cold days of late winter. Live crawfish fished deep in creek channels and off mainstream bluffs are ideal, but most use smoke, chartreuse and orange 1-to-3-inch jelly grubs or deep-diving crawfish crankbaits. Big bronzebacks actively nose around for crawdads where the bottom has a good mix of rock and clay. A good way to determine if a smallie has been rooting around for crawdads is to check the outside of its belly for red clay stains.

Smallmouth bass spawn slightly earlier here than in most upstream lakes, usually between mid-April and early May. Spawning occurs in water 5 to 15 feet deep off of sloping rock, clay or gravel points in primary embayments like Little River and Poland, Little Turkey, Sinking and Ish creeks. Spinnerbaits and plastic worms are standard offerings for hot bedding-time action, along with flipping jigs and live bait. Following the spawn, bronzebacks slowly trek from the creeks toward points in the main river channel. This move takes several weeks. The fish utilize a diverse variety of cover, such as sloping gravel beaches, the old road and railroad beds that traced along the river, bridge rip-rap and some of the tremendous number of private piers and docks.

Several good postspawn baits work well, but at least one well-known angler uses nothing but a chartreuse and black half-ounce spinnerbait with No. 6 copper blades. These are particularly effective "stair-cased" down rip-rap and points or fished horizontally over gravel or sand beaches and old rail and road beds. When bass fishing at Fort Loudoun Lake, never pass a pier or piling without ripping a spinnerbait past it.

June is a special time for taking smallies here. Top-water action off points and around bushes is first class. One reason is optimum surface temperatures, but perhaps more important is the lake's legendary willowfly hatches. These large, pale-colored adult mayflies spend most of their lives in a nymphal form burrowed in the lake bottom. Mass evening hatches are incredible sights. Literally millions of winged adults dot the lake's surface and nearby bushes.

Smallmouth bass (and most other fish, from bream to catfish) noisily slurp the surface for these abundant, protein-rich morsels. It's a fly rodder's smorgasbord. Popping bugs or large, light-colored dry flies such as a No. 10 Light Cahill or No. 8 Ginger Quill are not only highly effective but also a treat to fish.

For smallmouth bass fishermen, July through October is generally regarded as the "graveyard shift" season. Most serious angling for all species switches to the starlite time. Then the best brown bass fishing can be found off sloping bluffs and drop-offs and clay or rock points along the old river channel. Since the completion of Tellico Lake the injection of cool water has shifted the best hot-weather angling downstream. Try from the Choto Bend area all the way to the rip-rap around the dam. You won't be disappointed, although we may be when we catch you on our favorite spots. Jig'n'rind combos in brown, black and purple are preferred by the moonbeamers, although it's questionable whether pork puddin' really outperforms the venerable plastic worm.

Following the fast October turnover, autumn bass fishing at Fort

Loudoun is excellent. Daytime fishing is good using crankbaits like the "Firetiger" Model A Bomber along mainstream flats and rip-rap. (During October keep an eye out for "celebrating" boat captains returning from football games.)

Fort Loudoun's largemouth bass are "hamburger" for local fishermen. They grow big and fast here. Five pounders are common and seven-pound hawgs are not unusual. Fishing for largemouth here is excellent 12 months a year, something that the local boys do a remarkably good job of keeping under their hats. Largemouth follow winter movement patterns similar to those of the smallies. By March they've concentrated in feeder creeks and mudflats where "dingy" water is available. Praters Flats (shown on most maps as the Ish Creek) is an excellent winter and early spring site for live bait or ¼- and ⅜-ounce, dual-bladed spinnerbaits in white or yellow. Slow retrievals along drop-offs and stump beds can be awesomely effective. Fishing in the creek embayments holds until late May, when the green bass spawning peaks. Crankbaits and flippin' around stick-ups or debris work well. Following this time the fish fin out along points.

The summer willowfly hatch is also fly-flicking time for largemouth bass, but by July the bucketmouths have retreated to feeding during the dark hours. The best hot-weather bassin' is found where Tellico Lake joins Fort Loudoun. Docks and piers are vital twilight feeding spots for big bass. Most competitive anglers seeking largemouth bass use plastic worms in blue (with sparkles), red or wine.

Fort Loudoun rates as the best catfish lake in East Tennessee. A 130-pound blue cat was taken here in 1976. These fish are common in the lake and tailrace below the dam, often exceeding 50 pounds. Channel are the most abundant catfish species, followed by large-growing flathead or old-fashioned yellow cats. Catches of 50 pounds per fisherman are not uncommon.

Excellent winter catfish angling can be had deep along the lake's main river channel upstream from Concord to the mouth of the Little River. Dangerous PCB pollution in the Little River embayment makes eating bottom feeders like catfish a potential health hazard. During spring and winter live baits like shad or worms or organic baits like chicken liver are good, although during mild weather flies are remarkably productive. Catfish respond to warming weather by fanning out in creek embayments, flats and coves, moving in 5-to-10-foot-deep water. Summertime night fishing in back coves, along the river channel and in the tailrace is super. During hot weather, live baits or stinkbaits are preferred.

One of the lake's most popular gamefish is the crowd-pleasing white bass. If ever a fish came off of the drawing board solely for the purpose of curing late-winter cabin fever, the stripe is it. In late February, Fort

Fort Loudoun Dam (built 1940–1943), farthest upstream of all main river TVA dams, brings the navigation channel to Knoxville, 45 miles distant. Fort Loudoun is 122 feet high, 4,190 feet long, and its lake covers 14,600 acres. Its powerhouse has an installed generating capacity of 135,590 kw in four units. TVA photo.

Loudoun's whites make their spring run up the French Broad and Holston river arms. Using white, red or yellow flies or light spinners, anglers will discover fast action in the area around the forks of the river. By late March the whites are back in the lake, where they can be caught surface feeding in many nondescript locations. Some night fishing for stripe is practiced in the Concord and Prater Flats areas.

Fort Loudoun's crappie fishing is overshadowed by that of nearby Watts Bar and Douglas lakes. But make no mistake, the calicos here are plentiful and easily caught. During cold weather, catches of 10 to 25 fish per day can be made near the Concord, Poland Creek and Praters Flats areas. At this time the fish are 15 to 20 feet deep and will take minnows or smoke-colored grubs.

Spring movement into shallower water occurs in early March. When mild weather holds for a couple of days and the lake's level is steady, torrid fishing in 3 to 8 feet of water around scrubs and dock pilings is available. In the early spring, trolling is particularly effective, as is jigging structure. Spawning occurs in April, but can be postponed well into May by weather and water conditions.

During the summer the calicos move into considerably deeper water off sloping main channel and feeder stream points. Minnows are the most popular bait then for still fishing over located fish. Local fishermen sometimes take old-fashioned Bomber or Mud Dog plugs, remove the hooks and troll this deep-running rig trailing flies tipped with minnows. Diving planes and downriggers are also effective, but not seen on this shallow lake as often as they are at Norris and Watauga lakes. These ploys are productive until October, when the action moves for a short period to the shallow-water flats.

Bream fishing is well established at this mainstream lake. Bluegill are the mainstay, but redear sunfish are also common. Spring finds the bream spawning in shallow back coves with gravel or sandy bottoms. Live bait or small, $\frac{1}{16}$-to-$\frac{1}{32}$-ounce jigs fished deep through bream nests are effective. Hot-weather action along Talliaferro, Choto and Parks bends is good using bait or fly-flicking bugs and wet flies.

Sauger fishing in the lake is good at times; in the dam's tailrace it rates among the best anywhere. The state record walleye-sauger hybrid, a 9-pound, 15-ounce lunker, was taken in the Fort Loudoun tailrace in 1983. It wasn't a stocked crossbreed but a natural mix.

Rattlesnake fish occupy Fort Loudoun's headwaters and tailwaters from January through March and can be caught by trolling or riffle casting $\frac{1}{4}$-ounce orange, green or yellow jigs. Good fishing often extends from the forks of the river upstream in the French Broad River arm to Douglas Dam. The same techniques, as well as live minnows, provide good action well into April below Fort Loudoun Dam.

During the summer these nomadic perch scatter like bats, although a few are always taken below the dam using the above-mentioned baits and ploys. Lake fishermen trolling for crappie or white bass occasionally encounter these wanderers.

Fort Loudoun holds a few surprise fish which by all rights shouldn't be finning around there. During the winter rainbow trout from Tellico Lake wander through the connecting canal into forage-rich Fort Loudoun. This seasonal sojourn occurs while the latter is cool, in the 40-to-55-degree range. Minnow-type crankbaits trolled or cast along the shoreline between the canal and the dam are the best offerings.

Striped bass and white bass–striped bass hybrids also ply Fort Loudoun Lake, although at this time neither is stocked. Downstream lakes Melton Hill and Watts Bar and upstream Cherokee Lake receive these non-natives, however. The lock system permits upstream migration, and smaller fish are sometimes washed through the Cherokee Dam turbines. During the summer, sporadic lineside fishing occurs in the headwaters near Strawberry Plains. Excellent lineside fishing is always available during the fall, winter and spring in the Fort Loudoun Dam tailrace.

In 1982 what would have been an all-tackle world record hybrid was caught in the headwaters of Fort Loudoun in the Holston River by Arthur Steel of Morristown. When caught, it weighed over 20 pounds, but unfortunately it was misidentified as a "pure" striper and Steel placed it in his freezer. Months later at a local taxidermy studio it was correctly identified as a hybrid, but it was too late to claim even a new state record at its reduced "freeze-dried" weight of 19 pounds, 12 ounces.

PART THREE

Tributary Impoundments

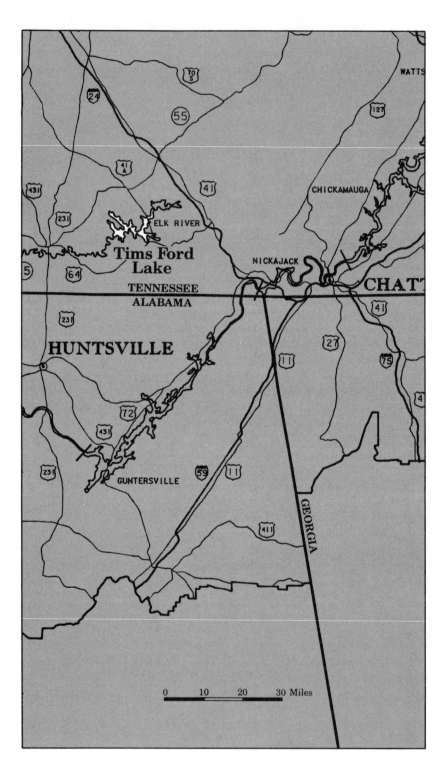

Tims Ford Lake

SIZE: medium

ACCESSIBILITY: very good

LOCATION: Tennessee (Moore and Franklin counties)

PRESSURE: moderate

PRIMARY GAMEFISH: largemouth and smallmouth bass, bluegill, striped bass, catfish

SECONDARY GAMEFISH: walleye, crappie, white bass

BEST MONTHS: March, April, May, June, October, November

BEST BAITS: live shad and minnows, deep-diving crankbaits, chicken liver, cut bait, plastic worms, pig'n'jig

BEST BET: fishing for striped bass using big top-water baits in May

Tims Ford is an off-the-beaten-path lake which receives only about a quarter of the recognition it deserves. This honey's biggest fans aren't complaining one bit, though. In fact, they would prefer that the sport fishery in Tims Ford Lake remain a well-kept secret.

Tims Ford is located on the southern edge of the Cumberland Plateau near Tullahoma and Winchester, in the heart of the Tennessee sippin' whiskey–making belt. The scenery in the surrounding countryside is second to none. Moore and Franklin counties front on the lake; the latter almost encircles this 10,600-acre impoundment.

Tims Ford Lake is formed by the impoundment of the Elk River, a clean, medium-sized flow. The dam, which was built in 1970, stands 175 feet high and is 1,484 feet across. The Elk River tailrace boasts a well-known rainbow trout fishery. The lake's winding, jagged shoreline totals 246 miles and stretches 34 miles to the headwaters. Tims Ford is classified as a storage-type impoundment and is subject to autumn drawdowns of up to 30 feet from full pool.

Tims Ford is a typical Cumberland Plateau lake in all respects other than the fact that it is not part of the Cumberland River drainage. The

Elk River flows southward into the Tennessee River at Wheeler Lake near Athens, Alabama.

Tims, as most local anglers refer to this emerald-green body of water, is a scenic, timber-lined lake. Resident giant Canada geese from nearby Woods Reservoir frequently "buzz" boaters here, adding a finishing touch few Volunteer State lakes can top.

Tims Ford has only one first-class dock and few commercial camping areas. Tims Ford State Rustic Park, located off the Mansford Road west of Winchester via TN 50, rates as one of Tennessee's nicest public facilities. Other public parks along this lake include Estill Springs Park near the community of Estill Springs and Winchester City Park located near Winchester on the Boiling Fork Creek embayment. There are five boat-launching ramps located around the lake perimeter.

The lake's bottom strata consist of gravel and rock; clay, gravel and rock; rock and clay; and clay. Most shoreline areas are steep and rocky. Notable exceptions include the headwater flats above and below the Estill Springs Bridge (US 41), the "Loop" area near the mouth of the Hessey Branch embayment area, the Winchester City Park area in the Boiling Fork Creek embayment and Shasteen Bend. Stump beds and deep submerged standing timber are moderately plentiful. Feeder streams are numerous on this spider-shaped lake.

Fishing Information

Tims Ford possesses a diverse cool/warm sport fishery which features top-notch smallmouth bass and striped bass fishing. Largemouth bass, crappie, white bass, bluegill, Kentucky bass, plus channel, blue and flathead catfish, are all well represented here. Trophy-class rainbow trout prosper in the Elk River downstream from the dam.

Smallmouth bass are a prime drawing card here. They prosper in the cool, rocky creek embayments and along the main river channel. Forage, which consists primarily of shad, chubs and suckers, is modestly plentiful.

Anglers fond of fishing rocky main river channel and creek points for ole Mr. Smalljaws will find themselves hard pressed not to fall in love with Tims Ford Lake. Mile for mile, few lakes in the country have more of this sort of structure.

Unlike most notable East Tennessee smallmouth bass fisheries, Tims Ford is a little slower "turning on" following winter. Cold-weather angling does occur here, and at times swimming $\frac{1}{16}$-ounce motor oil–colored grubs can be productive, but this lake simply does not have a well-developed cadre of frozen-fingered bronzeback hunters.

March offers brisk action along points. Jigs worked slowly down the steep grades or crankbaits drawn across bars and subsurface ridges near

Tims Ford Lake offers quality angling for several species of fish.
TVA photo.

the shoreline are sure to provoke arm-tugging strikes. At this time pre-dawn through late morning provide the best fishing.

Brown bass spawning begins as early as late March here and extends through April. Feeder creek embayments are the primary mating sites, with 5-to-15-foot depths preferred. Fly'n'rind in yellow, white, fox squirrel, and black are deadly. Small, copper-blade spinnerbaits are also effective, as are spring lizards and nightcrawlers.

May offers exceptional top-water smallmouth and largemouth bass angling opportunities. Bagley's Bang-O-Lure or the Rapala Floating Minnow can't be topped when tossed in alongside willows or under lakeside sweet gums or hickories. The cool temperatures common to this lake apparently extend the surface season, which is good during the early and late hours all this month.

As in other Tennessee smallmouth bass fisheries, summer's arrival signals a changeover for serious fishermen to the "graveyard shift." Night bassin' is a well-defined art here, using "black lights" indentical to those used to illuminate fluorescent poster art. Coupled with nylon fishing line, such as Stren's Blue Fluorescent monofilament, these 6-to-12-volt tubular lights make even six-pound test line easily visible.

Why go to all this trouble? Well, successful night fishing on deep-structure lakes such as Tims Ford requires a deft touch, and then some. Walking an ⅛-ounce jig down a 20-foot-deep rocky point isn't easy, because one must keep his line taut in order to feel "suck-in" strikes. Big, cautious bass immediately spit out even tasty morsels when they detect deception in the form of line tickling their lips.

With illuminated line even slight twitches look like jerks. When night fishing with this technique, anglers watch their lines like hawks. The instant it appears to move in an unnatural way, they take in the slack and drive the hook point home. These lights have enabled even novice anglers to take lunker smallies from Tims Ford Lake.

Night fishing, using brown-brown, black-black, brown-purple and brown-black spider jig and pork rind combos, lasts well into late October. Following the November turnover, crankbaits are highly effective off points.

Largemouth bass occupy an important predatory niche in Tims Ford Lake. Shallow back-cove areas are the place for getting the jump on late-winter hawg action, and live minnows fished on the bottom are difficult to surpass here between late February and April. Tourney-following purists, however, usually opt for plastic worms in pearl, red and black-firetail. Hurricane Creek between the mouth of Turkey Creek and Graves Branch is a solid starting point for spring lunker largemouth action.

Largemouth bass top-water action follows the same pattern as that for its smalljaw cousin. Surface angling for greenies is particularly profitable when lake levels get into shoreline trees and shrubs. Flippin' beneath overhanging shoreline greenery and in debris (or scum lines) is also productive. Mann's electric blue Augertail worm is an excellent choice for flippin' here, as are purple, blue or red spider jigs.

Following the advent of hot weather, Tims Ford hawg hunters begin to put their efforts into the twilight hours. Deep-running crankbaits like the Rapala Shad Rap or Bagley's Balsam Bee are effective when "sliced" across points. Deep-structure fishing with worms and jigs with light 6-to-8-pound-test line is an honored ploy here, and for good reason—it will work when all else fails.

Texas-rigged black or blue worms inched down the shoreline may not be life's most exhilarating experience, but it is without question the most productive hawg-fooling technique around. The same holds true for jigs, with or without pork rind chunks.

During hot weather, many direct the bulk of their bass fishing here to between the hours of 2:00 a.m. and 7:00 a.m. Then largemouth (and smallmouth) bass move to the shoreline to forage. Although they are always cautious, that's the time to nab a wall-hanger.

Moonlighting for largemouth bass holds until fall. Then worm fishing in creek embayments and casting medium- and deep-running crankbaits provide good daylight fishing for six to eight weeks.

Those familiar with Tims Ford's vigorous lineside fishery rate it among the nation's best. Stripers in the 17-to-25-pound range are relatively common, and it takes a 30-plus pounder to attract attention. Forage, in the form of gizzard shad, has always been plentiful. Excellent water quality and numerous cool summer havens add up to a rockfish fishery where the sky is the limit.

Winter angling for big linesides has never been as popular on this windy plateau lake as at Norris or Percy Priest lakes. Still there are a few who defy subzero wind-chill factors for a chance at a trophy-class striper. For these warmly clad anglers, the Elk River arm is the only place to be, particularly the mouth of Hessey Branch and the Estill Springs Bridge.

The number-one ploy is trolling large, lively shad along breaks in the old river channel; tossing large, silver-colored, deep-diving crankbaits or half-ounce leadheads tipped with a white firetail twister grub is a close second. This is one of the few places where bank-restricted striper fishermen do as well as their boat-fitted counterparts.

Tims Ford Lake's rockfish remain in this semiriverine setting well into April. Little, if any, striped bass reproduction is thought to occur here, but the instincts of these saltwater transplants urge them to nose forward into moving water.

Lengthening daylight and warming water temperatures combine to draw these fish back downstream into the impoundment. This doesn't happen until after a brief stint of May surface-fishing action, however, which is good along the clay points between Boiling Fork and Rock creeks. Large top-water baits such as pencil poppers or Redfins are dynamite when fished off of dingy points where postspawn stripers are chasing shoreline-spawning shad.

During hot weather striped bass seek out cool havens nearer and nearer to the dam. Depths in excess of 35 to 45 feet are common by late July. Deep-water trolling using either live bait, such as shad or bluegill, or big white and red bucktails works like a charm. This impoundment also holds several deep-water man-made fish attractors along proven striper migration routes on the old river channel. These are located near Marble Plains Church, Jollys Rock point, the Old Mansford Bridge crossing, the mouth of Anderson Branch and off the southern end of West Maple Bend.

The lake is noted for its sometimes brisk summertime "jump" striper action in the headwaters of cool feeder creek embayments: notably, Lost, Kitchens and Lick creeks.

Big striped bass prowl the depths of Tims Ford Lake. Winter is a prime time to go after these gamesters.

Tims Ford receives average to slightly above average marks as a crappie fishery. Ample submerged cover in most hollows and feeder creek embayments makes it fairly easy to locate good spring action, and because this lake has a full complement of top-flight predators, most calicos taken are fairly large. On the other hand, though, even on the best days, catches in excess of thirty slabs per angler are uncommon.

Winter crappie fishing is limited at Tims, although following mild breaks in the weather it can be productive. During winter local calico chasers rely on 1/16-ounce smoke- or motor oil-colored grubs. Coupled with 4-to-6-pound-test line and a sensitive graphite or boron spinning rod, these baits can be effectively tightlined over the 25-to-35-foot-deep structure preferred by slabsides. Anderton and Cooper branches and the Hurricane Creek embayment are the most consistent cold-weather fishing locations.

Even though Tims Ford is located atop the Cumberland Plateau, its crappie spawn comes off at about the same time that it takes place at Chickamauga or Nickajack lakes. March almost always produces a week or two of productive papermouth fishing. Tightlining jigs or minnows 15 to 20 feet deep works well, as does trolling white 1/8-ounce Roostertail spinners.

Shallow-water spawning peaks by mid-April. Dollflies, grubs or minnows bobber fished 2 to 6 feet deep over brush, drop-offs or stumps all work well. Even during the height of crappie-bedding activity, total catches per day seldom exceed 20 to 30 fish, but the presence of jumbo-sized slabs more than makes up for the slower action.

Most die-hard slabside fans make a quick transition to the "grave-yard" shift around early June. High-intensity lights beamed downward on the lake surface attract newly hatched shad schools, which then get the attention of predators like crappie or white bass. Minnows dunked beneath the light rays is the most widely recommended ploy; however, vertically jigged one-ounce gold Hopkins spoons or Dardevle's one-ounce Cope-Cats are equally effective. Productive hot-weather crappie areas include the Kitchens, Hurricane and Lick creek embayments areas.

Tims Ford has proven to be a consistent producer of hand-sized blue-gill. There aren't many finer ways for twiddling away a balmy summer evening than drifting along this lake's numerous bluffs fishing for blue-gill.

In late April and early May bluegill nesting occurs all along the shoreline. Shallow backwater areas, notably the headwaters of Lost, Hurricane, Turkey, Dry and Boiling creeks, produce the best catches. Crickets, redworms and $\frac{1}{32}$-ounce beetle spinners are the top baits and lures.

Following the spawn many of the biggest 'gills move into deeper water along rocky bluffs. Here terrestrial insects spangle the surface, where they are easily picked off. Standard bluegill baits work well, but if you're a fly rodder, flicking sponge-body flies is truly first-class fun. An added bonus is often a surprise, tackle-busting bronzeback.

Catfish species found in Tims Ford Lake include blue, flathead and channel, the last being the most popular and most commonly available. Winter angling for whiskered fish is best along the old river channel between the dam and the mouth of Boiling Creek. Trotlines baited with cut shad, chicken guts or liver work well.

Catfish move into shallow water at approximately the same time as crappie spawn. In fact, most perch anglers take several one-to-two-pound channel cats while vying for calicos. All three catfish species spawn in back coves and the headwaters of most feeder streams between late May and early July.

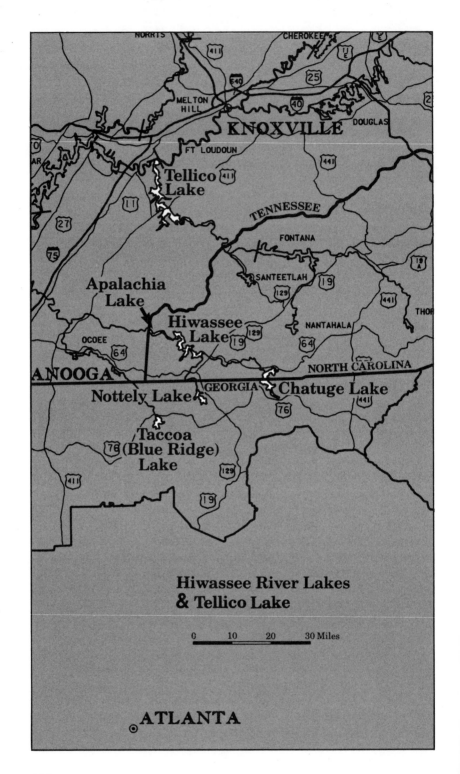

Hiwassee River Lakes
& Tellico Lake

0   10   20   30 Miles

Hiwassee River Lakes

The Hiwassee River system includes eight medium to small impoundments. Due to extensive pollution in the Ocoee River system in southeastern Tennessee, only five of these offer notable gamefish angling: Blue Ridge, Nottely, Chatuge, Hiwassee and Apalachia lakes.

All of these are classic mountain lakes featuring steep rocky clay shoreline, sharply sculpted feeder creek embayments and generally cool dispositions. They drain the Tennessee River Valley's southeastern-most corner—the end of the rugged Southern Appalachian Mountains. Most of the Hiwassee River's drainage is publicly owned U.S. Forest Service land, including the Nantahala National Forest in southwestern North Carolina and the Chattahoochee National Forest in northeastern Georgia.

The Hiwassee River lakes support diverse fisheries, although forage is sometimes a problem in several. Cover is another nemesis on most of these lakes. Each lake undergoes dramatic annual drawdowns, often in excess of 80 to 100 feet. Stumps left behind when these lakes were formed have largely disappeared, although a concentrated effort to add man-made brush piles and similar structure is well advanced here. Because these mountain lakes have quite a lot in common, it would appear easy to lump them together, but from an angling standpoint, that's impossible. Each is entirely different from the others.

Apalachia Lake

SIZE: small
ACCESSIBILITY: fair
LOCATION: North Carolina (Cherokee County)
PRESSURE: light
PRIMARY GAMEFISH: smallmouth bass, bluegill, rainbow trout

141

SECONDARY GAMEFISH: white bass, largemouth bass, catfish
BEST MONTHS: May, June, July, August, October
BEST BAITS: live minnows, nightcrawlers, jigs, cheese balls, deep-
diving crankbaits, small spinners
BEST BET: fishing for rainbow trout with cheese balls along the lake's
bluffs at night under a lantern in late May and June

Apalachia Lake is a very scenic lake, with emerald-green water that reflects the surrounding wooded ridges like a shimmering mirror. It's a remote lake by any standards, with limited access and very scant development along its shoreline.

Apalachia Dam was built between 1941 and 1943; it stands 150 feet high and is 1,308 feet across. Counting upstream, it is the first dam on the Hiwassee River system and is located only a few hundred feet from the Tennessee line. At full pool the lake level stands at 1,280 feet above sea level and covers 1,100 surface acres. This relatively short and narrow lake is just under 10 miles long and has 31 miles of shoreline. The maximum drawdown is eight feet.

Apalachia is one of the most isolated lakes in the TVA system. A series of rugged ridges keep it at arm's length from the "civilized world." These include the Unicoi Mountains to the north and the Burger, Pack and Payne mountains to the south. All of the lake frontage except a small area near New Prospect and a north-shore area upstream from the dam is under the control of the Nantahala National Forest.

The lake is accessible by car by only a couple of minor county roadways. Murphy is the nearest town. There are no commercial boat docks, campgrounds, or recreation areas along the lake, although Forest Service rules permit campers to stay at undeveloped areas for up to 14 days. There is one public boat-launch ramp located at the lake's headwaters near Hiwassee Dam.

Apalachia Lake is best described as a big slow river passing through a wooded canyon pass. Even its feeder creek embayments are relatively insignificant. It's icy cold, clear, and infertile. At its widest, the lake is barely a quarter mile wide, and for most of its length it is less than half that width. Rock and gravel are the primary bottom strata.

Fishing Information

Apalachia is better for pleasure boating than for serious fishermen looking for a place to ply their trade. Its low nutrient base and frigid disposition make establishing quality fishing for almost anything very difficult. Smallmouth bass and rainbow trout are the primary gamefish, followed by a few bluegill. Even when conditions are optimum, the lake rates mediocre.

Apalachia Lake holds lots of trout. Summer is the best time to visit this remote impoundment.

During June and July fly fishermen working trashlines with Royal Wulffs and Black Gnats take trout between Hiwassee Dam and the Hamby Bend area. Trolling spinners or medium-sized shad-style crankbaits is also effective in this vicinity at this time.

Smallies are most abundant in the lake's lower end. They also have a definite preference for back-cove areas over main channel points. These fish are small, with a two pounder being about the top of the line. Grubs, live baits and crankbaits are the most consistent offerings. During hot weather, bream fishing can be quite good along the shoreline in the lake's lower one-fourth. Fly fishing big bobbers is fun and productive, as are crickets fished three to five feet under a bobber.

—Hiwassee Lake

SIZE: small
ACCESSIBILITY: good
LOCATION: North Carolina (Cherokee County)
PRESSURE: moderate to light
PRIMARY GAMEFISH: bluegill, smallmouth bass, catfish, crappie

SECONDARY GAMEFISH: white bass, walleye, rainbow trout,
  largemouth bass, muskie
BEST MONTHS: April, May, June, July, August, October
BEST BAITS: live minnows and shad, hair jigs, deep-diving crankbaits,
  plastic worms
BEST BET: fishing for smallmouth bass using fly and rind combos
  along the lake's rocky points at night in late June

Hiwassee Lake in western North Carolina offers fair to good fishing for
a handful of gamefish species, plus an opportunity to view some of the
South's most superb mountain scenery. Despite its relatively "pocket"
size, Hiwassee is a surprisingly diverse lake that's full of surprises. The
lake is formed by the impoundment of the Hiwassee and Nottely rivers,
which drain almost a thousand square miles of northern Georgia and
parts of western North Carolina.

The dam, a concrete structure built between 1936 and 1940, stands
307 feet high and is 1,376 feet across. At full pool the lake covers 6,090
surface acres and stands at 1,523 feet above sea level. This long winding
lake measures over 22 miles from dam to headwaters and has 163 miles
of shoreline. Full pool is usually achieved in late spring or early summer,
and the winter drawdown is approximately 75 feet. The creation of this
lake submerged an earlier dam located on the Nottely River a third of
a mile upstream from its confluence with the Hiwassee.

The lake is ringed by some of the South's most majestic mountains.
The Fort Butler Mountains border its headwaters to the southeast, while
the Scott, Fain and Blackwell mountains and Buck Knob and Abbot
Top are located along Hiwassee Lake's northeastern areas. Ghormley
and Hibbert mountains, John Ish High Top and Panther Top line the
southern shoreline. Hiwassee is surrounded by the Nantahala National
Forest on all sides except for a long tract of the southwestern shoreline
near the dam and the area around Murphy. This is the only TVA lake
which borders Indian reservation land. The Henson Donation tract of
the Eastern Band of Cherokee Indians is located along the headwaters
of the Hanging Dog Creek embayment.

Development along Hiwassee Lake occurs in patches, notably the
town of Murphy on the Hiwassee River arm and the area south of the
dam. The lake is accessed by US 19-129, which crosses the Hiwassee
River arm at Murphy approximately 20 miles upstream from the dam.
NC 1326 (Joe Brown Highway) accesses the northern shoreline.

Murphy is the largest nearby town. There are three commercial boat
docks and five public boat-launch ramps. Lakeside camping is permitted
at the Forest Service's Hanging Dog Recreation Area. Day-use areas
include the Forest Service's Cherokee Lake Recreation Area and TVA's
Micken Branch Recreation Area and Hiwassee Dam Preserve.

Hiwassee Lake is a scenic lake that offers good fishing. TVA photo.

The lake enjoys good to very good water quality. A winding narrow lake, it averages only a couple of hundred yards wide along its entire length, with the exception of a small wide area in the lake's lower reaches. Hiwassee is a very deep lake which at times is relatively devoid of oxygen at extreme depths. The bottom is composed of granite rock and gravel and red dirt and clay.

Fishing Information

First and foremost, this is a smallmouth bass fishery. North Carolina's record smallie, a 10-pound, 2-ounce whopper, was caught here in 1953. Naturally most fish caught here are not in this class; in fact, a five pounder is a trophy, and anything over three pounds deserves a little chest pounding. The average fish is more like 10 to 11 inches long, but these are moderately plentiful.

Like all of the North Carolina highland lakes described in this guide, Hiwassee is stocked annually with threadfin shad. These bite-size forage fish are ideal food for smallie, bream, largemouth bass and other predators. Since they are very warm natured, they survive only the mildest winters and must be reintroduced each spring. Threadfins are the key to keeping the fishing quality of these lakes at their present levels. These high-elevation lakes simply don't receive enough nutrient run-off to sustain good fishing without the threadfin stocking program.

Hiwassee's smallie rate below the brown bass opportunities available at a number of other TVA lakes, but it's the best show in town at this highland lake. Little cold-weather fishing occurs here, but by April the local fishermen are using live minnows to probe the courses of feeder creek mouths. This is productive until early May, when spinnerbaits fished in the back-cove areas are the most effective ploy.

Mid-May is the season's best fishing along main river channel out-croppings and feeder creek embayment points. Top-water action occurs early and late, while crankbaits, grubs and live baits like big minnows and crawdads are effective at other times. Unlike at most TVA lakes, night fishing doesn't occur here to any great degree. A few fish are caught during June and early July, but, for the most part, catch rates plummet until October, when smallies are active along the shoreline in 5 to 10 feet of water.

Largemouth bass are also available in Hiwassee Lake, but they too are small. Most serious bigmouth fishing begins around late April, when the temperatures in major backwater areas like Grape and Persimmon creeks warm. Plastic worms and live minnows are the standard offerings. The best fishing occurs in mid-June, when these fish can be taken on crankbaits fished around man-made fish attractors.

White bass are probably the lake's most consistent fishery. During mid-March big whites in the 3-to-5-pound class ascend the headwater rivers to spawn. Stripe in this class cause a lot of excitement in the Nottely and Hiwassee river arms, where shoals, bridge pilings and other obstacles provide spawning structure. Quarter-ounce white and red bucktails and small Roostertail spinners fished across the current work well in this environment. Night fishing for hot-weather stripe is rare, but keep an eye out for surface breaks which occur sporadically throughout the lake between May and September.

The Little Tennessee and Hiwassee rivers were once populated by muskellunge. In 1971 the North Carolina Wildlife Resources Commission stocked the Hiwassee River with muskie. Later, tiger muskie, a cross between a northern pike and a muskie, were released in Hiwassee Lake, followed by a planting of Ohio River–strain muskie at the lake in 1984. At this writing it is not believed that a reproducing muskie population exists at Hiwassee comparable to the one at Fontana, although huge briarmouths over 20 pounds are occasionally taken. Trolling big plugs and bottom fishing with big creek chubs off points have accounted for most fish taken by anglers going specifically for muskie (many are caught accidentally by bass fishermen). There are no bonafide muskie hot spots, although there does seem to be a relationship between catches and the weather. Like duck hunting, the best muskie fishing is when winter weather is at its most miserable.

There's an interesting story concerning how smart Hiwassee Lake's muskie are. Two bass anglers spotted a grey squirrel bounding down the steep lake shore and then leaping out atop a stump that was exposed above the lake surface about eight feet from its banks. A hickory nut atop the stump had attracted the squirrel's attention. Once it had the nut, though, the squirrel discovered that the return distance to dry land was too great to leap without the aid of a running start. The squirrel rounded the stump's flat surface a couple of times and then slipped off into the water to swim back.

Suddenly a huge muskie erupted beneath the squirrel and both disappeared. The two bass anglers who'd been watching the squirrel were aghast at what they'd seen. While they discussed this amazing sight, they saw the muskie reappear and then gingerly replace the hickory nut atop the stump.

Hiwassee Lake gets mixed reviews for its panfish. It offers good fishing for robins (redbreast) and bluegill, but its black crappie offerings are only fair at best. Man-made fish attractors are the best April through July hot spots for all three, while shaded bluff areas provide good bluegill catches in hot weather.

The lake also has a very good channel and flathead catfish fishery. These are caught mostly in warm weather with chicken liver and other natural baits fished in back coves and off main channel points during the late evening and twilight hours.

Walleye are also caught in fairly good numbers. These fish are combination river and lake spawners, meaning that during the spring and late winter some of the walleye population mate upstream in the rivers, while others procreate in the lake along rocky outcroppings. Most of the walleye taken here are caught during the spring by anglers along the shoreline using quarter-ounce feather jigs or live minnows. Hot-weather catches are scarce, and summertime night fishing for marble-eyes is much rarer here than at nearby Fontana Lake. During the fall some fairly good catches are made in the shallows after surface water temperatures drop.

—— *Chatuge Lake*

SIZE: small
ACCESSIBILITY: good, fair in winter
LOCATION: N. Carolina (Clay County) and Georgia (Towns County)

PRESSURE: moderate
PRIMARY GAMEFISH: bluegill, largemouth bass, whiterock hybrid bass, catfish, crappie
SECONDARY GAMEFISH: white bass, walleye, rainbow trout, smallmouth bass
BEST MONTHS: April, May, June, July, August, October
BEST BAITS: live minnows and shad, hair jigs, chicken liver, deep-diving crankbaits, plastic worms
BEST BET: fishing for crappie using hair jigs tipped with minnows over the lake's man-made fish attractor brush piles in late April

Chatuge Lake was created in 1942 with the completion of Chatuge Dam in the Hiwassee River. It is the third of three TVA structures built on the main stream of this mountainous river system. Upstream from this impoundment, which straddles the Georgia–North Carolina state line, the Hiwassee River drains a 189-square-mile area in northwestern Georgia's Chattahoochee National Forest and western North Carolina's Nantahala National Forest. The river's headwaters form on Brasstown Bald (4,784 feet above sea level), the highest point in Georgia.

The earth and rock fill dam, which stands 144 feet high and is 2,850 feet across, was built at a cost of $9.3 million. It is a flood control and electricity production facility, with the lowest generating capacity in the TVA system. At full pool the lake stands at 1,927 feet above sea level and covers 7,050 surface acres. It extends 13 miles from the dam to the headwaters and has a total of 132 miles of shoreline. Autumn drawdowns average only about 20 feet.

Chatuge is a mountain lake, pure and simple. The lake is almost equally divided between the two states. It is rimmed on the east by Galloway Mountain and Garland Ridge in the Nantahala National Forest and Lloyd Mountain and Hollifield Ridge in the Chattahoochee National Forest. Cherry Mountain in the Nantahala towers to the west and Ramey and Ivy mountains and Long Ridge in the Chattahoochee form its southern skyscape. Towns County, Georgia, encompasses the lake's southern half, while Clay County, North Carolina, borders its northern edge.

The lake differs from most highland impoundments, which snake between narrow cliff passages. It is generally wide and sports large islands. When viewed from above, it has a definite "cresent moon" shape. The shoreline is composed of rock, clay and gravel and in many places is generally steep, although there is an abundance of mudflats.

Water quality rates moderately good, although turbidity is more pronounced here than on most similar lakes. Most natural fish cover is rock or quickly disappearing old stumps. Man-made fish attractors have been placed in several areas in the lake. These are vital to most fishing success.

This is one of the most highly developed and accessible TVA mountain lakes. Unlike many highland lakes, Chatuge has numerous lakeside homesites. It is also very accessible via automobile. US 64 borders its northern shoreline, and US 76 accesses it from the south and its eastern headwaters. The lake's eastern shoreline can be reached by NC 175–GA 75 (same roadway), while the western area is accessible via NC 69–GA 17 and GA 288. Hiwassee, Presley and Young Harris are the nearest Georgia towns, while Hayesville and Shooting Creek are the nearest North Carolina towns.

There are 11 commercial boat docks and 8 public boat-launch areas. Public camping is available at TVA's Chatuge Dam Reservation (North Carolina) and Towns Creek Recreation Area (Georgia), the U.S. Forest Service's Jackrabbit (Nantahala) and Lake Chatuge (Chattahoochee) recreation areas, and Towns County Park (Georgia). The Georgia Mountain Fair grounds are located adjacent to the Towns County Park. This autumn event is well worth visiting. Popular day-use-only areas around the lake include Clay County Park (North Carolina) and Chatuge Woods County Park (Georgia).

Fishing Information

Chatuge Lake offers diverse fishing opportunities which include largemouth and smallmouth bass, whiterock (white bass–striped bass hybrids), bluegill and redbreast bream, white bass, channel and flathead catfish, rainbow trout, crappie, and walleye. Chatuge's forage base is composed of gizzard shad, bluegill and yellow perch. Interestingly, the gizzard shad found here were stocked by mistake. Either North Carolina or Georgia inadvertently stocked these fish thinking they were stocking threadfin shad. Neither wants to take credit for the gizzard shad's now permanent presence, and, amusingly, each blames the other for this bait fish's presence.

During the early 1970s Chatuge had a reputation as a white crappie hot spot. Although their overall numbers are somewhat reduced at this writing, good stringers can still be taken there, thanks in part to new man-made fish attractors. These brushy concoctions don't increase the number of fish a lake can support, but they can concentrate the available fish in easily identifiable areas. Many of Chatuge's attactors were airlifted in by helicopter.

Winter crappie fishing can be very good at times. The best fishing centers around the Bell and Hog creek embayments. Vertical jigging minnows or small hair flies 10 to 20 feet deep along creek drop-offs is the best method, followed by trolling. Prespawn crappie fishing is also

Among TVA's mountain lakes, Chatuge has one of the best largemouth bass fisheries.

good in these areas, and in the Long Bullet Creek embayment and Philadelphia Church Cove. The fish are 7 to 12 feet deep at this time, and the same techniques work well.

Spawning occurs in late April to early May. Brush-pile fishing is without question the most productive approach. The Towns County Park, Philadelphia Church and Ledford Chapel areas are all good during the crappie nesting period. Minnows fished under bobbers work well. Hot weather crappie fishing is spotty, and most catches are incidental.

Chatuge is universally regarded as a first-class catfish hole. Most fish are taken during the hot-weather months, although crappie and bass fishermen mop up pretty good on channel cats when fishing brush piles and mud flats during April and May. Choice hot-weather fishing spots include the rip-rap around the US 76 bridges, the main channel points near the dam and the Chambers Cove area.

Chatuge is an above-average smallmouth bass lake. There are plenty of 1½ to 2 pounders, and 4 to 5 pounders are not unusual. Georgia's record smallie, a 7-pound, 2-ounce specimen, was taken here in 1972. The lake's smallies are the subject of TVA acid rain research. Studies have revealed that some of the mountain lakes in this region have smallmouth bass that display spinal deformities among 12 to 15 percent of the population. At this writing acid rain is not the proven culprit. Habitat and genetics are also suspect.

Excellent early winter bronzeback fishing is available in big creek embayments like Wood, Bell and Long Bullet. Live bait or medium-to-small jigs worked along sloping shale shoreline are the best cool-weather ploys. Angling for these fish dips during January and February, but in early March things start clicking again. The extreme mouths of feeder streams are the place to be. Big, dark live minnows snaked along with the flow will bring a limit of brown bass to the net quicker than anything. Later in April, when the water warms, try spinnerbaits in these areas, and in backwater areas.

May usually holds two to three weeks of prime top-water smalljaw action. Points along the main river channel or major feeder creeks are tops for working a shad-style surface bait. At night later during summer these areas are good bets for fishing plastic worms or leadhead spider jigs. Brown, purple and blue are the top colors, and pork rind is often used. Autumn action rates good, especially mid-October. Deep- and medium-depth crankbaits worked parallel to the shoreline are difficult to top for good smallie catches.

Chatuge also holds a fair number of largemouth bass and spotted bass. Largemouth bass in the 1-to-2½-pound class are the most common, although hawgs over five pounds are often taken. Late March is the starting time for going after these fish. The flats in the Long Bullet and Shooting creek embayments are solid bets for early season action. Big minnows are difficult to top, but spinnerbaits and plastic worms worked slowly along the bottom are excellent green fish getters.

Creek action dominates angling for these fish well into May, when they move closer in to the shoreline to look for nesting areas. Medium-depth-running crankbaits in silver, red and chartreuse are good at this time, followed by strawberry or grape worms. Late May also finds these fish willing to strike topside baits during the late evening and early morning. Hot-weather action is best at night using plastic worms or jigs around the mouths of coves and inlets and along the main river channel.

The abundant white bass are a popular species in this lake. Late winter and early spring, when these fish ascend the Hiwassee River, provide the best fishing. Torrid spawning-run action centers between the GA 75 and Streakheal bridges. Jigs or minnows cast out and quartered across the current are deadly. Trolling upstream is also effective. Stripe return to the lake by mid-May. Surface fishing for whites is popular, around the Long Bullet and Bell creek embayments. Night fishing is productive near the US 76 bridges and Clay County Park.

Whiterocks were stocked in the lake by the Georgia Department of

Natural Resources to curb the proliferation of big gizzard shad. This fishery is still in its infancy, but things are already going great. Whiterocks up to eight pounds were showing up in 1985, and these fish are expected to double that poundage. These fish are bonafide roamers. During the spring they are taken in the headwaters in the company of white bass. Hot weather finds them available in the jumps and at night under lantern lights. Small whiterocks are more likely to run with white bass than those over five pounds, which tend to school together in deeper water. The deep-water attractors located at Brown Island, Hog and Shoot creeks are good bets for year-round whiterock action. Big shad or live bluegill drift fished are impossible to top.

Chatuge Lake once had a good reputation as a walleye fishery, and indeed a few fish in the three-to-seven-pound class are regularly taken by crappie or stripe fishermen. Why this fishery has declined isn't known, although it is likely the lake will be restocked with walleye in the very near future.

Stocking trout in Chatuge doesn't have a bright future. Chatuge is not classed an optimum trout lake, although good catches were, and still are, made. When federally reared rainbow trout were abundant and readily available, they were stocked here regularly. At this time trout aren't planted by either state, although a few wash down from nearby mountain streams. Fishing deep with corn or nightcrawlers at the base of the dam at night is the best bet for trout action.

⎯Nottely Lake

SIZE: small
ACCESSIBILITY: good, fair in winter
LOCATION: Georgia (Union County)
PRESSURE: moderate to light
PRIMARY GAMEFISH: bluegill, smallmouth and largemouth bass, white bass, walleye
SECONDARY GAMEFISH: catfish, crappie
BEST MONTHS: April, May, June, July, August, October
BEST BAITS: live minnows, crickets, grub-style jigs, red wigglers, deep-diving crankbaits, plastic worms
BEST BET: fishing for bluegill in late evening using crickets along the lake's bluffs in July and August

Nottely Lake is one of those overlooked bodies of water that offer good fishing. It features good largemouth and smallmouth bass angling, plus chances for several other species. It's a very scenic lake with an abundance of public access areas.

Nottely Dam was completed in 1942, only one week beyond six months from the day the project began. Modern planning engineers must marvel at this speedy rate of construction. The dam impounds the Nottely River, a tributary of the Hiwassee, which drains a 214-square-mile area of northern Georgia. It's an earth and rock fill structure, 184 feet high and 2,300 feet across. At full pool the lake is 1,779 feet above sea level and covers 4,180 surface acres. It extends 20.2 miles from the dam to its headwaters and has 106 miles of shoreline. Winter drawdowns average almost 45 feet.

Like other Hiwassee River impoundments, this too is classed as a "mountain lake." It is bordered on the east by Cobb and Loftis mountains and Bowling and Anderson knobs. Davenport Mountain forms a considerable portion of the lake's western scenery, while Brackett Knob is found along the edge of the western headwaters. The lake is surrounded by the Chattahoochee National Forest Purchase Unit, although the only land under the U.S. Forest Service's control is lake frontage property. Fortunately, this has allowed Nottely Lake to escape the intensive development crunch so evident at nearby Chatuge Lake.

Nottely Lake is located in Union County, Georgia; Blairsville is the nearest town. There are four commercial boat docks on the lake and four public boat-launch ramps. Public camping is available at TVA's Poteete Creek Recreation Area. Day-use areas can be found in the Dam Reservation area.

This a typical highland impoundment complete with numerous stretches of rock bluff shoreline, long narrow feeder stream embayments, and a snaking, riverlike headwater area. It enjoys moderately good water quality despite the heavy farming and development along the Nottely River upstream from the lake.

The bottom strata are composed of clay, rock and gravel. This is the primary gamefish cover aside from a few stump beds, old building foundations and an impressive sprinkling of man-made shoreline and deepwater fish attractors, or brush piles. One notable exception is the scattered colonies of canary grass introduced here to provide aquatic shoreline cover. This northern native can withstand being submerged for periods in excess of 40 days. It is ideal on cover-poor lakes like Nottely because to spread, this plant must be cultivated.

Fishing Information

Nottely Lake's fishery is largely composed of big, topflight predatory fish. It has a long-standing reputation as a trophy largemouth bass fishery, although in recent years this has faltered somewhat and could continue to change. The lake also offers trophy striped bass fishing. Its secret is a tremendous forage base of gizzard shad. Threadfin shad are stocked periodically.

In years past, big largemouth bass were Nottely's calling card. It has never been noted as an easy lake to fish, but then lunker bass don't come easy anywhere. Inconsistent yearly spawning success is one reason larger fish dominated the lake's largemouth bass age-class structure. More medium and small largemouth bass are now being caught there, but this could possibly be a result of increased competition from two near relatives—the spotted and smallmouth bass. Both are on the increase.

Spotted, or Kentucky, bass were not found in Nottely until relatively recently. This newfound species was imported from other nearby Georgia impoundments, probably by some unknown fisherman who took it upon himself to stock the fish here. Since that time there has been a virtual explosion of the Kentucky bass population. Georgia's state record spotted bass, a 7-pound, 12-ounce beauty, was caught here in 1972. If the growth of the Kentucky bass population continues its present course, and it probably will, these fish are likely to be the lake's dominant black bass representative.

Winter largemouth bass fishing rates fair. The headwaters of several major feeder creeks hold sometimes active concentrations of bass. These include Camp, Youngcane, Conley and Ivylog creeks. Live baits inched along meander drop-offs can't be topped. Hardware casters can sometimes have good success using chartreuse fly and rind combos or plastic worms. This pattern holds relatively steady until March, when rising water creates warm shallow areas.

Spinnerbaits and medium-depth-diving crankbaits in white, green and yellow are recommended for early spring fishing action, although anglers good at bottom walking plastic worms can always do moderately well along gravel bars and off points. Flooded canary grass areas deserve a special note. Fishing this type of cover can be exciting and productive. Forage fish are attracted to this 12-to-18-inch-high grass, which also provides predator fish with ambush cover. When fishing submerged grass, don't limit your efforts just to skipping along the top of the weed line. Also work baits along the bottom through these growths. Later, particular attention should be given to the shoreline edges, where shallow, easily spooked fish can be caught on buzzbaits. This type of fishing occurs between late April and early June. The shoreline canary grass has also proven to be remarkably productive at night.

Twilight bass fishing at Nottely is productive from the beginning of hot weather until late fall. Point fishing with plastic worms, pig'n'jigs and deep-diving crankbaits has accounted for a lot of taxidermy work. If you aren't getting the kind of results you'd like, try slowing down the presentation; these hawgs have a reputation for avoiding fast-moving baits.

Kentucky bass are usually caught in mixed bag stringers with large-mouth bass, although they are also consistently caught along rocky shoreline on twistertails and grubs. This area also hosts an increasing number of smallmouth bass. Creek mouths hold winter and early spring smallie concentrations. Live baits are the top offerings, followed by black or smoke-colored grubs. Following the spawn the best smallie and spotted bass fishing is along the main channel between the mouth of Youngcane Creek and the dam.

Striped bass were introduced to Nottely Lake in the sixties to reduce crowding by large gizzard shad. Stripers have been successful in converting a portion of the shad into silver-bound pounds of gamefish. Fish in excess of 40 pounds have been taken here, which rates the project a success, although in years past the lake has had unexplained striper die-offs.

Nottely is an excellent winter rockfish lake. Try drift fishing along river channel drop-offs between river mile 30 and the US 76 bridge. Headwater fishing begins in early December and progressively moves upstream until March, when these fish are sometimes taken in head-water shoals alongside spawning white bass. Drift fishing with big shad is the best early-winter and mid-winter tactic. Later, when these fish are in moving water, jigs are difficult to top. Nottely's stripers can't reproduce in the river, although this doesn't quell their enthusiasm for spawning.

Following the spawn there is a brief period of fairly decent top-water action in early May along clay points. This is followed by a move to summer schooling patterns which progressively draw these fish closer to the deep water near the dam. Between June and September these fish ply 10-to-40-foot depths, and they're difficult to locate without an electronic depth finder. Live bait and big bucktails are the favorite summer baits. Striper chasers should closely examine TVA maps for the locations of deep-water man-made structure.

Nottely is a bonafide hot spot for catfish. Channel and flathead catfish are the main fare, although a few white cats are sometimes taken. Georgia's state record flathead catfish, a 51-pound, 15-ounce monster, was caught here in 1969. Catfish can be taken here year-round. Impressive winter catches are made by trotline fishermen working the main channel between Chastain Branch and Youngcane Creek. The dam area upstream to Camp Creek is good to red hot during early spring. Hot-weather whiskered fish angling rates among the finest anywhere. All backwater areas, such as the backsides of inlets, coves and feeder creek embayments, are worthy of wetting a hook. Jug fishing is probably the most effective way to fish an entire cove, but still fishing at night with a nice bonfire and cool drinks is tops in this writer's opinion.

Bluegill and redbreast bream are abundant here, and during the spawn large specimens can be taken. Traditional May spawning areas include shallow, gravel-bottom backwater areas. Fish the bottom with natural baits or small leadhead grubs. Following the nesting period big "bullgill" station along shaded bluffs. They can be easily caught, but they're deep, usually 8 to 15 feet down.

In recent years Nottely's crappie have been coming on strong. The lake has never been known as a topflight slabside producer, and still isn't. This could change, though, if these fish continue their population boom. One of the secrets to the heavier stringers of crappie has been the installation of brush piles. These don't increase the numbers of fish, but they do concentrate them, especially during the spawn. Another secret to the crappie's return (as well as the overall good bill of health this lake presently enjoys) is the dynamic nature of its gizzard shad population. All age groups are well represented, rather than a top-heavy load of bigger gizzes. In March, April, and May crappie fishermen should concentrate their efforts around Nottely's fish attractors, particularly those in vicinity of Ivylog Creek.

Trout and walleye are also occasionally encountered by anglers fishing here. Trout are not stocked, but they occasionally wash down from upstream mountain creeks. Walleye were once relatively well represented at Nottely, but at this time it must be termed a remnant fishery. Those taken are incidental to other fishing activities, and are big, between four and eight pounds.

—— Taccoa Lake

SIZE: small
ACCESSIBILITY: good
LOCATION: Georgia (Fannin County)
PRESSURE: moderate to light
PRIMARY GAMEFISH: largemouth and smallmouth bass, bluegill, walleye
SECONDARY GAMEFISH: crappie, white bass
BEST MONTHS: April, May, June, July, August, October
BEST BAITS: live minnows, nightcrawlers, jigs, hair flies, deep-diving and medium-depth crankbaits, plastic worms, small spinners
BEST BET: fishing for white bass with hair flies or small spinners in the lake's headwaters from early to late April

Taccoa Lake is one of three TVA impoundments found in the state of Georgia. Blue Ridge, as most local fishermen refer to it, is a scenic highland lake rimmed by ridges that constitute the southern-most tip of the Appalachian Mountains. It's an old lake, and one that sports an established fishery which at times is very productive and at other times, very frustrating.

Blue Ridge Dam is an earth-fill structure that stands 167 feet high and 1,000 feet across. It sits atop the Taccoa River, which drains a 232-square-mile area of mountainous northern Georgia, much of which lies within the Chattahoochee National Forest. At full pool Taccoa is 1,691 feet above sea level and covers 3,290 surface acres. Minimum pool is 1,590, a difference of over 100 feet. The lake extends 11 miles and has 65 miles of shoreline.

Blue Ridge Dam was built by the Tennessee Electric Power (TEP) Company, which began construction in late 1925 but soon discontinued its efforts and left the site idle until 1929. The dam was completed the following year. TVA acquired this and three other TEP Company facilities in 1939.

Taccoa Lake is located wholly in Fannin County. The Chattahoochee National Forest (Taccoa Ranger District) surrounds the lake and controls shoreline frontage except for the Dam Preserve and one nearby small tract. Hickoryland, Long, Davenport, Green, Rich and Tickanetly mountains form the lake's craggy shoreline. There is one commercial boat dock and three public boat launches. Camping is permitted at the U.S. Forest Service's Lake Blue Ridge and Morganton Point recreation areas. Both areas are very nice, particularly Morganton Point, which offers a scenic beach and rockhounding opportunities for various minerals including staurolite.

The lake's northern shoreline is accessed by US 76, its eastern banks by GA 4. Blue Ridge is the largest nearby town, while Chattanooga is located 60 miles to the east via US 76 and I-75 and Atlanta is situated 90 miles to the southwest via US 19.

Blue Ridge Lake is almost a mile across at its widest point, which is just upstream from the dam area. However, much of the lake is narrow and bluff lined. The bottom strata are composed primarily of rock, gravel and clay. The lake sports steep shoreline in most areas, although there are a few flat areas in the tributary embayments.

Fishing Information

Taccoa enjoys a good reputation as a smallmouth bass and walleye fishery. It's a clear lake, which experienced fishermen know translates into special fishing approaches for these two keen-eyed gamefish. White bass; channel, white and bullhead catfish; and bluegill and black crappie are also available.

The lake has a dense population of ¾-to-2-pound smallmouth bass.

When conditions are right, a moderately good bass angler can take several dozen smallies in a single day. The lake also holds a fair number of trophy-class 5 to 6 pounders. Early spring is the best time to tangle with this lake's bronzebacks. Cold-weather angling is moderately good, but during the winter months Taccoa rates as one of the coldest locations in the TVA system.

Lengthening periods of daylight during March put a spark of life in Taccoa's smalljaw bass. Many local experts regard this time as the season's best. Early season smallie tactics and baits are simple, yet require quite a lot of practice to master. Most fish are in feeder creek embayments holding 8 to 20 feet deep. Live baits like nightcrawlers and spring lizards work well, but most anglers prefer artificial offerings. Small ¼-to-⅛-ounce grubs and jigs in grey, white, red and blue bounced along the bottom are always good bets. In late April these fish are shallower, usually in 3-to-8-foot-deep areas in the rear of coves and embayments or occasionally out along points. Spinnerbaits, medium-depth-diving crankbaits and plastic worms are the best bets then until hot weather sends the bass deep.

Beginning in early June the best bronzeback fishing is available either during the very late evening and early morning or on moonless nights. Twilight bass can be shallow or deep. Live baits or pig'n'jig combos in green, blue-black, black or brown are excellent jigging choices. Taccoa drops quickly during late summer, and by autumn the best brown bass are found off main channel and primary feeder stream points. Medium-depth-diving crankbaits, plastic worms and jigs are the best offerings for the period from turnover through cold weather.

Taccoa Lake also sports a mediocre largemouth bass fishery. Those taken here are generally large, up to six pounds. They respond slower to warming trends, but can be taken on plastic worms in the shallow flats of creek embayments during April. Otherwise, these fish follow roughly the same movement patterns as the smallies.

Walleye were stocked in Blue Ridge Lake shortly after the lake was created. Goggle-eye in the ¾-to-1½-pound range are abundant, although it's not uncommon to take specimens up to 8 pounds. These fish are regarded by many as the lake's most outstanding sport fishery. These are "lake-oriented" walleye, meaning they spawn in the lake and seldom leave still water for riverine adventure. The lake has a gizzard shad, yellow perch and bluegill forage base upon which these voracious predators feed. Spawning occurs during late winter, and as noted, there is little riverine walleye fishing similar to that found in the headwaters of other TVA impoundments, such as Norris Lake. Although the spawn provides little excitement, mid-March shoreline fishing can be excellent from the vicinity of the dam upstream to the Charlie Creek embayment

Most mountain lakes hold good-eating, large-growing walleye.

to the west and the Star Creek embayment to the east. At this time the walleye are hungry and active, feeding in 3-to-8-foot depths along the shoreline. Live minnows, nightcrawlers and small jigs cast to the shoreline from a boat and "staircased" down steep clay banks are most effective combinations.

Most fish are caught very early or very late under dim light conditions. This type of fishing holds until late May or even early June. During the remainder of the season walleye hover at 15 to 20 feet in the daytime and feed shallow only under the stars. Night fishing accounts for the lion's share of the fish taken at this time. Most are taken near the dam area using minnows fished under lanterns suspended over the water. Nighttime trolling is also effective, as is day trolling with downriggers.

At one time muskie were stocked in this lake. Georgia's record book brairmouth, a 38-pound beauty, was taken here in 1957. At this writing, though, there isn't much of a muskellunge fishery to speak of in Taccoa.

There is a better than average bluegill fishery, though, and Taccoa has one of the Tennessee River drainage's most productive redbreast fisheries. Spring bream fishing begins in back-cove areas around the middle of April. Shallow two-to-five-foot depths are the rule into June. Spawning occurs in backwater areas with a fine gravel or hard clay base. The Charlie Creek area is always a good starting point. Following the nesting period the best bream fishing is in the evening around shaded bluffs near the dam or along the main river channel and major feeder creeks.

Taccoa doesn't rate very high as a crappie lake. A few good stringers are taken during the height of the spawn, in mid-April, off of the man-made brush piles, but this is regarded as a spotty slabside fishery.

The lake does have a very good white bass fishery. During March these fish race up the Taccoa River in great numbers, where they're caught along eddies, shoals and bridge pilings. They return to the lake in early May, and for the rest of the summer roam the impoundment in large schools. Break fishing action can occur anywhere almost anytime a hungry group of stripe locate a surface-traveling shad school. Small surface plugs cast into the middle of such a top-water melee are pat bets for action. Night fishing with minnows or hair jigs under a lantern is also productive. Little winter fishing for stripe is practiced here, although at this time a few are always available in the river and suspended schools can be found along feeder creek drop-offs.

Catfish are plentiful. Channel cats are the most numerous, followed by a fair number of white catfish and bullhead. Commercial fishing is forbidden at Blue Ridge, but sport fishermen can trotline or jug fish. During the spring excellent catches are made along the shoreline on the lake's lower end using natural baits or stinkbaits. Cats move into backwater areas around June, where they can be caught. During hot weather the best catches are at night using chicken liver for bait.

Taccoa is not rated as a trout fishery, but anyone visiting there who's fond of these gamesters should take a look at the tailrace trout fishery downstream from Taccoa Dam. Big rainbow and brown trout are taken there regularly. There is also an outfitter there who specializes in river trout trips.

Tellico Lake

SIZE: medium

ACCESSIBILITY: very good, few marinas

LOCATION: Tennessee (Monroe, Blount, and Loudon counties)

PRESSURE: light, but gaining in popularity

PRIMARY GAMEFISH: largemouth and smallmouth bass, bluegill, crappie, walleye

SECONDARY GAMEFISH: rainbow and brown trout, white bass, sauger

BEST MONTHS: March, April, May, June, October

BEST BAITS: live minnows, nightcrawlers, spinnerbaits, deep-diving and medium-depth crankbaits, plastic worms

BEST BET: fishing for largemouth bass with medium-depth crankbaits around stick-ups in late April

The Tellico Lake project was launched in the sixties during the heyday of TVA. The federal agency's power and popular support were at their zenith. Historians may someday point to the creation of this lake and the subsequent death of one of the East's finest trout rivers as the beginning of TVA's ultimate demise.

As a youngster, I remember bumper stickers reading "Dam the Little 'T'" and others saying "Save the Little 'T.'" Emotions ran high to preserve thousands of acres of rich productive farmland, irreplaceable Cherokee Indian archaeological and religious sites, and Tennessee's finest trout honeyhole. Conservationists tried without success to halt this seemingly senseless project, but bureaucrats backing the pork barrel project paid no heed. Even when the discovery of the snail darter stymied TVA efforts, construction at the dam continued unabated.

The final nail in the conservationists' coffin came when an eleventh-hour amendment in Congress sponsored by a local politician exempted the Tellico Dam Project from the Federal Endangered Species Act.

161

Within days the water behind the dam rose and the Little "T" was history.

Although Tellico Lake has been around less than a decade, it has already proven to be a major addition to the Volunteer State's impressive collection of lakes. Completed in 1980, Tellico Dam stands 105 feet high across the Little Tennessee River, only a few hundred feet upstream from its junction with the Tennessee River. Unlike most TVA dams, Tellico has no generating capacity. A canal connecting the lake with Fort Loudoun Lake passes its power potential through to Fort Loudoun Dam's hydroelectric turbines. At full pool, the lake stands 813 feet above sea level and covers 16,500 surface acres. It extends 33 river miles to the base of Chilhowee Dam. Unlike most headwater tributary lakes, Tellico does not undergo a dramatic autumn drawdown. It fluctuates at the same rate as its Siamese twin, Fort Loudoun Lake.

Blount County fronts the north shore of Tellico Lake from its headwaters to river mile 30. Monroe County encompasses the lake from that point on both sides to river mile 18, where Loudon County forms its common boundary thereafter to the dam. Lenoir City, Loudon, and Vonore are the nearest towns. Limited access to the northern headwater shoreline is provided by US 129, while TN 72 and 95 extend additional north-shore access. TN 72 also accesses the south side of the lake.

The lake has 1 commercial boat dock and 11 public boat-launch ramps. Fort Loudoun State Park is located on the lake in Monroe County. TVA maintains a dozen recreation areas. Camping is permitted at Lotterdale Cove and Notchy Creek recreation areas. The new 2,000-acre Tellico Lake waterfowl refuge at Chota Peninsula opened in mid-1986.

Tellico's water quality rates among the valley's finest. The lake was formed primarily by the clean waters of the Little Tennessee River, which drains the Great Smoky Mountains National Park and Pisgah, Nantahala and Cherokee national forests. Its major feeder streams, Citico Creek and the Tellico River, also have high water quality. Although this lake is ringed by the Smoky and Tellico mountains, it is not a mountain lake like Watauga or Chatuge. Rather it is a moderately shallow lake with lots of mudflats and standing timber. The river and feeder creek channels are the lake's deepest water. These areas are usually flanked by extensive stick-ups and stump-lined flats. The bottom strata are primarily mud, gravel and some rock. Lake vegetation is nil. Brush and standing timber are abundant and figure prominently in fishing strategies.

Fishing Information

Tellico is more like two lakes. Its headwaters begin directly beneath Chilhowee Dam; here rainbow and brown trout, plus large walleye, abound. Downstream, the lake waters spread and warm. A shallow, warm-water fishery exists here. The line between the two is most distinct during the warm-weather months.

Tellico's outstanding largemouth bass fishery was one of this lake's most welcomed attributes. Lunker hawgs are taken here year-round. Winter bass fishing is concentrated deep along old creek meanders, notably Clear and Baker creeks. Here brown-brown and brown-black pig'n'jigs or pork and rind combos work like charms. Spring arrives early here in comparison to many area lakes. Tellico's shallow flats and ample structure are too much for the local bucketmouths to resist when the sun begins warming these 2-to-6-foot-deep areas. Movement to the shallow areas often occurs in early March. Twistertail grubs, light-hued spinnerbaits and plastic worms are always good bets.

Rising spring lake levels continue through April. At this time flippin' purple, brown, or chartreuse spider jigs is preferred. May beckons in a top-water extravaganza. Buzzbaits and top-water baits are deadly worked near heavy structure. Fly rodders can have a ball here casting big hair flies. Summer bassin' continues in the timbers, although in this season the night hours are the most productive. Worming is worth trying, as are medium-depth-running crankbaits like Shad Raps and Rebel Crawdads. The best night bass action is in the area between Hall Bend and Mizell Bluff and the vicinity of the Island Creek embayment.

When Tellico Lake was created, it was little more than enlightened conjecture to say that it would support a decent trout fishery. During the lake's first couple of seasons tales of mammoth brown trout of up to 17 pounds were common. Today trout are still caught at Tellico, although not in this size-class. Winter finds these scattered from the headwaters to the dam and spilling over into forage-rich Fort Loudoun Lake via the connecting canal. Trolling spoons and shiner crankbaits near points and submerged islands works well. Warming water temperatures trigger trout migration upstream to the old Little Tennessee River channel immediately below Chilhowee Lake. When hydroelectric production is occurring, drift fishing using corn, worms, salmon eggs and grasshoppers is good. Trolling and casting plugs are good at all times. Autumn finds Tellico Lake's trout beginning to stir. "Jump" action, identical to that common to white bass, occurs downstream at the mouth of the Tellico River. Fall is also when mature brown trout make spawning runs up Citico Creek. Bottom fishing big shiners and casting medium-depth-diving crankbaits along the embayment headwaters are the best approaches.

Prior to the construction of any dams on the Little Tennessee River, this flow had quite a reputation for its river-run walleye fishing. Dam construction stymied these fish. The creation of Tellico Lake, however,

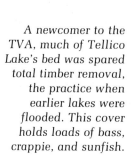

A newcomer to the TVA, much of Tellico Lake's bed was spared total timber removal, the practice when earlier lakes were flooded. This cover holds loads of bass, crappie, and sunfish.

enabled the reestablishment of this perch fishery. Walleye in the 8-to-10-pound class are occasionally taken, but limits are not common. The best year-round walleye fishing occurs in the headwaters between Harrison Island and the Tellico Blockhouse. This section of the lake is always within their preferred temperature range. Trolling spoons, 5-inch Rebel Floater Minnows or Hellbenders works well during all seasons. Night fishing using minnows under lights is productive from July through early October in the area between Harrison Island and Bacon Bend, but few partake.

Tellico Lake's bluegill fishery has been a pleasant surprise, particularly for fly flickers. Platter-size bluegill are always abundant during the fair-weather months. Bedding occurs as early as April and can extend well into June. Most prefer bobber fishing with crickets or redworms. The best show in town, though, is in the old standing timber using a willow wand and popping bug. Popping small cork, hair or bugs near exposed wood structure will almost certainly be met with a cat-quick take. Color and pattern are not nearly as important as casting accuracy and patience. Try to place your fly as near as possible to a likely looking brush or limb. If a strike doesn't occur on impact, allow the fly to sit idle for a few minutes.

Tellico Lake is rarely noted as a good crappie fishing place, but those familiar with its calicos know it's a secret worth keeping. Ample structure and an adequate forage base combine to make these fast-growing sunfish plentiful. Winter crappie fishing can be outstanding here in the area between the connecting channel and Jackson Bend. Vertical jigging with motor oil, yellow, or smoke-colored jelly grubs fished over wood cover is almost always productive. Trolling creek meanders is also effective at times. Bedding action begins in late March when seasonal conditions chime correctly. Again, timber and brush are the hot spots, with 3-to-7-foot-deep water being the key depth zones. Live tuffies, dollflies and small twister grubs all work well. Most regulars here suspend their offerings under a bobber. Summer calico action is a spotty, hit-and-miss affair. Some good hot-weather catches are made at night minnow fishing under a lantern light, although this technique is not utilized as much as one might expect. Summertime catches of crappie can be made here vertically jigging minnows right against flooded timbers.

Catfish found here include flathead, blue and channel cats. For those familiar with this lake's whiskered fish population, there is only one place to try your luck—the connecting channel. Trotlines baited with chicken liver worked near the channel mouth are seldom retrieved without enough whiskered fish to feed a medium-sized crew.

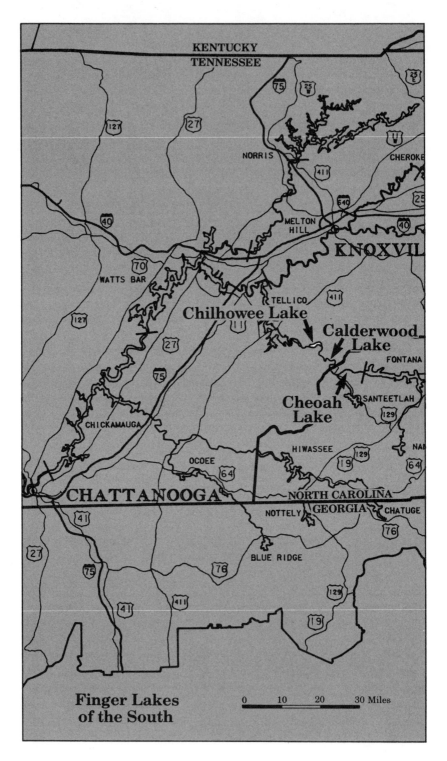

**Finger Lakes
of the South**

0   10   20   30 Miles

166

Finger Lakes of the South

Wine connoisseurs fond of New York State white and sparkling wines probably believe the country's only "finger lakes" are those glacial afterthoughts found in the Empire State. Not so, and if you don't believe this, just look at the Great Smoky Mountains National Park's southern edge.

Found here are three slender, snaking lakes—Chilhowee, Calderwood, and Cheoah—the "Finger Lakes of the South." Chilhowee is entirely in Tennessee, Cheoah is in North Carolina, and Calderwood is located astride their common border. Unlike nearly all other nearby man-made lakes in the Tennessee River drainage, this string of Little Tennessee River impoundments is not part of the gigantic Tennessee Valley Authority system. Each is owned and operated by Tapoco, a subsidiary of the Aluminum Company of America (or Alcoa).

These are old impoundments. Cheoah was completed in 1919, Calderwood Dam was finished and ready to operate in 1930, and Chilhowee was finished in 1959. Located between the Great Smoky Mountains National Park and Nantahala and Cherokee national forest (as well as corporate properties), the lakes are virtually undeveloped. There are no marinas, few restaurants and gas stations and very little lodging available near these lakes. While this is certainly an inconvenience of sorts, the surrounding natural setting more than makes up for any hardship.

All three impoundments have scenic qualities that man's handiwork can hardly match, and more important to anglers, each holds loads of brightly silvered trout. It would be easy to lump these lakes together, but each differs from the other in a variety of ways.

Sound interesting? You bet it is!

——Chilhowee Lake

SIZE: small
ACCESSIBILITY: good, no marinas
LOCATION: Tennessee (Monroe and Blount counties)
PRESSURE: moderate to light
PRIMARY GAMEFISH: bluegill, rainbow trout
SECONDARY GAMEFISH: catfish, brook and brown trout, largemouth
  bass, walleye, smallmouth bass
BEST MONTHS: May, June, July, August, September, October
BEST BAITS: nightcrawlers, dry flies, jigs, cheese balls, shallow-depth
  crankbaits, small spinners, wet flies
BEST BET: fishing for rainbow trout with dry flies along the lake's
  floating trashlines downstream from Calderwood Dam in June

The first "Finger Lake" is Chilhowee, a 1,747-acre impoundment and
the only body of water in this group solely in Tennessee. Until the late
seventies Chilhowee Lake was the final indignation the Little "T" bore
before emptying into the Tennessee River just downstream from Fort
Loudoun Dam.

At that time, what was thought by many to be the finest trout river
in the eastern United States was spawned forth beneath the shadow of
Chilhowee Dam. Brown trout over seven pounds were common, as growth
rates were excellent due to the fact this tailrace river flowed over a rich
limestone base.

We last fished that river only two weeks before the gates were closed
at the controversial Tellico Dam, drowning the river forever. It was a
bright autumn day, and we arrived just as the turbines at Chilhowee
Dam were shut down. Our party of four caught almost 300 trout, re-
leasing many fish over 19 inches long. This was a golden farewell to a
24-carat trout river.

Chilhowee Lake is the most diverse, accessible, and popular of the
Finger Lakes. The dam stands only 68 feet high; however, it backs up
a lake over nine miles long. At its widest point, Chilhowee Lake is almost
a mile across, five times wider than Calderwood at its widest.

It is also a remarkably shallow mountain lake, seldom reaching over
50 feet deep. For most of its course it is less than 20 feet deep, with 10-
foot-deep water common along the shoreline. Chilhowee's headwaters
are wedged between two vertical rock cliffs, a sight well worth boating
up the lake to view.

Chilhowee Lake has no marinas, but it does have three public boat-
launch areas. The first is located at the mouth of Abrams Creek, the

Small spinners for trout and white bass.

second is located one mile upstream from the first, while the third is located at the mouth of Tabcat Creek, five miles upstream from the dam. All three are easily visible from US 129.

Camping is permitted on the lake's south shore on properties owned by Tapoco and the Cherokee National Forest. Camping also occurs on the north shore downstream from the Panther Creek embayment area. We would not recommend the latter for two reasons. First, the area is gravel covered and virtually devoid of trees or other vegetation. Second, this area is regularly frequented by thugs, hoods, and other unsavory sorts. Anyone buying this book certainly would not be at home around these gents and lasses.

Fishing Information

Chilhowee is actually two lakes: one being a cold-water trout fishery located in the lake's upper half, and the other a warm-water lake beginning around the mouth of Tabcat Creek. The cold-water fishery is maintained by the regular influx of icy, clean water from upstream Calderwood Dam.

Trolling for trout is popular and productive, as is night trout fishing; both are practiced here just as on the upstream lakes, although by greater numbers of anglers. During the summer the lake is alive with lights as all sorts of fishing and pleasure craft dot its course, vying for tasty trout.

Fly fishermen will be delighted to discover that this lake offers sea-

TVA's Finger Lakes all boast excellent rainbow trout fishing.

son-long summertime long rod trout action in the trashline. Lines of debris beginning at the base of Calderwood Dam extend unbroken from shoreline to shoreline. Viewed from above, these trashlines resemble bathtub rings as they slowly wash down the lake, disappearing approximately five miles downstream.

The debris holds large numbers of beetles, bees and other terrestrial food items which are of considerable interest to Chilhowee Lake's big rainbow trout. Trout cruise the trashlines gingerly picking off insects. Fly flickers using large nymphs or beetle patterns sit in the bows of their boats or canoes watching the lake's mirrorlike surface to detect approaching feeders.

Once a trout begins prowling a debris line, it will follow it from one end to the other, rhythmically surfacing every 10 to 20 feet. The trick is to gauge your quarry's surface pattern and attempt to drop your fly where it will surface next.

Admittedly, this is a hit-or-miss angling technique, but it can be awesomely effective. One fly fisherman from nearby Maryville who has been flicking to the trashline trout for many years confided he took over 30 trout in excess of 20 inches from Chilhowee Lake in a single month.

Bluegill and catfish are abundant along the shoreline on the lake's lower half. Natural baits are the most popular way for taking these fish. Chilhowee is an excellent largemouth bass lake, although it is seldom noted as such. While fishing there in 1983, we saw one angler hook into a seven-inch stocked trout one afternoon, only to have a 10-pound hawg engulf the panicked trout. The bass was successfully landed by the fisherman.

Most bass fishing takes place downstream from the Tabcat Creek launch area. Top-water lures and spinnerbaits are recommended early in the season, while plastic worms and live baits work best following July. Little fishing takes place here during cold weather.

Chilhowee also sports a little-known walleye fishery. Like the bass, these fish are most common in the "second lake," or lower half. During the spring quite a few marble-eye are caught along the shoreline and around the mouth of Tabcat Creek by trollers. Between May and September nearly all walleye fishing occurs at night using minnows under a lantern extended over the water. Limits are generally uncommon, but big fish in the five-to-nine pound class are regularly taken.

—— Calderwood Lake

SIZE: small
ACCESSIBILITY: fair, year-round
LOCATION: Tennessee (Monroe and Blount counties) and North
    Carolina (Graham and Swain counties)
PRESSURE: very light
PRIMARY GAMEFISH: smallmouth bass, bluegill, rainbow trout
SECONDARY GAMEFISH: catfish, brook and brown trout
BEST MONTHS: May, June, July, August, September, October
BEST BAITS: nightcrawlers, dry flies, jigs, cheese balls, shallow-depth
    crankbaits, small spinners, wet flies
BEST BET: fishing for rainbow trout with small spinners along the
    lake's bluffs in late June

Calderwood Lake is one of the South's least-known gems. Located between Cheoah and Chilhowee on the Little "T," this 536-acre impoundment offers superb trout fishing. Unlike its upstream counterpart Cheoah Lake, though, Calderwood offers more angling opportunities than just trout.

Bream fishing along the shoreline in Calderwood's lower end can be explosive during the summer months. Natural baits fished one to four feet deep are sufficient, but if your tastes are a bit more difficult to stimulate, try using a popping bug.

Channel catfish are also abundant in this lake, and while these fish rate high as tablefare from almost all waters, whiskered fish from this gin-clear lake are the mildest in flavor we have ever eaten. Bank fishing for cats is productive, as are trotlines. Limb lining from the lakeside trees is loads of fun and when conditions are right will net more fish than two men can handle.

Calderwood Dam stands 213 feet high, but is less than 200 feet across; during the summer this arch-shaped dam resembles a concrete wedge driven between two green sofa pillows. It is a deep lake, with depths over 190 feet deep in the lake's lower end along the river channel, which winds over eight miles back through rugged, remote ridges.

This lake fluctuates, like Cheoah, usually on a daily basis. The lake's level is dependent on upstream generating activity. The Cheoah River enters the lake at its headwaters only a few hundred feet downstream from Cheoah Dam, although the two are unrelated.

Santeetlah Lake is created by the impoundment of the Cheoah River. If you're not confused now, add to this the fact that although the Cheoah

Mixed bag: a fine stringer of large- and smallmouth bass.

River resurfaces downstream from Santeetlah Lake and is a "textbook" tailrace flow, it is not affected by power generated using Santeetlah Lake's stored water. This is accomplished at the Santeetlah Powerhouse on the south shore of Cheoah Lake.

The Cheoah River drains a large section of the Nantahala National Forest. Other key feeder streams entering Calderwood Lake include Parsons Branch, a medium-sized trout stream draining the Great Smoky Mountains National Park, and Slickrock Creek, one of North Carolina and Tennessee's premier brown trout streams. This stream's 10,700-acre watershed is shared by the Cherokee and Nantahala national forests and is protected by the national wilderness system.

The Tennessee–North Carolina state line bisects this lake less than two miles downstream from Cheoah Dam. According to a long-standing reciprocal agreement between these adjoining states, both states' fishing licenses are honored on the entire lake and Slickrock Creek.

The lake's northern shoreline is National Park Service domain, and there is neither roadside camping nor designated backcountry campsites along Calderwood's length. The lake's southern shore is shared by the U.S. Forest Service (Nantahala and Cherokee national forests) and Tapoco. Camping is permitted for reasonable lengths of time and under relatively liberal restraints on both properties, although commonly acknowledged courtesies such as no littering, permanent structures, large fires, cutting standing timber, and so forth, are required of those using these properties.

Calderwood Lake is the most remote and difficult to access of the Smoky Mountains Finger Lakes. Roadside access from US 129 is available only at the crossing of this two-lane highway immediately downstream from Cheoah Dam and at a gravel road which leads off of US 129 to Calderwood Dam. The latter is a steep roadway difficult to negotiate during inclement weather. There are no marinas or other facilities on this lake.

Fishing Information

Fishing pressure on Calderwood is light. Both the Tennessee and North Carolina fishery departments stock this lake with brook, rainbow and brown trout. Food is in short supply, but because fishing pressure is also scant, many of the lake's stocked trout live out their lives here, achieving considerable size. Brown and rainbow trout in excess of 10 pounds are taken each year.

This is a bit ironic for those old-timers who remember when this lake was created during the thirties. At that time fishery folks believed such high-elevation lakes could only be sterile, oxygen-depressed deserts. This notion was carried over well into the TVA era. When Norris Lake was constructed during the mid-thirties, hatcheries for warm-water fish species were also built to "try" to establish some sort of fishery in that 35,000-acre lake.

Following the impoundment of the Little Tennessee River at Calderwood Lake, no one checked to see if fish could exist in that lake, no one except the local fishermen, who discovered that trout from the tributary mountain streams migrated into the lake where they quickly grew fat. For almost ten years the secret of this lake's excellent trout fishing was shared only by a small group of anglers.

When it was discovered trout could live in tailrace rivers and deep mountain impoundments, regular stocking began here. To the dismay of many local anglers, the quality of this lake's trout fishery actually dropped (in their opinion) due to the planting of fish from locales other than the mountain streams.

Fishing for trout at Calderwood Lake during the summer is easier if a depth finder and downrigger for trolling are available. This is particularly true in the lake's lower end. Night fishing in the lake's upper third is also popular and highly productive, not to mention lots of fun. A word to the wise: even on the hottest August nights you can catch a nasty head cold in this frigid ravine.

When night fishing here, suspend a lantern over the water and either vertically jig spoons or still fish lively minnows a few feet deep. Trout are very shallow at times, while for reasons unknown to this scribe, they can sometimes be very deep.

During the spring dry flies and terrestrial patterns are productive along the abundant tree-lined shore. Seeing a four-pound rainbow cartwheeling through a blooming redbud tree will certainly get your attention if the beautiful scenery around this highland lake hasn't already grabbed you.

—— Cheoah Lake

SIZE: small
ACCESSIBILITY: good
LOCATION: North Carolina (Graham and Swain counties)
PRESSURE: light
PRIMARY GAMEFISH: rainbow trout
SECONDARY GAMEFISH: brown and brook trout, bluegill
BEST MONTHS: April, May, June, July, August, October
BEST BAITS: deep-diving crankbaits, dry flies, red wigglers, dough
    balls

BEST BET: fishing for rainbow trout using live bait and drift fishing
with the current in late May

Cheoah was the first impoundment built on the Little Tennessee River,
predating the creation of the Tennessee Valley Authority by almost fifteen years. It was completed in 1919 by its present-day owner, Tapoco,
a subsidiary of the Aluminum Company of America (or Alcoa). Tapoco
owns and operates Cheoah, Santeetlah, Calderwood and Chilhowee dams
and lakes.

Cheoah Dam's hydroelectric capabilities are quite substantial despite
its age, with the bulk of the power being consumed by Alcoa for the
production of aluminum. This old dam is visible where US 129 crosses
Calderwood Lake near Tapoco.

Cheoah Lake extends approximately 10 miles behind 189-foot-high
Cheoah Dam. Despite the dam's impressive height, much of the lake is
silt filled; its winding main channel and the area near the Santeetlah
Powerhouse are the lake's deepest zones.

The lake begins immediately downstream from Fontana Dam's tailrace and accounts for approximately 595 surface acres. Unlike upstream
Fontana and most other western North Carolina highland impoundments, Cheoah is not a storage-type reservoir. Its limited capacity is
quickly achieved whenever Fontana Dam's hydroelectric turbines are

*Lead jig, doll, or hair fly. This is the most productive and
widely used bait in the TVA system.*

in operation. Extended periods of upstream power generation automatically mean reciprocal turbine activity at Cheoah Dam.

The Finger Lake area along the Little Tennessee River was one of the primary cultural centers of the Overhill Cherokee. These tribes were forcibly removed from the eastern United States during the late 1830s. By the time of the War of Northern Aggression (1861–65), this area was completely settled, although it was never crowded. The Little Tennessee River's course was a natural route for railways, and logging trains made daily treks out this way by the end of the nineteenth century. Only rising lake waters halted timber operations in a number of otherwise remote watersheds like Slickrock Creek. Today this area is fully forested and displays a wild look seldom found around southern manmade lakes.

Cheoah is fed year-round with cold, clean water from several mountain streams. This fact makes it one of the coldest, if not the coldest, impoundments south of the Mason-Dixon Line. In addition, icy water from Santeetlah Lake several miles away arrives at Cheoah Lake via a pipeline, descending 663 feet before emptying at the Santeetlah Powerhouse, approximately 5.4 miles upstream from Cheoah Dam.

Cheoah is located on the border of Swain and Graham counties. Robbinsville and Fontana Village are the nearest major towns. It is accessed by NC 28 and US 129.

There are no commercial docks or launches on Cheoah Lake, but there are two unnamed public boat-launch ramps. The first, and most popular, is located at the Santeetlah Powerhouse, which is accessible from Tapoco via US 129, across Calderwood Lake, and left onto Meadow Branch Road. At approximately four miles this gravel road arrives at the Santeetlah Powerhouse and ramp.

Tapoco is a very small outpost, primarily operated for Tapoco employees, families and support personnel. Scona Lodge, a historic mountain hideaway, is located here, and although several attempts have been made to reopen this quaint turn-of-the-century establishment, unfortunately at this writing it is not open.

Camping is permitted along the lake's southern shoreline, which is held jointly by Tapoco and the Nantahala National Forest. Extended stays of over ten days are not allowed, nor is littering, cutting down green or dead trees, or other related behavior. Many areas along the lake's southern shoreline are accessible only by boat.

Fishing Information

Trout are the lake's primary gamefish, and this lake is stocked regularly by the state of North Carolina with rainbow, brown and brook trout. Although food is not as abundant here as in Fontana, Cheoah's trout grow reasonably fast and achieve larger sizes. Twelve-to-sixteen-inch rainbows and browns are common, and larger brown trout up to five to seven pounds are available in good numbers. The brookies usually do not grow longer than a foot, but by southern stream standards this is large.

Cheoah's headwaters are actually a tailwater river and are very productive during brief periods following turbine shutdowns at Fontana Dam. There is something magical about a tailwater river descent following shutdowns. Aquatic insects (though sparse) emerge regardless of the time of day, and trout seem to come out of the woodwork. Fly fishing with streamers, dries and nymphs or spinner fishing is good at this time, along with small spinners, floater and minnow plugs and a variety of baits.

Limited natural reproduction occurs each spring in the Twenty Mile Creek drainage area. During this season many successful anglers concentrate their efforts along this narrow embayment, fishing near the bottom.

Trolling minnow-type plugs, dollflies, small spinners or live bait, many anglers convert otherwise slow angling periods into productive times. Most trollers use brisk speeds and concentrate on either the main river channel or close to the shoreline. Suspending bait in the tail of boils at the Santeetlah Powerhouse is productive, but for safety reasons boaters should not get too close to this facility.

Shoreline fishing is very popular during the spring, particularly near the Twentymile Creek embayment and Santeetlah Powerhouse, as well as along US 129 and NC 28, which often pass close to the lake.

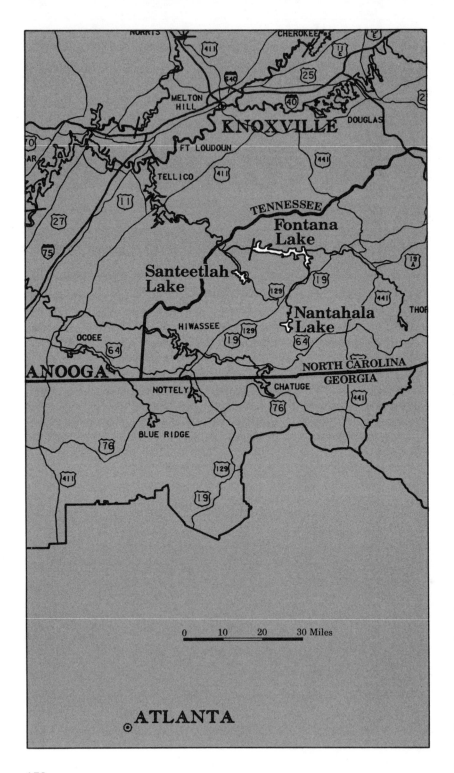

Fontana Lake

SIZE: medium

ACCESSIBILITY: good, fair in winter; few marinas

LOCATION: North Carolina (Graham and Swain counties)

PRESSURE: moderate to light

PRIMARY GAMEFISH: bluegill, smallmouth and largemouth bass, white bass, walleye

SECONDARY GAMEFISH: brown and rainbow trout, catfish, crappie

BEST MONTHS: April, May, June, July, August, October

BEST BAITS: live minnows, hair jigs, spring lizards, pig'n'jig, nightcrawlers, deep-diving crankbaits, plastic worms

BEST BET: late evening fishing for walleye using minnows along the lake's steep shoreline around Fontana Village in May

Perched almost 2,000 feet above sea level, Fontana Lake is one of the highest impoundments in the seven-state Tennessee Valley Authority. This 10,530-acre lake is wedged between the Great Smoky Mountains National Park and the Nantahala National Forest. During the summer months when the surrounding countryside is dominated by forest green and cloud-dotted, pale blue skies, this emerald-green lake appears natural, sometimes giving the impression of being the gem in a fine piece of jewelry.

Development along this impoundment is limited. In 1985 there were six marinas along the lake's shoreline, which offered the standard array of boat dock services (gas, snacks, boat rentals, launching ramps and, in some cases, guide service).

There are no significant aquatic weeds here, and little in the way of fish-holding structure other than rock and gravel. The fish-attractor program carried on by TVA and North Carolina is an attempt to provide man-made structure, usually in the form of downed trees or brush piles.

Framed by the Smokies, Fontana is a very scenic lake. TVA photo.

These sites concentrate fish 9 to 19 times greater than unmanipulated shoreline.

Fontana Dam impounds the Little Tennessee River, which drains western North Carolina. The Little "T" is formed by such well-known Carolina rivers as the Tuckasegee, Nantahala and Oconaluftee.

This is a storage-type impoundment which is drawn down over 50 feet each year. The lake is held at a low level during the autumn and winter to accommodate potentially heavy seasonal rainfall. Lake levels begin rising during the early spring, with full pool (1,709 feet maximum) usually being achieved between May and July. A gradual drawdown usually begins in mid-to-late July, although all the above water level data are dependent on annual rainfall, as well as power and downstream navigational needs.

The construction of Fontana Dam began overnight following the nation's entrance into World War II in late 1941. The Tennessee Valley Authority was nearly 10 years old when the Fontana project began, and a number of projects in the Tennessee River Valley had already begun.

High-voltage power needs at defense plants in nearby Alcoa, Tennessee, for warplane construction, as well as a top-secret project taking shape in Oak Ridge, Tennessee (where the first atomic bomb was assembled), were the impetus behind the dam's crash building program. Many thousand of acres of bottomland and ridge country were purchased from local residents, many of whom were less than willing to turn over family holdings to the federal government. Much of this land became the lake and immediate surroundings, although a total of 44,204 acres acquired from the mountain folk was later deeded over to the Great Smoky Mountains National Park. Today this property forms the sometimes controversial north-shore Hazel Creek area. An additional 11,667 acres acquired along the lake's southern shoreline was later transferred to the U.S. Forest Service.

Less than a month after the bombing of Pearl Harbor the first construction crews began arriving at the sleepy mountain hamlet known as Fontana Village. Legislation passed by Congress prior to the hostilities for a dam atop the Little Tennessee River in Graham County, North Carolina, had paved the way for the project's beginning.

This legislation was not adequate warning, though, for what was to ensue. Survey crews arrived first, followed by building crews, which immediately began putting up housing for the soon-to-arrive 7,000 construction workers and support crews which worked on the dam 24 hours a day, seven days a week.

Building Fontana Dam was an engineering accomplishment of no small merit. It ranks as the tallest dam east of the Rockies, standing 480 feet high, yet it took only slightly over two years to complete. The project cost only $71 million, a mere fraction of what such a gigantic undertaking would cost today.

Even today Fontana Lake is considered a backwoods area, but over 40 years ago, few had even heard of this place whose claim to fame was the fact it was the site where the last known mountain lion in the southern mountains had been killed in the 1920s.

In order to accommodate the influx of thousands of construction workers, engineers, support personnel and their families, housing, dormitories, cafeterias, stores, laundries and even movie houses and schools were built. The construction camp took the name Fontana Village. Even during the war era when gas rationing and extremely poor mountain roads slowed most travel, well over one million Tennessee and North Carolina residents made the trip here to witness this much-heralded building project.

The completed Fontana Dam gave TVA a new, ready-to-operate hydroelectric and flood control facility and a white elephant construction ghost town. Even before the project's completion, federal and state officials had realized Fontana Village's recreational possibilities. The war years were an inopportune time to kick off a tourism project, however, and for several years only dam maintenance crews resided there.

Guest Service, Inc., a Washington, D.C.–based nonprofit corporation which had experience in operating recreational ventures in a number of western national parks, leased the Fontana Village complex from TVA during the late forties and has operated it as a family vacation site since that time.

We have stayed at Fontana Village many times over the years. Return trips to that quaint, low-development area are an annual event now. Two things about Fontana Village make it different from virtually every other Southern Appalachian vacation spot.

First, much of the rustic beauty found here when Fontana Village was a backwoods construction camp still exists. The worker cabins and cottages have been remodeled and are now guest lodging, but their rough-hewn character still glimmers through. The old cafeteria still serves up homemade fruit pies and biscuits and gravy, just as it did daily 40 years ago, and the old movie house, which once flickered Bogie and John Wayne movies across its silver screen, still shows the latest movies. Modern amenities abound, but much of the village's former self is openly visible.

Second, Fontana Village is located in close proximity to the finest treasure house of the southern highlands. One has only to walk a few hundred feet to enjoy the region's lush flora. The Appalachian Trail passes directly through the village, while other trails and noteworthy backcountry destinations are easily reached.

With the low-key approach and the area's total lack of competing development, staying here gives one the strong feeling of having stepped back in time 50 years.

Fishing Information

Fishing is without question Fontana Lake's number-one drawing card. Angling is nearly always very good here, and the lake's setting amid such splendid mountain scenery makes even those occasional fishless days easy to bear.

For a mountain lake Fontana Lake sports a surprisingly diverse gamefish fishery. Angling for smallmouth bass, walleye, white bass, rainbow and steelhead trout, muskie (and tiger muskie) and bream is on a par with lakes anywhere. Catfish are also plentiful, and fishing for largemouth bass, brown trout, red breast bream and crappie rates fair to good.

Much of Fontana Lake's nationally recognized fishing reputation can be traced to the lake's smallmouth bass fishery. While everyone has his own opinion about which gamefish is the top battler when stung by a hook (and I might add I'm a dyed-in-the-wool trout fisherman), most angling surveys end with the smallmouth bass at the top of the list, and rightfully so. The acrobatics these chunky muscle-bound fish perform when they are hooked are enough to inspire even the most jaded trout fisherman.

Fontana Lake, with its steep, rocky shoreline and year-round cool water temperatures, is picture perfect bronzeback habitat. Bronzebacks in the 10-to-14-inch class are the usual fare, but big smalljaws in the three-pound class are always a possibility, and tackle busters in the four-to-six- and even seven-pound class inhabit every rocky point.

The best smallmouth bass fishing occurs between mid-April and late June. This timeslot encompasses the smallie's early season awakening, their movement into small feeder creek areas and the nesting time along the gravel shoreline areas.

Bait fishing with live, 3-inch minnows is a productive early season ploy, while later in the season such crankbaits as the Rebel deep-running Crawdad or the Bomber II are lethal when worked adjacent to the shoreline. Throughout this period these bass are relative shallow (2 to 10 feet deep) and easily accessible to the average angler.

Hot weather and "long day sunshine" send the smallmouth bass deep from July through September, with average depths being 10 to 35 feet deep during the daylight hours.

Then these fish can be taken on red, purple or black plastic worms, as well as brown, black or purple spider jigs with No. 101 Uncle Josh pork rinds. Because deep-structure fishing with these bottom-chunking baits is difficult and usually frustrating for inexperienced anglers, many Fontana Lake bass fishermen turn to the twilight hours, when the brown bass return to the shallows to feed.

Nighttime fishing for smallmouth and largemouth here can be out-standing. A variety of baits ranging from deep-water hardware to me-dium-depth-running crankbaits and even top-water baits are used during the night hours. Live baits, particularly spring lizards or nightcrawlers fished off rocky points, are also good nocturnal bass takers. These varied nighttime fishing methods are consistently used by knowledgeable local bass anglers throughout the autumn months.

Largemouth bass are readily available throughout Fontana Lake despite the fact that this impoundment is seldom touted for its green hawg fishery. Granted, the bigmouth bass are not caught as frequently as the smalljaws, but they are actively sought here by bass tourney anglers seeking to accumulate quick poundage during competition.

Techniques used to take Fontana's bronzebacks work well for ole bucketmouth. Holding areas for both are closer on Fontana Lake than on most lakes due to the lake's steep-walled character. There are a few mudflats in the headwaters preferred by the warmer-natured largemouth bass during the spring, but generally speaking these fish frequent the

Drifting big, live minnows along feeder creeks is a sure-fire bet for early spring smallie action at Fontana Lake.

same general areas, which in turn makes the tactics and baits used for the bronzeback quite effective for its larger-growing cousin.

Fontana Lake has a long-standing reputation as an outstanding walleye fishery. These large-growing perch were native to the Little "T" drainage prior to the lake's creation and have prospered here. Late winter finds these river-spawning fish in the swift headwaters of the Little "T," Nantahala and Tuckasegee rivers. Tramping the river banks casting green or yellow, quarter-ounce, leadhead jigs or live minnows along the rocky bottom is the best way to catch a mess of spawning-run marble-eyes.

Following the spawn, these fish return to the lake by April, feeding in 2-to-13-foot water near the shoreline. While they are shallow, cast night crawlers, minnows or green ¼–½-ounce, feather jigs to the bank and "staircase" those baits down. These techniques are good through late spring, when warmer weather sends the walleye progressively deeper. Trolling creek embayments, especially Hazel and Forney, is super-effective.

During the summer months most serious walleye fishing occurs under the stars in the lake's lower one-fourth. Vertically jigged spoons or dollflies, as well as dabbled live minnows, under a lantern extended over the water is a bonafide trick for taking these delicious fish. The areas immediately adjacent to the dam and Eagle Creek are top spots for lantern fishing for walleye, which get up to seven pounds here.

Many anglers visit this lake to explore its underrated trout fishery. Rainbow trout in Fontana originally descended from the well-known trout streams Hazel, Noland and Forney which empty into the lake; subsequent stockings of these fish have produced a first-class lake rainbow trout fishery. The recent introduction of steelhead rainbow trout by North Carolina fishery managers has resulted in a relatively new fishery for these "sea-run" 'bows, which hopefully will achieve greater growth than the stream-oriented rainbows common to Fontana's open-water environment. The lake also has a little-fished-for and generally overlooked brown trout population.

Late winter and early spring find these cold-natured exotics in the headwaters of the lake's numerous feeder streams. This is spawning time for the trout (except the browns), and swift-moving water is required for mating success. While actual spawning takes place in the streams, good rainbow trout catches can be made in the creek mouths, where these fish "stage" in large numbers prior to entering the current.

Small spinners and a large variety of live baits, as well as small, silver-hued shallow- and medium-depth-running crankbaits, are all good at this time. These fish are not overly aggressive in the early season, but persistence and keeping your bait wet will usually net enough fish for a shore lunch.

Santeetlah Lake

SIZE: small
ACCESSIBILITY: fair
LOCATION: North Carolina (Graham County)
PRESSURE: moderate to light
PRIMARY GAMEFISH: bluegill, smallmouth and largemouth bass, walleye, catfish
SECONDARY GAMEFISH: rainbow trout, white bass, crappie
BEST MONTHS: April, May, June, July, October
BEST BAITS: nightcrawlers, hair jigs, deep- and shallow-depth crankbaits, live minnows, plastic worms
BEST BET: fishing for smallmouth bass using live minnows or top-water plugs along the lake's points during the early morning in June

Santeetlah Lake is the sort of honeyhole that when an outdoor writer sells a story that reveals it to the world of hungry fishermen, the hapless scribe gets hate mail from the local fishermen who've been keeping it a secret. This is not to say this lake is a Shangri-la where all snake-bitten anglers can go to change their luck. If you're experienced at fishing at night for walleye and smallmouth bass in mountain lake settings, however, this lake is worth investigating.

Santeetlah Lake is created by the impoundment of the Cheoah River, which drains a 176-square-mile watershed that includes the Snowbird, Unicoi (Stateline Ridge) and Cheoah mountains. Most of this tract is located within the Nantahala National Forest, which in turn contains the rugged Slickrock Wilderness Area (formerly part of the Santeetlah and Tellico wildlife management areas) and the famous Joyce Kilmer Memorial Forest. The latter holds the Southern Appalachians' finest remnant stands of cove hardwoods and is a must visit for anyone fishing at this lake.

At full pool the lake covers 2,850 surface acres. The dam, which was built by Alcoa between 1926 and 1928, stands 215 feet high and is 1,054 feet across. It has a hydroelectric generating capacity of 45,000 kilowatts, but the powerhouse is not located at the dam. Water from the lake is piped several miles away to a powerhouse on the banks of Cheoah Lake.

Santeetlah Lake is not a TVA impoundment and therefore does not offer anglers the unlimited access and recreational facilities common to TVA lakes. While Alcoa controls many aspects of the lake, however, the U.S. Forest Service owns a vast portion of the lake frontage. There is some development around the lake, notably at Santeetlah and the Cheoah District Ranger Station area. Public camping is available at the Forest Service's Cheoah Point Recreation Area and Horse Cove Recreation Area (which is a short distance from the lake). Day-use areas include the Forest Service's Snowbird Recreation Area. Camping is permitted on federally held lands; however, there are private clubs and other holdings around the lake where uninvited guests are not welcome.

Santeetlah, Robbinsville, and Fontana Village are the nearest towns. The lake's eastern shoreline is traced by US 129. Paved Forest Service and county-maintained roads encircle the rest of the lake. There are no commercial boat docks, but there are two public boat-launch ramps.

Like most mountain reservoirs, Santeetlah's most outstanding feature is its main river channel, which is formed in the lake by the confluence of Tulula and Snowbird creeks. The primary bottom strata are rock, gravel and red clay.

Fishing Information

In 1963 a surprised angler lifted an equally surprised 14-pound, 15-ounce largemouth bass from Santeetlah Lake. This fish is still the biggest bucketmouth bass ever taken in the Tar Heel State. How representative is a 15-pound bass for this lake? Well, in all truthfulness, not very—but it did happen.

Santeetlah's reputation for surprises supersedes everything else written about this lake. It holds fairly decent populations of largemouth and smallmouth bass. Like most of the other Tennessee River Valley lakes at such lofty elevations, however, this is not a rich lake and growth rates for major gamefish are slow. North Carolina Wildlife Resources Commission data indicate that four-year-old smallmouth and largemouth bass average only 13 and 12 inches long, respectively. At Pickwick Lake on the Tennessee River, fish of this age-class would be 18 and 19 inches long.

The lake's black bass population is hamstrung by low forage and lack of cover. The state stocks the lake each year with threadfin shad, which helps relieve the baitfish problem somewhat. Cover is another

Santeetlah Lake is a real sleeper that few other than local walleye fishermen frequent.

dilemma. During the drought of the mid-1980s when the lake level reached a record low, the local Graham County Sportsman's Club spent considerable time and money "furnishing" the exposed dry lake bed with many brush piles. These should prove a boon to a lake virtually devoid of this sort of natural fish cover.

A few local bass anglers fish this high-elevation impoundment for smallies and hawgs in cold weather. They concentrate their efforts on feeder streams and use live baits. These areas are the best places to be from the onset of cold weather until late April, when the bass move out along rocky points. At this time surface plugs and spinnerbaits are most productive. The hot-weather months provide spotty fishing success, although a few fishermen have good luck during the early and late hours inching plastic worms along the bottom. Autumn fishing gets high marks, with the fish falling into late spring–like patterns.

Santeetlah Lake has a good reputation as a walleye fishery, with a knack for shelling occasional leviathans. The state record walleye, a huge 13-pound, 4-ounce specimen, was caught here in 1966. Like the lake's record largemouth bass, this fish is not really representative of the walleye available here, however. Growth rates for Santeetlah's walleye are comparable to those recorded for black bass: about 16 inches at four years of age. This slow rate of growth is the primary reason minimum-size restrictions on North Carolina's mountain lake walleye were removed a few years ago. During the spring walleye are caught in fair numbers on minnows around the mouth of West Buffalo Creek. They then appear to move down the lake as the season progresses. By late May the best fishing is at night under lanterns near the dam using small spinners, nightcrawlers or minnows.

Crappie are available at Santeetlah, but they are not the lake's strongest card. There are a fair number of rainbow trout, plus a few big mossy-back browns. These aren't stocked, but wash down from numerous feeder streams which offer outstanding moving-water fishing for 'bows and browns. The lake's trout follow the same basic movements described for walleye, except two to three weeks earlier.

Channel catfish are relatively abundant at Santeetlah. Jug fishing the side coves is a popular and productive way to spend an evening here. Spring fishing rates fair, but hot-weather fishing in the backwater areas can be outstanding in late evening and at night.

Nantahala Lake

SIZE: small
ACCESSIBILITY: fair
LOCATION: North Carolina (Clay County)
PRESSURE: moderate to light
PRIMARY GAMEFISH: rainbow trout, smallmouth bass, bluegill
SECONDARY GAMEFISH: brown and brook trout, catfish, walleye
BEST MONTHS: April, May, June, July, August, October
BEST BAITS: deep-diving crankbaits, nightcrawlers, live minnows,
    dough balls, crickets
BEST BET: fishing for rainbow trout at night using nightcrawlers
    under a lantern along the lake's bluffs in late July

Nantahala Lake is the easternmost body of water covered in this guide book. The lake is formed by the impoundment of the Nantahala River, which is a Cherokee Indian word meaning "Land of the Noonday Sun." It's an appropriate name for a lake created over a river gorge that once got sunlight only at noon.

Like Cheoah, Calderwood, Santeetlah, and Chilhowee lakes, this impoundment is owned and controlled by Alcoa. The dam is 250 feet high and 1,042 feet across. At full pool the lake covers 1,575 surface acres and measures 4.6 miles long.

Nantahala is a super-cold lake with very good water quality but a low nutrient base. Its bottom strata are granite rock, granite gravel and red clay and dirt.

The lake is bordered to the southwest by the Valley River and Tusquitee mountains and to the northeast by Cooper Ridge Bald, Jarrett Knob and Jarrett Bald of the Nantahala Mountains, over which the famed Appalachian Trail passes. The nearest towns are Andrews and

Franklin. The lake is accessed by a paved county-maintained road (Macon Co. 1310) which connects US 19 at a point near Andrews to US 64 near Franklin.

There is negligible development along this highland impoundment and no public camping areas or commercial boat docks. There are two "semi-official" boat-launch areas: at Rocky Branch and Big Choga Creek. The lake is fronted by lands under the control of Nantahala National Forest for slightly over half of its length. The rest is under private ownership.

Fishing Information

Nantahala Lake is a classic mountain lake. It's deep and clear and offers the fish residing there a very limited amount of food. Annual stockings of threadfin shad help the fishery along, but don't do enough good to provide high-quality fishing.

Smallmouth bass are Nantahala's best card, but this fishery rates only fair to good. This is followed by mediocre largemouth bass fishing. Each grows slowly here. Spring fishing for both is sometimes pretty good in the Big Choga and Jarrett creek embayments, where live baits and small spinners are the standard offerings. Later in the season grubs and plastic worms worked along side-water areas work well.

Walleye fishing used to be pretty good at Nantahala Lake, but at this time it rates poor. Trout are no longer stocked here, but the lake does get a fair number of wash-downs from the mountain streams. The big rainbow and brown that ply the lake can be taken by trolling big spoons. May through July and October are the best times to try your hand at these sleek speedsters.

Nantahala has a little natural structure, and at this writing has not received much in the way of man-made fish attractors. This will change, as the North Carolina Wildlife Resources Commission has the lake scheduled to receive the "full treatment" in the near future.

Lack of structure and cover are limiting factors for Nantahala's panfish, particularly black crappie, which are small and scarce. Despite an overall lack of needed cover, however, the lake sports a surprisingly good bluegill and redbreast fishery. Most pre-June fish are caught in back-cove areas. During hot weather 4-to-8-foot depths along the bluff areas are the best bets.

There's pretty good channel catfish fishing here, and those caught are very good eating. Late spring and summertime catfish angling is one of the lake's best points. The headwaters, around the mouth of Big Choga Creek and near the base of the dam are the best places to try to fool a whiskered fish with a glob of nightcrawlers or cut bait.

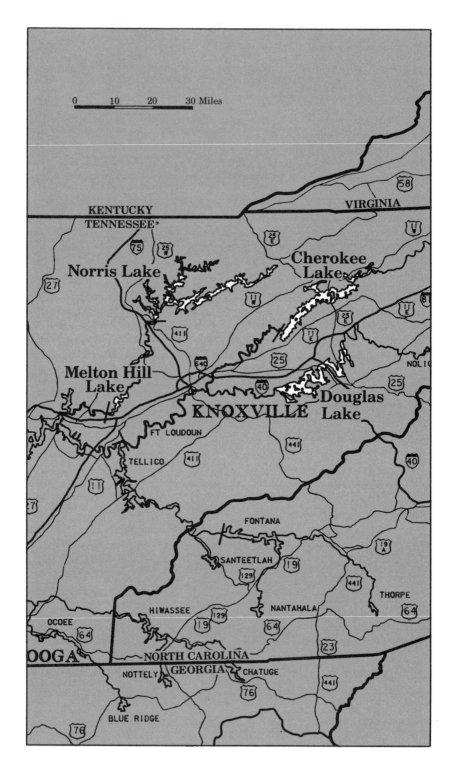

192

Melton Hill Lake

SIZE: relatively small

ACCESSIBILITY: very good

LOCATION: Tennessee (Roane, Anderson, Knox, and Loudon counties)

PRESSURE: moderate

PRIMARY GAMEFISH: crappie, bluegill, largemouth and smallmouth bass, catfish, northern pike, striped bass

SECONDARY GAMEFISH: white bass, sauger, muskie

BEST MONTHS: January, February, March, April, May, June, October

BEST BAITS: live minnows and shad, red wigglers, hair jigs, top-water plugs, crankbaits, spinnerbaits

BEST BET: live bait or shallow-running crankbaits fished along the hot water discharge canal at TVA's Bull Run Steam Plant for northern pike and striped bass

Casual inspection of Melton Hill Lake would indicate that this 5,690-acre impoundment of the Clinch River differs little from a dozen other East Tennessee lakes. Initial impressions can be misleading, however. This lake is fed by a frigid flow originating from beneath Norris Dam, which permits it to support an extremely diverse fishery.

Like other waters fed by cool-water rivers, Melton Hill has a top-heavy, but varied, predatory fishery. Largemouth and smallmouth bass, striped bass, white and whiterock bass (a striped bass–white bass hybrid), muskie and northern pike prowl this weedy impoundment. It hosts Tennessee's only northern pike fishery. Crappie, catfish and bream are also available in respectable numbers.

Melton Hill Lake is located on the Clinch River near Oak Ridge. Four counties share parts of its shoreline: Roane, Anderson, Knox and Loudon. Located approximately 53 miles downstream from Norris Dam, the lake is 44 miles long and at full pool has 173 miles of shoreline.

Completed in 1963, Melton Hill is considered a relatively recent addition to the TVA system. The dam is 1,020 feet across, and a navigation lock allows commercial and recreational craft access to Melton Hill from Watts Bar. This is a shallow tributary lake, measuring only 100 feet deep at the base of the dam. Drawdowns do not exceed 6 feet.

Like nearby Ft. Loudoun Lake, in many places Melton Hill has a townlike atmosphere. The lake's size and location appear to be a limiting factor in the development of commercial interests such as docks and resorts. There are only two commercial docks here: Oak Ridge Marina in Oak Ridge on Melton Lake Drive and Kerns Boat Dock on Ferry Pike in Oak Ridge.

The south shore offers considerably greater public access than the north shore, which is blanketed with dwellings. There are 10 public boat-launch areas on the southern shore compared to six on the opposite side. Melton Hill, Hickory Creek and Guinn Road parks in Knox County, Oak Ridge Municipal and Chestnut Ridge parks in Anderson County and the TVA Melton Hill Dam Reservation in Roane and Loudon counties are the primary public-use areas along the lake.

Melton Hill's bottom contour and shoreline characteristics are more like those encountered at Tennessee River mainstream impoundments than at its sister tributary lakes. Gently sloping grades separate scattered "river bend" flats and deep, winding creek meanders. The outer edges of these bends have proven to be key structure points for a number of gamefish species. During the lake's construction most standing timber was removed. Old foundations and stump beds are considered important to fishing success.

Fishing Information

The most important single factor for fishermen to be aware of is the lake's widespread milfoil infestation. The minimal drawdown helps create ideal conditions for this aquatic weed, which during the summer often covers entire coves and even feeder creek embayments by late summer. Some areas become so badly clogged that boat travel is impeded.

The milfoil's arrival at Melton Hill, as at other Tennessee River Valley impoundments, has been a mixed blessing. On the plus side, the grass generates oxygen and provides cover for both predators and their prey. It also provides excellent feeding grounds for the lake's large population of giant Canada geese, which in recent years have been hunted on a quota basis.

On the other hand, milfoil can limit the amount of fishable water. Some anglers curse the grass, accusing it of limiting their selection of angling techniques and lures. Others, however, have discovered it is one of the keys to this lake's unique variety of angling experiences.

Large northern pike are available at Melton Hill Lake.

Melton Hill Lake's forage base consists primarily of shad. Winter kills are common here, although the warm-water discharge from TVA's Bull Run Steam Plant provides a superb cold-weather refuge. Unusual thermal conditions are the second key to understanding why this lake holds such a diverse, yet limited sport fishery.

A joint TWRA-TVA venture brought about the introduction of northern pike into Melton Hill Lake during the late seventies. These cool-water predators are not native to the Tennessee River drainage system. This lake's combination of shallow, weedy habitat and year-round cool temperatures, however, made their introduction a logical addition.

Most anglers think of these toothed predators as Canadian fish, and indeed most of North America's premier northern angling is found there. In fact, Melton Hill Lake is the northern pike's southern-most abode. Only one other southern state maintains an ongoing northern pike management project.

At times fishing for these savage fish can be excellent here. In winter the northern sometimes rampage the weedlines. Those wishing to vie for trophy-class northern here can find no better starting point than the area around TVA's Bull Run Steam Plant. Several recent state record northerns have been caught there during winter's coldest weather.

Warm water emitted from this facility attracts large concentrations of bait fish, which in turn serve as a magnet for predators. While fishing at this steam plant, one may have designs on northern pike, but the catch can include anything from a whiterock hybrid to a muskie. Between mid-December and March, this area is a bonafide mixed-bag hot spot where feeding white bass, catfish, drum, largemouth bass and other desirable fishes are likely to congregate. It is located off US 25W approximately six miles south of Clinton and seven miles east of Oak Ridge via TN 62.

The hottest wintertime ploy for Melton Hill's big northern was perfected by Ray Jones of Oak Ridge, who's probably caught more lunker pike from the Bull Run Steam Plant area than anyone. His favorite cold-weather northern technique is swimming a seven-inch-long, metallic "rainbow"-hued Rebel Floating Minnow parallel to the thick grass line. This bait is fished briskly beneath the surface, with the rod tip held high. There's nothing bashful about a northern pike's megaton take.

Spring's warming scatters these fish into the shallows, where northerns generally spawn. Farther north, May and June are traditional mating months, but it is not known if they have reproduced here yet.

These are solitary, territorial predators fond of stationing near stumps, brush, deadfalls and of course aquatic weeds. They rarely stray far from the comforts of such structure-rich, sheltered areas. Because these fish are slight feeders, and meet each day with an empty stomach, more northern pike are caught during the very early hours. The best rule of thumb for northern pike is to make sure everything tossed is either flashy or makes a racket.

A number of techniques and baits work well on warm-weather water wolves. Bass anglers working buzzbaits briskly near weeds are often surprised by washtub-size swirls. Buzzbaits retrieved across or near milfoil beds are always good between spring and late fall, particularly at dawn.

During the summer northerns are most common in the lake's upper half. Large top-water baits such as the Arbogast Jitterstick will attract a pike's attention when worked near grass lines. The same is true of medium-depth-running crankbaits such as the Cordell Redfin, which should always be fished outside of the weeds!

A few anglers have discovered how deadly live bait is on these fish. Large, 5-to-6-inch minnows cast into the middle of grass "holes" or still fished under a bobber are effective. If you try this, make sure you have a strong enough line to work a 2½-foot-long load of TNT from a tangled mess.

Melton Hill Lake also boasts a slightly above average largemouth bass fishery. Keeper-sized bass are plentiful, and 5 to 7 pounders are not uncommon. Hawg hunting here lags a little in comparison to most lakes, rarely becoming noteworthy until mid-March. Then fishing bottom structure with large, live minnows or casting fly'n'rind combos in the feeder creek embayments of Bull Run and Beaver creeks and Grable Branch is brisk.

The grass flats warm quickly by late April and quickly begin to provide excellent spinnerbait, top-water, buzzbait and fly rod popping bug bassin' opportunities. When feeding, bass patrol adjacent to the milfoil and rest in its tangles. Baits worked alongside the fringe areas are often met with savage strikes.

Hot weather triggers some fish, such as largemouth bass, to migrate to the headwaters between the Chestnut Ridge and Eagle Bend areas. The normally heavy summer generating schedule at Norris, which begins after July 4th, sends Melton Hill a steady influx of cool water. This cool flow snakes under the warm surface, creating a shallow, but distinct thermocline.

Mid- and late-summer warm water temperatures push these fish deeper, as well as upstream, where cooler havens exist. Pig'n'jig combos and rubber worms are good then. Many anglers have discovered flippin' around shallow stump beds and dock pilings to be awesomely effective. Late evening shallow-water action has become something of a tradition here during "hot times." Several years ago when it was Don's job to write a weekly fishing report for the *Knoxville Journal,* he discovered that Melton Hill produced as many, if not more, reports of late summer lunker largemouth bass as other surrounding impoundments.

Melton Hill Lake sports white, striped and white-striped hybrid bass. Whites are native to the Clinch River and thrive here. Excellent cold-weather catches are made at the Bull Run Steam Plant. There is also a largely ignored spring run up the Clinch River to the vicinity of the TN 61 bridge.

Striped bass and hybrids inhabit this lake primarily because the TWRA's modern Eagle Bend Hatchery, which is located on its headwaters in Clinton, makes periodic, sometimes unscheduled releases of these exotics.

Melton Hill's winter lineside fishing can be very good. Like the lake's other high-octane predators, stripers and hybrids are drawn to the shad concentrations at the steam plant's discharge channel. Quarter-ounce leadheads tipped with white and red twister grubs trolled or cast are the top striper and whiterock tricks.

March and April are transitional times which must be at least mildly frustrating for Melton Hill's mature striped and hybrid bass. Following their instinct to reproduce, both species begin swimming toward moving-water areas. The Clinch does not provide suitable habitat for a successful striper spawning run (the hybrids are sterile), but this hardly deters either's efforts.

Runs upstream as far as the TN 61 bridge are common. More than a few fishermen have been awed by the sight of a 25-pound lineside finning in a shallow shoal.

Stripers scatter throughout the lake in May. By June large schools can be found near the dam. Trolling or still fishing, using big bream for bait, is effective.

Every Tennessee lake holds sizable catfish, and Melton Hill is no exception. Little attention is paid to Mr. Whiskers during winter, but beginning in spring they are sought after by many; the Gallaher Bend, Carbide Park, and Solway Bridge areas consistently produce good catfish catches. Summer cat hunters turn to the twilight hours, although late afternoon "jugging" is becoming increasingly popular here.

Melton Hill Lake is not known as a place to go for loading up on slabsides. Nearby Watts Bar Lake's well-known crappie fishery overshadows that of this impoundment. The lake does hold crappie, though, and between late March and mid-May it is capable of shelling out stringers in the 40-to-80-fish range.

The best early season calico fishing is concentrated in the Bull Run Creek embayment and the flats off Gallaher Bend. Smoke-colored grubs and minnows are the best crappie offerings here. Trolling is the most effective approach, although tightlining deep structure is also productive.

Spawning time finds these fish in brush and stump bed areas. Baits jigged along under a bobber work well. Scattered, but modestly productive crappie fishing continues throughout the summer here. Try fishing minnows 10 feet deep wherever wood and brush structure is found.

Bluegill are super-abundant here. Between March and October these feisty fish can be taken almost anytime in and around the milfoil beds. Live baits such as redworms, crickets and Japanese beetles are deadly.

Norris Lake

SIZE: medium-large

ACCESSIBILITY: very good, fair in winter

LOCATION: Tennessee (Grainger, Campbell, Claiborne, Union, and Anderson counties)

PRESSURE: heavy to moderate

PRIMARY GAMEFISH: smallmouth bass, striped bass, catfish, white bass, walleye

SECONDARY GAMEFISH: sauger, lake trout, crappie, bluegill, whiterock hybrids

BEST MONTHS: April, May, June, November, December, January

BEST BAITS: live minnows and shad, jigs, deep-diving crankbaits, spinnerbaits, plastic worms, nightcrawlers

BEST BET: drift fishing with big, live shad in the Blue Fox Dock area for trophy striped bass in late November

Norris is one of three major TVA tributary lakes (along with Douglas and Cherokee) running roughly along a northeastern axis. It was the pilot project, after which the dozens of TVA dams now dotting this well-watered valley followed. Norris Dam was completed in 1936 and was named in honor of George W. Norris, a Nebraska New Deal–era senator who befriended and fought for the TVA concept. The dam's completion came just in time to play a key role in helping to control the disastrous Mississippi and Ohio river floods of 1937.

Norris Dam sits 265 feet high atop the Clinch River and is 1,860 feet across. It backs up a lake which at full pool covers 34,200 surface acres along its 72-mile length. Norris Lake has approximately 800 miles of shoreline and during the winter months is annually drawn down almost 75 feet.

The lake is actually formed by two rivers: the Clinch and the Powell,

Norris Dam, begun in 1933 and completed in 1936, was the first dam built by the TVA. Located on the Clinch River in eastern Tennessee, it is 265 feet high and 1,860 feet long. Its reservoir has a storage capacity of two and one-half million acre-feet of water, of which 1,922,000 is useful, controlled storage. The power installation consists of two 50,400-kw units.

the latter being the lesser. Both drain watersheds located primarily in southwestern Virginia. On the map this impoundment has a dual snaking, or V-shaped, appearance. Although the Clinch River arm is larger, the Powell River embayment is important in its own right, extending 56 miles to its headwaters.

Norris Lake winds through five counties: Anderson, Union, Grainger, Campbell, and Claiborne. Despite the lake's close proximity to Knoxville, it has an attractive, uncluttered tree-covered shoreline that approaches the primeval beauty encountered along the lakes of southern Canada. Development, particularly new subdivisions, may soon change this, but there are still numerous areas devoid of human presence.

Norris has a well-developed marina business and is popular with both local residents and visiting boaters and fishermen. There are 20 marinas on the lake, and services range from plush to Spartan. Exceptional public access and park areas surround the lake.

Norris Dam State Park, located near the dam site off US 441, and Big Ridge State Park, four miles off TN 33 via Maynardville, are well-developed facilities that offer developed campsites, meals and cabins, as well as a smorgasbord of recreational activities and programs. Other park areas include the Norris Municipal and Anderson County parks.

Hunters have long acknowledged the TWRA's Wildlife Management Areas at Norris to be among East Tennessee's finest gun sport hot spots. A large tract of land once well known as the "Central Peninsula" but now referred to as the Chuck Swan Wildlife Management Area (WMA) separates the Powell and Clinch river arms. This now-wooded former farming area sports excellent populations of raccoon, wild turkey, white-tailed deer and other wildlife. The Cove Creek Peninsula WMA, which separates Cove and Big creeks, is located near the dam. It also offers big- and small-game hunting opportunities.

TVA maintains a number of "Small Wild Areas" (SWA) along the lake. These areas feature unique flora around caves and ravines, as well as picturesque waterfalls and scenic views. Trails offer access. The Small Wild Areas at Norris include Hemlock Bluff SWA, located on Loyston Point; Monk's Corner SWA, located on the Powell River arm off Lead Mine Bend Road; Stiner Woods SWA, also located off Lead Mine Bend Road; and the River Bluff SWA, located just downstream from Norris Dam.

Norris Lake has few wide spots, but it contains an abundance of coves and secluded hollows. A large portion of the lake's northwestern and southeastern shoreline is steep and rocky. Flats do exist, though, mostly in coves and feeder creek hollows. Rock, gravel and clay points, creek meanders and man-made brush piles are key structure areas. Sycamore, Davis, Lost, Cedar, Mill, Big and Cove creeks are the primary feeder creek embayments.

Norris is colder than its downstream cousins, and its water quality gets excellent ratings, although it is considered a relatively infertile fishery. Its forage base of gizzard and threadfin shad, which is rather slim, is the most limiting factor upon a top-heavy predator population.

Like other tributary impounds, Norris is classed as a deep-water lake. Its bottom consists of gravel, shale, clay, rock and mud. Aquatic vegetation is nil, and as at other early TVA projects, all standing timber was removed before the lake's initial flooding. Only scattered stumps and stump bed "forests" remain, and with each passing season these become increasingly scarce.

Norris Lake was one of the first impounds to receive experimental man-made "fish attractors." The fact that this lake, like so many other TVA impounds, has a problem with steadily deteriorating submerged organic structure prompted fishery biologists to attempt a remedy. Both forage fish and many types of gamefish concentrate around cover, giving anglers easier access to greater quantities of fish.

The answer proved to be astonishingly simple. Old discarded car tires are banded together and stood upright and topped with small downed trees; the entire structure is secured to the lowest point in a cove or feeder creek embayment. These attractors are built according to a number of patterns, such as long lines or square "checkerboards," ranging in size up to an acre. Their presence here, as at other lakes, is marked by a buoy.

Fishing Information

Norris supports a diverse, exciting sport fishery with warm, cool and cold habitats. This is somewhat ironic to old-timers who remember the controversy surrounding this lake's creation. Because the lake is so deep, some biologists felt it might not be able to support reproducing gamefish populations. When the dam was being constructed, a warm-water hatchery was built below the dam to provide Norris Lake with fish. It quickly proved to be a "white elephant." Found here is some of Tennessee's best angling for smallmouth bass, walleye, and striped and whiterock hybrid bass. Crappie, largemouth and Kentucky bass, various catfish species, white bass, muskie, sauger and bream are all represented here.

Rainbow and brown trout are common in the Clinch River tailrace, and 'bows occasionally show up in the deep water near the base of the dam. This does not mean that Norris has a trout fishery, but this should soon change, as lake trout were introduced here in 1985. These fish are expected to do as well here as at Dale Hollow Lake, where they have proven to be a huge success.

Muskellunge, or muskie, were once stocked here in large numbers, but these fish are definitely fewer today than in past seasons. Still, the lake is noted for holding some of the country's biggest tackle-breaking muskie. In 1983 a 42-pound, 8-ounce state record muskie was taken here. That's a trophy anywhere.

One of America's best year-round striped bass fisheries is available at Norris. Good water quality, ample lake size and favorable year-round water temperatures combine to permit the striped bass to grow large here. The present lake record lineside, a 49½ pounder, was taken here in 1978. Stripers over 30 pounds are common.

Amazingly, though, such monster stripers may not be Norris Lake's best. While probing this lake with electro-shocking equipment during a fishery survey, TWRA crews surfaced a striped bass which was estimated to have been heavy enough to top the present world record for landlocked striper, which stands at 59 pounds, 12 ounces.

Striped bass fishing at this old TVA impoundment is a year-round sport, with some of the hottest action occurring during the dead of winter. The late Jim Simpson of Maynardville was Norris Lake's lineside angler "emeritus." He caught 30 to 40 pounders so often that his very presence on the lake drew crowds to watch him systematically undo whoppers.

The cold-weather months of December through February were Simpson's preferred time for going after trophy-class stripers. He worked the main river channel near the lake's headwaters in the Clinch River arm. Jim's favorite bait changed little with each progressing season. It was almost always large live gizzard shad—big, lively 7 to 10 inchers, which he netted in a circular throw net, tossed with deadly accuracy.

Simpson was a perfectionist, and he knew having an attractive bait was vitally important for fooling five-to-eight-year-old linesides. His shad were treated with as much care as a newborn babe. Every precaution was taken to ensure these abundant, but surprisingly fragile bait fish were safely removed and put into a well-aerated tank. Each shad was gently lip hooked and never spiked through vital body areas.

During the winter, Jim's favorite technique was "drift fishing," although proper position was maintained by thrust delivered by an electric trolling motor. His usual winter rigging consisted of five heavy spinning outfits with loosely set drags, strung with 8-to-12-pound-test line.

Four rods draped directly over the boat's side, set at whatever depth his video depth reader indicated his quarry occupied. The fifth rod was used as a trailer, "long lined" 35 to 45 feet behind the boat. It probably accounted for slightly fewer than half of the rockfish he landed.

During winter, Norris Lake's striper prefer to locate near the headwaters along the old Clinch River channel. Mild weather finds them 10 to 15 feet deep, while cold weather can drive them twice this deep. During cold weather some Norris Lake striper addicts do well vertically jigging large spoons, while others troll big bucktails. At Norris, however, the shad always possess a mystic power over these fish.

Norris Lake's spring striper action is on a par with that found anywhere. Most action occurs along clay points and inlet mouths from the Black Fox Church area upstream to the mouth of Sycamore Creek. Wintertime striped bass ploys are used through April.

A big change in technique occurs during mid-May, when a brief period of shoreline striper top-water action occurs. Large surface-diving plugs such as the Cordell Redfin are then tossed right against clay points and retrieved slowly, creating a distinctive V wake. The results can be heart stopping!

Norris's linesides reschool by late May and slowly begin migrating deeper and closer to the dam. Despite their size, these nomadic schools are not always easy to locate; once pinpointed, however, the odds of hanging into a tackle wrecker are good. Tactics depend greatly upon the depth of the fish, which in turn is largely determined by surface temperatures.

Stripers like 68-to-72-degree temperature zones. This preference becomes very distinct as they grow past the 15-to-20-pound size. They will seek out such zones even if they are devoid of forage fish. At Norris Lake this is not a problem because cool areas generally permit access to food. Such areas can be deep, however, up to 60 to 80 feet deep, making catching fish here difficult without special know-how and equipment.

During late summer stripers are usually concentrated between the Loyston Sea area in the Clinch River arm and the base of the dam. Downriggers have proven exceptionally well suited for taking stripers deeper than 20 feet.

One of Norris Lake's best-kept secrets is its premier smallmouth bass fishery. Bronzebacks in the four-to-six-pound class are plentiful, and if you know your smallies, the odds of taking such a fish are great.

Many local experts feel Norris's best smallmouth bass action occurs

Norris Lake is nationally known as a consistent producer of big striped bass.

while most fishermen are still toasting their stocking feet beside a woodstove. February's blustery, cold weather may appear to hold nothing more than the promise of frostbitten fingers, but this is when old small-jaws goes on the prowl.

Crayfish react to late winter's extended daylight with accelerated molting activity, which makes these preferred smallmouth bass forage items more available. Soft jelly crayfish baits such as Mann's Cajun Crawdad painstakingly inched down a 20-foot-deep clay and gravel point are deadly.

Another highly recommended cold-weather ploy is anchoring off such main river channel points and still fishing with live minnows. This is a game of numbers and patience. Rule number one is: It is difficult to have too many lines out in different directions or at various depths. It's sort of like trying to cover bets on all the numbers and colors of a roulette wheel.

Rule number two is: Get comfortable. While this method can produce trophy-class bronzebacks, it can also be a waiting game. Dress warmly and bring along your favorite needlepoint project.

Smallmouth move into shallower abodes by late March and are then caught on medium-depth-running crankbaits. April finds Norris Lake's brown bass contemplating spawning. Back-cove areas are actively sought out, and holding depths are surprisingly shallow, usually no deeper than five feet. Spinnerbaits run briskly beneath the surface are effective, as are surface baits.

May is the prime time for top-water action, but this lake's best smallmouth bass hunters have already made a switch from day to nighttime angling. Brown, black or purple pig'n'jig combos are the number-one nighttime Norris smallie bait, followed by plastic worms and live spring lizards. The wee morning hours can be most productive well into late fall.

Pig'n'jig combos are also effective on the lake's nocturnal largemouth bass, but the plastic worm is rated tops by most. Strawberry, black fire-tail, electric grape and black are the top takers. Worked slowly over old building foundations, worms are lethal.

Norris holds loads of largemouth bass, but not as many as such better-known East Tennessee hawg honeyholes as Douglas or Watts Bar. Lunkers are seldom over six pounds, and these are not that common.

Working medium-depth-running crankbaits around rocky points, creek mouths and sloping clay points is the best largemouth bass ploy in late winter and early spring. This technique works well into May when early and late surface action supersedes. Largemouth bass drop deeper fairly quickly, taking to 15-to-20-foot depths by mid-June.

Night bassin' for all black bass species is popular here until October.

Autumn's winds turn the lake over then, permitting a wide range of spinners, crankbaits and buzzbaits.

Norris is a much better walleye lake than many suspect, and its sauger population is virtually untouched. This is one of the few lakes holding viable populations of both perch family members.

Each January spawning walleye and sauger ascend the Clinch and Powell rivers heralding in some of Tennessee's best river-run action. This spawning run sometimes lasts into early April and progresses upstream to the Cracker Creek area on the Clinch and Stiner Woods area on the Powell. Walleye up to 8 to 12 pounds are taken here.

Following the spawn these fish return to the lake, where they scatter. For most, postspawn fishing for walleye and sauger means trolling jigs, minnows or green twister grubs at night all such places as the Loyston Sea's Bear Hole area. A few do well minnow dabbling under lanterns, and mid-summer twilight top-water turn-ons are not uncommon.

Another popular springtime river-spawning fish, the spunky white bass, is abundant here. March and April spawning runs up both headwater rivers draw "elbow room only" crowds. Dollflies, small spinners and minnows are year in, year out stripe catchers.

Like the walleye, these fish return to Norris Lake following spawning activity. They spend the summer and winter prowling open water ripping apart bait fish schools. Between June and August, top-water "jump" action can occur just about anywhere, with the Hickory Star area traditionally providing excellent break-fishing action. Night fishing for these gregarious gamesters under lantern light is also productive. The area between Big Creek and the dam is preferred by many night white bass fans.

Crappie fishing is not Norris Lake's strongest card, but at times, such as during the height of the spring spawn, it garners a good rating. Norris does have a bonafide reputation for always shelling out big slabsides, with 15 inches being common.

The best calico fishing is usually 10 to 15 feet deep over stump beds or man-made attractors. Chartreuse and motor oil–hued grubs and minnows are the top local calico takers. Trolling works reasonably well, but is not particularly popular here. Some decent postspawn, deep-water catches are made in the Mill Creek embayment area.

Bluegill are available throughout this old lake during the warm-weather months. Hand-size bream can be caught, but acquiring a cooking "mess" can require considerable culling. The late May bedding time provides Norris's best bluegill action. Shallow back-cove areas, such as those around the Hunting or Davis creek embayments, are prime locations. Redworms, crickets or beetlespinners are the top baits.

Hot weather bluegill fishing is consistently brisk along almost any shoreline area. Those seeking to tangle with "bull" bream will find the bluff areas interesting. Big bream hold in deep rock crevices waiting to ambush fallen terrestrial insects. The trick is to position your boat adjacent to a cliff and fish your bait deep without a floater. Cast against the rocks and allow the bait to tightline drift downward, up to 15 feet. The pay-off can be a tasty bluegill fish fry.

Norris is a good catfish lake. Blue, flathead and channel catfish are all available here, with the last being the most abundant. Winter action is concentrated along the main river channels 25 to 30 miles upstream from the dam. Trotlines baited with stinkbaits or chicken liver often produce heavy whiskered fish catches. Spring through late summer is the favorite catfish angling time for most. Back-cove areas and creek embayments are bottom fished using nightcrawlers, cut shad and, of course, chicken liver.

Douglas Lake

SIZE: medium-large

ACCESSIBILITY: very good, fair in winter

LOCATION: Tennessee (Cocke, Hamblen, Jefferson, and Sevier counties)

PRESSURE: moderate to heavy

PRIMARY GAMEFISH: crappie, bluegill, largemouth bass, catfish

SECONDARY GAMEFISH: white bass, sauger

BEST MONTHS: March, April, May, June, September, October

BEST BAITS: live minnows, hair jigs, twistertail grubs, deep-diving and medium-depth crankbaits, spinnerbaits

BEST BET: tightline jigging or minnow fishing over sunken brush piles for crappie in Mud Creek during late April

There's no better explanation for Douglas Lake's superb crappie fishing than to concede it must be held in high favor at the Crappie Lord's Golden Hall. Each spring ton upon ton of mild-tasting calicos are caught here. Enough so that this World War II–era impoundment always finishes far ahead in catch rates over its neighboring East Tennessee crappie fisheries.

The irony of all this is that no one really knows why Douglas Lake's slabside catch rate has such a dominating lead. Perhaps the local custom of kissing and tossing back the season's first crappie is the answer.

Douglas is a scenic lake tucked in alongside English Mountain, a 3,500-foot-high ridge system bordering the Great Smoky Mountains National Park. There are no state parks here, but there are numerous very nice commercial campgrounds and marinas.

Cocke, Jefferson, Sevier and Hamblen counties front this 41-mile-long TVA impoundment. Historic Dandridge, the Volunteer State's second oldest municipality, is located along Douglas Lake's main channel. Davy Crockett, one of the American frontier movement's best-known folk heroes, posted his marriage bond at the nearby Jefferson County Courthouse.

Prior to the creation of Douglas Lake in 1942–43, steam-powered, shallow-draft river boats ran commercial shuttle services along the French Broad River between Dandridge and downstream Knoxville. This service continued until shortly before the dam's construction.

Douglas Dam stands 202 feet high and 1,705 feet wide and is a product of the accelerated construction characteristic of other war-era projects. This 30,400-acre lake is fed by three major rivers which converge at its headwaters: the Pigeon, French Broad, and Nolichucky. All three begin in the western North Carolina highlands.

Douglas Lake's water quality is surprisingly good in most respects, despite extensive upstream agriculture, industry and urbanization. Only the Pigeon River, which is shamelessly desecrated by Champion Fibers at its Canton, North Carolina, papermill, has a destructive pollution problem. At this writing the states of Tennessee and North Carolina are locked in a legal fight over this flow's disgraceful situation.

Douglas Lake's bottom strata consist of extensive mudflats, sloping slate and clay points, steep rock-faced bluffs and numerous long feeder creek meanders. The lake's annual drawdown is 62 feet, thus halting any upstream invasion of aquatic plant life. The lake has 555 miles of shoreline.

Fishing Information

Douglas Lake has a good balance of forage fish, rough fish and gamefish. Crappie are the impoundment's most important and popular gamefish species, followed by a grossly underrated largemouth bass fishery. White bass are extremely common, as are bluegill and warmouth bream.

Until recently, the lake's sauger fishery was one of upper East Tennessee's finest, particularly during the sixties and seventies. The apparent demise of the sauger fishery here is not fully understood, although some professional fishery managers speculate this situation could be either a normal cyclic low or a side effect of the present high number of white bass, which may be presenting competition for spawning success.

In recent years the Tennessee Wildlife Resources Agency has undertaken walleye stockings in the Nolichucky River near Erwin. At this writing it appears their efforts have taken hold, reestablishing these native perch. Catches, while still unpredictable and sporadic, have produced adult, spawning walleye.

Douglas Lake sports both channel and flathead catfish populations. Drum, or sheephead, are plentiful, and actively sought here by some. Deep at the dam's very edge, rainbow trout are occasionally taken.

It is not uncommon for crappie fishing to turn on at this lake as early as January. When a string of mild, sunny days peeks through normally frigid January weather, the result is often a stint of first-class calico fishing. Unfortunately, this sometimes leads to a conflict of interest between anglers suffering from cabin fever and the duck-starved local waterfowl gunning cadre. Those few misdirected northern ducks who end up in mountainous East Tennessee find Douglas Lake's exposed wintertime mudflats simply irresistible!

Cold-weather crappie angling can be aided by a good electronic bottom-reading device. During the cold-weather months slabside schools are usually tight and stationary at 20 to 30 feet deep on points over stumps.

Vertically jigging jelly grubs or live minnows is preferred by most. Trolling for calicos is a universal religion here—winter, spring, summer or fall. During winter, the Nina, Stumpy Cove and Swann Bridge areas are top-notch crappie honeyholes.

Spring lake level rises and an urge to procreate combine to put the slabsides on shallow slate points and cocklebur-covered cove basins. When the lake achieves full pool early, unbelievably good spawning action can be found in the lake's black willows and buck bushes.

During the height of the spawn, bobber-fished flies, grubs, and minnows worked 1 to 5 feet deep over slate or brush or in the treetops are the most popular offerings. One-day party catches of 500 to 700 fish are certainly not uncommon when all the necessary conditions are in line.

Excellent shallow-water spring calico fishing occurs near the Willow Branch campground, Swann Bridge and Muddy and Indian creeks and from the Inspiration Point Resort area down the lake to the Flat Creek embayment area near Eden Church.

Summer and autumn slow Douglas Lake's crappie catch rate. Trolling 15 to 30 feet deep utilizing a downrigger is growing in popularity yearly as more and more East Tennessee anglers become acquainted with these "Yankee" deep-water–probing devices. Minnow dabbling under lantern lights, which has been practiced here for decades, is also productive.

Largemouth bass fans would be hard pressed to find a better hawg lake anywhere in Tennessee than Douglas Lake. "Keeper"-sized bass are abundant, while 3 to 4 pounders are common. Larger bass are fewer and further between, however; the unofficial lake record is just under 10 pounds.

In May 1985 the Tennessee BASS Federation held its annual championship tourney here, with anglers representing all corners of the Volunteer State, from Memphis to Bristol. When the smoke had cleared following the two-day event, a record-breaking 1,278 pounds of largemouth bass had been caught and released. That's a heap o' bass any way you slice the pie, but even more revealing about Douglas Lake's bass fishery was the fact that the largest hawg taken was under 6 pounds.

Douglas Lake has a reputation as a "worming" lake. Red or strawberry during spring, purple or grape at other times is the accepted rule of thumb here. Many prefer to cast brown-brown, brown-black, black-black and purple-brown-black pig'n'jig combos. For these heavyweights, seasonal considerations have little bearing on either color or technique selection. Either bait works well when the bass suspend over shelves.

White or yellow spinnerbaits produce well during warm weather, while medium- and deep-running crankbaits are also good. Organic structure is a premium item on this denuded old impoundment, so don't pass any without casting.

Late May almost always offers excellent dawn and dusk top-water bass action. Standard surface baits such as the Rebel Floater Minnow, Bang-O-Lures, Skipjacks or the Dalton Fish are all good choices.

Hot weather has two effects on the bass here. First, warming water and intense light drive the bucketmouths deep, up to 35 feet. Second, it sparks their nocturnal instincts. Twilight bassin' has long been popular here. Deep-water–fished rubber worms, pig'n'jigs and other slowly fished baits are standard night baits.

White bass virtually disappeared from this lake during the late sixties. Today, however, they are enormously abundant. These gregarious fish begin ascending the French Broad and Nolichucky rivers to spawn as early as February. Excellent river fishing using white-red or yellow grubs or flies, shiny spoons or small spinners is available at the river's mouth and Enka Dam on the Nolichucky River or upstream from the Rankin bottoms to the Rankin Bridge area on the French Broad River.

Whites begin appearing back in the lake by mid-April. They reoccupy Douglas Lake's every nook and cranny within a few short days. Evening "jump," or surface, action is available over mudflats through July, and sometimes later. Another popular hot-weather white bass ploy is night fishing. As when fishing for crappie (most combine their efforts for both species), lanterns are extended out over the water and minnows or flies are jigged 10 to 20 feet deep. The Swann Bridge area is known for producing heavy stripe stringers then. Winter white bass action on Douglas Lake rates spotty and attracts little attention, although angling for these schoolers can be good if suspended fish can be located.

Catfish anglers will discover that this lake is a slightly above-par fishing hole. Main channel trotlines near the headwaters produce well during the late winter and spring months. Stinkbaits, cut shad and chicken liver are the best year-round offerings.

Late spring finds the cats in hollows and coves, although many fishermen still concentrate their efforts on the old river channel. During hot weather, the twilight hours at Indian and Muddy creeks are always outstanding whiskered fish producers.

Late winter sauger and walleye spawning runs up the 'Chucky and French Broad are regarded locally as sure signs Ole Man Winter is exiting East Tennessee. Walleye have become increasingly common upstream to Enka Dam (and beyond). Spawning sauger have traditionally taken both river arm routes. Mating sauger are sometimes found in the French Broad River as late as May and as far upstream as Hot Springs, North Carolina.

Large green or orange twister grubs are the top baits for the walleye and sauger spawning runs. Fishing for these big river-run perch is not easy because the river rocks will snatch your baits before a fish can find them. When these fish "move in," however, limits often come fast, many times in less than a half hour.

Following the spawn, both species return downstream to the lake, where they scatter like monkey dung. Few anglers seriously seek out either fish. Incidental walleye and sauger catches do occur, however, particularly during the spring crappie-bedding season. Trollers and night lantern fishermen make most of these scattered catches. There is little question that good hot-weather angling for these fish does exist, but to this scribe's knowledge, no one has ever taken on the task of unraveling either fish's summertime patterns.

The bluegill is Douglas Lake's leading sunfish species. Winter bluegill action is rare, but by spring these gamesters have moved into high gear. Spawning occurs as early as mid-April here and bedding areas are usually located in sheltered back-cove areas where bowl-shaped shallow areas exist.

The best summer action is available at 8-to-15-foot depths along the lake's main river channel bluff areas. Crickets, available near Sevierville, are the top bait, followed by wasp and hornet larvae and redworms.

Cherokee Lake

SIZE: medium-large

ACCESSIBILITY: very good, fair in winter

LOCATION: Tennessee (Grainger, Hamblen, Hawkins, and Jefferson counties)

PRESSURE: heavy to moderate

PRIMARY GAMEFISH: largemouth and smallmouth bass, striped and whiterock bass, catfish, bluegill

SECONDARY GAMEFISH: saugeye, crappie

BEST MONTHS: April, May, June, August

BEST BAITS: live minnows and shad, jigs, deep-diving crankbaits, spinnerbaits, purple and black plastic worms

BEST BET: night fishing for largemouth and smallmouth bass using crankbaits in the German Creek area during late June

Created in 1941, Cherokee Lake is the first of several impoundments on the Holston River system. At full pool it covers just over 30,000 surface acres and has almost 400 miles of primary shoreline along its 54-mile length. Cherokee Dam stands 175 feet high, and the lake's elevation at full pool is 1,075 feet above sea level. Full pool is usually achieved in late May, and the annual drawdown occurs in the early fall. Minimum pool is 1,020 feet above sea level. At 6,760 feet across, this concrete and dirt-fill structure is the second-widest dam in Tennessee; only Pickwick Landing Dam on the Tennessee River is wider. The project cost $36 million, a bargain equal to the cost of about a dozen modern-day grammar schools.

The lake was named in honor of the Cherokee Indians, the last tribe to freely roam the Holston River drainage. It's a scenic body of water, bordered on the north by the 3,600-foot-high sandstone Clinch Mountains and to the south by Crockett and River ridges. Grainger and Hawkins

213

counties border the lake on the north, and Hamblen and Jefferson counties, on the south. Morristown and Jefferson City are the nearest towns. US 11E and TN 113 trace along its southern edge, US 11W and TN 92 are the major access routes along the northern shoreline and US 25E crosses at river mile 75.

Cherokee rates among Tennessee's most accessible lakes. There are 11 commercial boat docks and 20 public boat-launch ramps. Camping is available at Panther Creek State Park, a 1,900-acre facility bordering the lake in Hamblen County, Cherokee Park, the Fall Creek Public Use Area, and the Cherokee Dam Reservation. The May Springs Recreational Area and Grainger County Park are "day-use-only" areas.

Like that of most old TVA impoundments, Cherokee's lake bed was stripped completely prior to its initial flooding. Little natural cover remains other than fast-disappearing stump beds and rock and gravel. The bottom consists of clay, slate, rock and gravel. Bluffs and steep shoreline are common, but so are shallow, gently sloping cove areas. Man-made fish attractors dot the lake bottom.

Cherokee's course is straighter than that of most tributary lakes. High rock cliffs characterize much of the old river channel's course. Numerous large islands in Cherokee account for 62 miles of shoreline. Cloud Creek is of historical importance, as a line running from its mouth to Cumberland Gap was the boundary between white settlers and Indian territory under the 1771 Treaty of Long Island.

Fishing Information

Cherokee Lake is one of the most popular fishing spots in East Tennessee, offering both variety and quality. One of the first places striped bass were successfully stocked, Cherokee is also the site of the nation's first striped bass–white bass hybrid fishery.

The gizzard shad and rough fish population here accounts for over 700 pounds per surface acre. That is the heaviest poundage per surface acre of forage and rough fish in the TVA system, and it made Cherokee an ideal location for a landlocked striped bass stocking program, beginning in the 1960s. The program was a success, despite the misgivings of some anglers concerned about crappie and black bass numbers. At the height of Cherokee's striper program hundreds of thousands of fingerlings were being stocked annually. Then the bottom fell out.

During the mid-1970s a combination of long-festering water quality problems and extremely hot, dry weather resulted in a striped bass die-off. Cherokee's water had long been rated among Tennessee's most troubled. For decades intensive industry upstream in Elizabethton, Kingsport and Johnson City, plus mercury leaching from abandoned salt mines in southwestern Virginia, had been causing pollution problems.

The headwaters of Cherokee Lake offer great winter fishing.

Another problem arose in the mid-1950s with the construction of the John Sevier Steam Plant less than ten miles upstream from Cherokee Lake on the Holston River. This coal-fired unit uses river water in its steam turbines. Because the river level fluctuates in response to hydroelectric production at upstream Patrick Henry Dam, sufficient water to operate John Sevier is stored. Much of the time the Holston's flow is sufficient to cause water to pass over John Sevier Dam. At times, though, water doesn't go over it. The entire flow is diverted into the steam plant and returned downstream in a superheated state.

This isn't a threat during the winter, when the influx of warm water concentrates fish. During the summer months, however, the hot water discharge is a bane. The heated water passing downstream stretches from bank to bank. Fish can escape by moving, but invertebrates like mussels, aquatic insects and other important life forms are trapped.

The problem doesn't stop there either. Normally during hot weather when a river enters an impoundment where the surface temperatures are in the high seventies to low eighties, the cooler river water slips beneath the surface and continues on. This so-called thermocline, or layering of water in different temperature bands, occurs in most Tennessee lakes. During hot weather fish seek out the cool, oxygenated water in the lower layers. In Cherokee the inflowing river water is as warm or warmer than the lake's surface water. Rather than slip beneath the surface, the Holston's flow spreads out over Cherokee Lake's surface. Extended periods of steam plant activity, extremely hot weather and low rainfall can combine to leave Cherokee Lake devoid of thermoclines and its temperature in the mid-eighties from top to bottom. The problem escalates when algae blooms occur in this fertile lake. When the algae dies, a lethal drop in the lake's dissolved oxygen level can occur.

In order to survive this stressful season, Cherokee's striped bass locate cool inflowing feeder streams, or "thermal refuges," as researchers refer to these havens. During particularly bad times, thousands of rockfish stack up like cord wood in submerged meanders, unable to leave to feed more than a few feet away. Under the worst conditions, die-offs happen.

Since the early eighties there has been a slight, but steady improvement in Cherokee Lake's water quality. In 1986 the Environmental Protection Agency ordered that a constant flow of water be maintained over John Sevier Dam. Hopefully, this will help reduce the heated water problem.

Striped bass are still stocked in Cherokee, although the rocks here are smaller than those caught from Norris or Tims Ford lakes. Growth rates are good until the fish reach the 25-to-30-pound mark; thereafter, few top the 35-to-38-pound mark. Trophy-class linesides at this lake are the most susceptible to heat stress. Hardier striped bass–white bass hybrids, simply called "hybrids," are now stocked in greater numbers. These easy-to-catch fish reach the 10-to-15-pound mark.

Catching striped bass and hybrids is a year-round sport. During the dead of winter good catches can be made bottom fishing live shad at the mouths of Caney and Cloud creeks and drift fishing suspended baits between the Malinda Bridge area and the steam plant. Trolling big white and red bucktails tipped with pearl-colored worms also works well then. Rocks and hybrids stay in the headwaters until late April.

During May excellent top-water action for linesides is available off of red clay and slate points in Cherokee's upper half. Floating 7-inch Rebels or Rapalas cast adjacent to the shoreline and retrieved slowly with a V wake are deadly. The German Creek area is the best top-water starting point.

Hot weather sends lineside schools migrating toward the dam. Groups splinter and stop over to feed in the Mossy, Panther, May Springs, Ray and German creek embayments. Holding depths vary from season to season, and even week to week, as these fish consistently seek out 72-to-74-degree zones. Live bluegill fished along creek meanders works well, as does trolling jigs or spoons, although downriggers are needed when the fish are deep.

This is one of the few places where night fishing for linesides is popular, probably an offshoot of the traditional night fishing for several species here. Half-ounce black bucktails with 6-to-8-inch black plastic worms or shad are the most popular twilight offerings.

Beginning in late September after the lake is drawn down, rockfish and hybrids move upstream along spring migration routes. At this time trolling and live bait fishing are effective. Striper school locations are closely monitored by area dock owners. During the summer where ten or more boats bunch up, it's a safe bet a striper school is nearby.

Anglers most familiar with Cherokee Lake know it is a fine smallmouth bass lake, despite the fact that little is heard about it. Bronzebacks in the 6-to-7-pound class are remarkably common. Smallmouth bass fishing is a year-round endeavor for many anglers. February is one of the "hottest" months for smalljaw action. Small grey, green or chartreuse grubs and live tuffies bounced along creeks and river channels work well.

Seasonal warming affects shallow back coves first, and that's where the best early spring smallie fishing can be found. From mid-March to early May, during the spawn, spinners and shallow-diving crankbaits tossed against the shoreline are effective. Following the spawn the bass scatter out along most gravel and rock points. Point fishing can be either very easy or extremely difficult. Ripping deep-running crankbaits over these submerged fingers is effective at times, but most area fishermen concede plastic worms or pig'n'jig combos coupled with a big dose of patience are the best approach. Preferred colors are black, purple, motor oil and wine. Weights and bait lengths vary, but not techniques. All must be fished slow and deep by inching the bait over the bottom, using seductive lift and drop or "steady, slow-return" retrieves. These feeding spots are utilized until hot weather, when the old river channel points become the primary holding zones.

Between May and October night fishing accounts for 75 percent of Cherokee Lake's serious smallmouth bass fishing. Big bronzebacks feed late, very late, and you can't catch them sleeping in bed. The baits and techniques are the same as those used at other times.

Cherokee is a better largemouth bass lake than most know. The lake record is old, but the record hawg weighed over 12 pounds. I've seen a few 10 pounders. Largemouth bass come on "slower" than their brown cousins, although during the winter a few bass are taken on live bait or small jigs fished along muddy creek embayments.

March signals a move into the newly filled shallows, where water temperatures are higher. Spinnerbaits, buzzbaits and shallow-running crankbaits and plastic worms work well in back coves through the end of May. Spawning is over then, and the hawgs move along the shoreline seeking cover such as stump beds, brush, old road beds, deadfalls, fish attractors and points. During the hot weather these fish move to progressively deeper water along the old river channel. At times there is first-class top-water action. Submerged building foundations are a fa-

Cherokee Lake produces mixed-bag catches of bass that you can brag about.

vorite haunt during the dog days. Angling during the graveyard shift is the best time. Plastic worms and pig'n'jig combos inched along deep structure are *the* nighttime bigmouth bass bait. During the fall worms and orange-colored crankbaits worked around rock and gravel points are effective. Small points near the mouths of feeder streams are particularly productive.

Cherokee Lake's catfish action rates high. Channel cats are the most numerous whiskered species, but blue cats are stocked periodically and one's odds for nabbing a big one are good. Very large flathead cats in the 35-to-40-pound class are taken each summer by trotline fishermen. When permitted, commercial fishermen make good catches during the cold-weather months. These hardy souls are about the only catfish anglers on the water then except for a few faithfuls who do quite well bottom fishing stinkbaits at the John Sevier Steam Plant. During hot weather jug and bank set fishing using cut bait and chicken liver are popular and productive at the German Creek, Cherokee Park and Cedar Hill areas and Slate Hill near US 25.

White bass are abundant in Cherokee and can be caught just about anywhere, anytime. During fall these fish migrate up the Holston River, where they concentrate downstream from the steam plant until mid-April. Jigs and minnows, trolled or cast, work well here. Catches of up to 200 fish per day are not uncommon. In late spring stripe move downstream. There they school and run the lake's open water at cove mouths and in back coves. Brisk action is often available when the white bass prey on schools of surface-swimming shad. Break fishing, as it is called, can net a lot of whites in a short time.

Cherokee has a checkered reputation as a crappie lake. Some years it is the hottest number in upper East Tennessee. During others it is colder than a dead mackerel. Black crappie are the dominant species in this rocky lake, but white crappie are also well represented. Most of the slabsides taken here are nice sized, averaging 2 to 3 pounds.

Late winter is a tough time to take on Cherokee's calicos, but it can be done successfully. Deep, long-line jigging with minnows or ⅛-ounce white jigs coupled with 4-to-6-pound-test line and ultra-sensitive fishing rod is the best approach. Spring crappie fishing often finds these fish slow to forsake deep water. Deep trolling with the aid of diving planes or downriggers, fishermen mop up in the Cedar Hill, Rocky Hollow, German and Fall creek areas. To be assured of good crappie fishing on Cherokee Lake, learn the location of all TVA-TWRA fish attractors. These tire and brush cover sites are excellent starting spots for year-round slabside action. Other man-made brush piles are not marked, but occasional checks around before the water rises will reveal their location.

Cherokee also sports a good bluegill and warmouth bream population. These fair-weather quarries are most available between late April and October. Live baits such as redworms and crickets are always good here. During the spring try back coves and feeder stream embayments. Exceptional hot-weather fishing can be found 5 to 10 feet deep along river channel bluffs.

Cherokee Lake once had a very good sauger fishery. This disappeared, however, when the John Sevier Steam Plant was built. During the early 1980s sauger-walleye hybrids were stocked, and these have proven successful. Saugeye, as most refer to these crossbreeds, grow fast, reaching 3 pounds in two years, and they are capable of topping the 10-pound mark in forage-rich fisheries like Cherokee.

Saugeye are easily caught on artificial lures and live bait. During the winter good catches are made from the Malinda Bridge area upstream to the steam plant. River action peaks in March, and thereafter these fish move downstream and scatter throughout the lake. This is still a young fishery, but at this writing, during other seasons, the Cherokee Dock–Fall Creek area appears to be preferred by the saugeye. Quarter-ounce green twistertail grubs and flies are the best lures and casting close along the shoreline and around rocky points is the best approach for late spring through autumn.

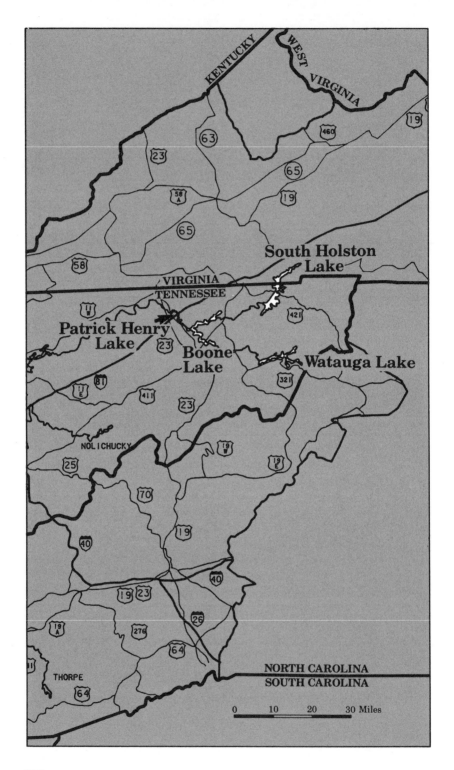

Fort Patrick Henry and Boone Lakes

Fort Patrick Henry and Boone lakes are upper East Tennessee's most urban fisheries. Both are located on the Holston River. Boone is the larger of the two, lying immediately upstream from Fort Patrick Henry Lake. Although Patrick Henry is smaller, it is considered the more scenic. Boone offers the better overall fishing, however.

Fort Patrick Henry Lake

SIZE: small
ACCESSIBILITY: very good
LOCATION: Tennessee (Sullivan County)
PRESSURE: heavy (pleasure boating heavy)
PRIMARY GAMEFISH: largemouth and smallmouth bass, striped and whiterock bass, catfish, bluegill
SECONDARY GAMEFISH: crappie, rainbow trout
BEST MONTHS: April, May, June, August, February
BEST BAITS: live minnows, red wigglers, jigs, deep-diving crankbaits, spinnerbaits, blue plastic worms
BEST BET: fishing for rainbow during June downstream from Patrick Henry Dam

This man-made lake was named in honor of an early Volunteer State outpost built near the South Fork of the Holston River. The fort itself, of course, was named in honor of the revolutionary patriot. Area anglers often simply call this lake "Pat Henry."

The dam stands 95 feet high and is 737 feet across. It was built in

1952 and has two hydroelectric units. At full pool Fort Patrick Henry Lake covers 872 surface acres and extends 10 miles, with 37 miles of shoreline. Elevation at full pool is 1,263 feet above sea level, with a drawdown to 1,258 feet above sea level.

The lake has a very limited storage capacity, and when hydroelectric production occurs upstream at Boone Dam, it is usually necessary to quickly follow suit at Fort Patrick Henry. The net result is constant 1-to-5-foot changes in water level. Being a "flow-through" reservoir, this lake has little time to retain nutrients upon which to build a really good forage base.

From the air Fort Patrick Henry Lake looks more like a river. At its widest point it is only a quarter mile across. The bottom is clay, mud and gravel, with a few rocky outcrop areas. This is one of the very few eastern lakes in the system hosting significant growths of aquatic weeds such as milfoil.

Sullivan County completely encircles the lake. Kingsport's suburbs flank the lake's tailwater reaches, while Bristol and Johnson City are only minutes away. US 23 follows the lake's southwestern shoreline, and I-81 crosses at river mile 12.5. There are two public boat-launch ramps and one commercial dock at Warriors Path State Park. This the finest state-operated park in upper East Tennessee. It offers excellent camping, as well as an array of other recreational opportunities.

Fishing Information

Fort Patrick Henry Lake is best known as a haven for sail and pleasure boating, water skiing and other similar pursuits. This is not to say some good angling, particularly for warm-water species, is not available here, but this lake is important recreationally to the bustling Tri-Cities.

Fishing success at Pat Henry fluctuates almost as much as its water level. Some species, like bass, are more cooperative at high tide, or when the lake is at or approaching full pool, while others such as bream respond better to angling efforts when the lake level is being dropped.

The largemouth bass is Pat Henry's top drawing card, and local fishermen accustomed to the lake's whimsical nature make good catches. During the winter the steady flow of cold water through the lake makes much of Pat Henry inhospitable to largemouth bass. On the other hand there are a number of coves along the lake's lower end which offer "refuge." Many of these side areas offer challenging weed fishing. Spinners and medium-depth-diving crankbaits work well in these areas.

Prespawn bass fishing here can be very good in feeder creek areas located downstream from I-81. This is also the area holding the best bedding action. Buzzbaits knifed alongside weed beds are deadly during periods of no generation. At other times jigs, spinners and crankbaits in white, orange and brown work well. Pat Henry's bass stay frisky and relatively shallow throughout the summer and autumn months. Using the above-noted baits, try fishing the main channel points when water is passing through the lake.

Many feel Fort Patrick Henry is one of the best and most overlooked bluegill lakes in Tennessee. Hand-sized bream are common. The 'gills occupy the same area preferred by the bucketmouth bass and follow the same basic seasonal movement patterns. Spawning occurs in shallow back-cove and feeder stream embayments around mid-May. Following this time, the best fishing is along the river channel where bluffs and shady areas are available. Crickets and worms are the most popular offerings, but if you're a fly fisherman, try dropping a sponge-bodied bug around the shoreline.

Most fishermen are not aware of the excellent trout fishing opportunities in Pat Henry's headwaters. Cold water released from Boone Dam creates year-round cold-water habitat downstream to the I-81 bridge. Rainbows up to nine pounds are not unusual. In fact, some feel this six-mile stretch is the best trout fishing in East Tennessee. A few brown trout are also taken here, along with occasional striped bass and hybrids washed down from Boone.

Drift fishing such baits as corn, nightcrawlers or cheese balls when Boone Dam is generating is a favorite ploy, followed by trolling shallow-diving minnow-type crankbaits and casting the shoreline with small

Fishing for white bass at the Holston River below Patrick Henry.

Mepps-style spinners. When there is no turbine activity at Boone, fly fishing the shallows using No. 10 to No. 18 dry flies or nymphs is productive, as is bait fishing on the bottom of deep holes.

There are a few crappie in Fort Patrick Henry Lake, but this is a spotty, generally insignificant fishery. This is not true of channel and flathead catfish, which are well represented here and grow to a fair size. The best fishing for these ugly fish is downstream from the interstate bridge, with June through September the prime time. Back coves, feeder stream embayments and the main river channel all provide good catches.

——*Boone Lake*

SIZE: small
ACCESSIBILITY: very good
LOCATION: Tennessee (Sullivan County)
PRESSURE: moderate to heavy
PRIMARY GAMEFISH: crappie, bluegill, largemouth bass, catfish
SECONDARY GAMEFISH: white bass, striped bass
BEST MONTHS: March, April, May, June, September, October
BEST BAITS: live minnows, hair jigs, twistertail grubs, deep-diving
    crankbaits, spinnerbaits, plastic worms
BEST BET: early April crankbait fishing along creek channels for
    largemouth bass

The pioneer explorer Daniel Boone canvassed much of the area presently known as the Tri-Cities (Bristol–Johnson City–Kingsport). This storage–flood control–power generation dam was christened in 1952. It is 160 feet high and 1,532 feet across and houses three hydroelectric units. At full pool the lake's surface stands at 1,385 feet above sea level and covers 4,310 surface acres. It extends 33 miles and has 130 miles of shoreline. Full pool is achieved each spring and by fall it is drawn down again approximately 50 feet to an elevation of 1,330.

The lake is formed by the impoundment of the South Fork of the Holston River and Watauga River, downstream from lakes bearing the same names. Boone Lake has a very distinct V shape. It is characterized by high rock bluffs along the winding primary river and numerous feeder stream coves. The bottom is composed of clay, gravel and rock. Much of the shoreline either has a steep gradient or is a sheer bluff, although there are back coves and some flats.

The lake's South Holston River arm and the northern edge of the Watauga River arm are located in Sullivan County, while the southern portion of the Watauga River arm is bounded by Washington County.

Kingsport, Johnson City, Bristol and Elizabethton are the closest towns. US 23 roughly parallels Boone Lake's southern edge, while US 11E (also 19W-411) crosses the Watauga River arm at river mile 9 and the South Holston River arm at river mile 33. There are 8 commercial boat docks and 10 public launch ramps but no public campgrounds around this popular lake.

Fishing Information

Boone is a surprisingly diverse warm- and cold-water fishery. Despite its pocket size it produces a proportionately great amount of fishing. The largemouth bass is the dominant black bass species. Largemouth account for about 90 percent of the lake's bass population, according to Tennessee Wildlife Resources Agency fishery biologist Doug Peterson, who rates Boone's bass population as "very good to excellent."

"The lake is rich in nutrients from agricultural run-off and municipal waste discharges," says Peterson. "Forage is abundant, and the growth rates for many species of fish here are surprisingly good."

Winter fishing is good in the lake's lower reaches in backwater areas from the Pier Dock and Sugar Hollow to the dam in the South Holston River arm and from Deerlick Bend and Snyder Creek to the dam in the Watauga River arm. Deep-water worming and jigging work well off clay and slate drop-offs, and live bait is also productive.

Around the end of March the green fish occupy feeder stream embayments and back-cove areas all the way up to Beaver Creek in the South Holston and around Knob Creek Dock on the Watauga river arms. Medium-diving crankbaits and spinnerbaits work best, with white, chartreuse and yellow the top colors.

Spawning occurs in May and sometimes as late as June. A favorite prespawn ploy is to flip or jig back-cove trashlines, where big bass position to ambush spawning shad. Brown, blue-black or orange-brown ³/₈-to-¼-ounce jigs dropped silently through shoreline debris and then vertically jigged are deadly on bass.

During hot weather the bass migrate out along the river arms. As the weather gets hotter and water temperatures rise, two things occur. Some fish find zones off main channel points where they can be comfortable. Others move further up into the river arms seeking cooler water which comes during periods of upstream generation. This group is usually shallower, but not quite as large.

Big, deep-running crankbaits capable of cutting depths over eight feet are prime summer offerings, followed by purple worms and jigs. Night fishing is also productive here, particularly when one of the upstream dams is passing water in conjunction with turbine activity at Boone Dam.

Bluegill grow large in Boone, and fishing for these bantam-weight battlers here is quite popular. Bedding occurs anywhere a shallow back cove offers a soft or gravel bottom. Later in the summer excellent catches of hand-sized bream can be made along the Mackyfield Bluff and Boring Ford areas in the Watauga River arm and Hick Bend and Devault Bridge areas in the South Holston River arm. Good fly fishing is also available in the flats around Indian and Devault bends in the Watauga.

Boone has been a real surprise for striped bass and hybrid fans. It's a moderately small lineside lake by Tennessee standards, but it has a heavy gizzard shad forage base in excess of 200 pounds per surface acre. Striper and hybrids are stocked at a rate of five per surface acre. In recent years 25 to 30 pounders have become routine, and fish up to 38 pounds are taken. A new Tennessee state record hybrid bass weighing 18 pounds, 1 ounce was caught here in 1985.

Winter striper fishing here is practiced by only a handful of fishermen. These either troll red and white bucktail jigs or drift fish live shad along the steep bluff drop-offs and creek mouths. Try the South Holston River arm between the old Rainbow Bridge area and Hicks Bend or the US 11E bridge and Pickens Bend area in the Watauga River arm. Holding depths for striper and hybrid average 5 to 25 feet.

Good spring striper action using the same approach is also available in these locations. In May the linesides move into shallow coves and tributary systems, where they feed upon spawning shad. Some top-water action is available, along with subsurface jig and crankbait fishing.

During hot weather striper schools fragment and go in two directions like the bass. Some move into 25-to-40-foot-deep water around the dam. Downriggers are helpful for catching these fish. Other striper schools move upstream into the river arms, where upstream cool water discharges provide habitat. Sometimes these fish can be found in surprisingly shallow water around the Hodge Island area in the Watauga and the Beaver Creek and Massengill Island areas in the South Holston river arms. Good catches are made trolling and drift fishing live shad or bluegill.

Boone Lake holds the best crappie fishing in the Tri-Cities area. It gets high ratings during the height of the spring run, when catches in excess of 75 to 100 fish per fisherman are not uncommon. Size fluctuates considerably, but numbers are almost always good. Winter slabside action is at its best following mild weather and minimum turbine activity in one or both river arms. Live minnows are the standard offering. These are bumped along brush, stumps and drop-offs in creek embayments. Candy Creek is a prime cold-weather spot in the South Holston, while Reedy Creek and White Branch are worth investigating in the Watauga area. Spawning usually peaks from late April through May. Cove areas downstream from the above-noted crappie hot spots are all worthy of mention, especially those with TVA-TWRA fish attractors. Following the spawn, crappie fishing really slows as these fish scatter. Some night fishing is available along main channel drop-offs.

Catfish are abundant in nutrient-rich Boone Lake. Channel cats are most numerous, and 10 pounders are common. Flatheads in the 40-pound class are common year-round, and a few blue cats are also caught. Little winter whiskered fish chasing occurs here, but there is considerable summertime catfish angling. Chicken liver, shrimp and cut shad and shad gut are the most productive local baits.

Sauger also occupy portions of Boone Lake, along with a fair number of white bass. These fish run the river in the late winter and spring. In the South Holston River the best white bass and sauger action occurs from the Sportsman's Dock upstream to Massengill Island. In the Watauga Indian Bend downstream to Boones Creek Dock is the best starting point for winter and spring white bass and sauger fishing. Quarter-ounce orange or green jigs tipped with minnows work well on the sauger, while light spinners and minnows are the top stripe takers.

Boone's headwater rivers offer some of the finest tailrace river trout fishing in the Southeast. Rainbow and brown trout inhabit both, and each produces loads of trophy-class fish. Don took a nine-pound brown from the South Holston River in 1983. During the winter (and sporadically during other times, too) a few trout are caught from Boone Lake. These catches are usually incidental to other types of fishing, particularly trolling for rockfish or crappie. A few people catch trout at the base of the dam during hot weather by bait fishing 40 to 65 feet deep.

South Holston Lake

SIZE: small

ACCESSIBILITY: very good, fair in winter

LOCATION: Tennessee (Sullivan County) and Virginia (Washington County)

PRESSURE: moderate

PRIMARY GAMEFISH: smallmouth bass, white bass, bluegill, rainbow trout

SECONDARY GAMEFISH: crappie, ohrid trout, catfish, largemouth bass, walleye, sauger

BEST MONTHS: April, May, June, July, August, October

BEST BAITS: live minnows, nightcrawlers, pig'n'jig, deep-diving crankbaits, plastic worms

BEST BET: fishing for smallmouth bass with jigs tipped with pork in the lake's downstream feeder stream embayments at night during July

South Holston Lake is located in extreme upper East Tennessee in a natural setting of spectacular dimensions. The many sheer rock bluffs and cliffs surrounding this impoundment give it a "glacial" look typical of lakes far removed from Ole Dixie. This 7,580-acre reservoir was created in 1950, and like its nearest TVA neighbor, Watauga Lake, it's a "mountain lake" sporting a diversity of cold-, cool- and warm-water fisheries. The lake is formed by the impoundment of the South Fork of the Holston River, which drains the Mount Rogers area of southwestern Virginia. The lake's headwaters extend into Virginia, making South Holston the only Tennessee River Valley lake in that state.

The Holston River's name is derived from its old Cherokee name "Hogoheegee." Early white settlers to the South Holston River Valley found game such as black bear, elk, white-tailed deer and buffalo plentiful, but it was beaver pelts which they sought. These were easily converted into shillings.

South Holston Dam, a dirt-fill structure, stands 285 feet high and is 1,600 feet across. It was built for storage, flood control and power production. At full pool, which is usually achieved in late spring, the lake stands at 1,742 feet above sea level and extends 24 miles with 168 miles of shoreline. The late summer or fall drawdown is between 60 and 100 feet.

South Holston Lake's bottom is composed of clay, shale, gravel and rock. There is little natural cover other than bars, rocky points, sporadic stump beds, and creek and river meanders. Intensive efforts to place man-made fish attractors in the lake's coves have been highly successful. Their status and location are available from TVA or state wildlife and fishery agencies.

The lake straddles the border between Tennessee and Virginia. Re-

South Holston Lake has an outstanding smallmouth bass fishery.

ciprocal fishing agreements between these two states to honor each other's licenses on most of the lake ended in 1983 and were not renewed. At this writing, however, efforts continue on the part of sportsmen in both states to have a new agreement enacted. Sullivan County encircles the lake's Tennessee portion, which accounts for approximately 75 percent of the full-pool acreage. Washington County encircles the Virginia portion of the lake. Bristol, Kingsport, and Elizabethton are the nearest towns. TN 44 parallels the lake's northwestern edge, while US 421 bisects it near river mile 58. VA 75 traces the lake's north shore, and numerous secondary roads, notably the Avens Bridge Road, provide additional headwater access.

The lofty Holston Mountains tower along the lake's southeastern shores, while rolling countryside borders much of its northwestern edge. Nearly all of the southeastern shoreline is under the control of the Cherokee and Jefferson national forests, which encompass the old game-rich Kettlefoot Wildlife Management Area. There are four commercial boat docks and nine public boat launches in Tennessee's part of the lake and three docks and three ramps in the Virginia end.

The U.S. Forest Service operates the Jacob Creek and Little Oak Mountain recreation areas around South Holston Lake. Both offer camping, but the Little Oak Mountain site is particularly nice and ranks among best publicly owned facilities anywhere. Public camping is also available at the Sullivan and Washington county parks.

Fishing Information

South Holston receives considerable fishing pressure from anglers residing within easy driving distance of its banks. Actually, because it has an undeserved reputation as a very tough lake to fish, it is often overlooked. This is too bad, as this impoundment is a delightful place to wet a line. It's an above-average smallmouth and white bass fishing hole, and it also offers excellent angling opportunities for rainbow trout. Crappie fishing can be very good during May, and bluegill catches rival those of any nearby lakes. Catfish are relatively plentiful, and largemouth bass caught from South Holston Lake sometimes top 8 pounds. Toss in sometimes very good sauger fishing and you can see why this scenic lake is so popular among local fishermen.

The lake's rocky shoreline harbors great quantities of pincer-equipped crawfish. There is nothing a smalljaw bass relishes more than these protein-rich crustaceans. The lake is loaded with 9-to-12-inch bronzebacks, and lunkers in the 5-pound class aren't unusual. Winter fishing can be good here, particularly in December. Small brown or smoke-colored grubs and live baits fished along steep bank areas in a rhythmic lift and drop are productive. Angling in the extreme cold weather of January and early February is sometimes productive when fishing on the crest of a front or during balmy weather; all but the most ardent fishermen forgo fishing here at this time, however.

Spring smallie fishing hits high gear in mid-April. Major feeder creek embayments in the lake's midsection are the best starting points. Spinnerbaits worked from the shoreline down to 10 to 15 feet are effective until early June. Jig fishing can also be good then, along with running medium- and deep-diving crankbaits. Spawning usually occurs in late April or early May. Sloping shoreline with a gravel or sandy bottom 5 to 10 feet deep is ideal for nest robbing.

Late May usually brings a brief two-week period of brisk top-water brown bass fishing. Places where the lake backs up around black willow trees in back coves and along rock bluffs are ideal locations to work Jitterbugs, Rebel Floater Minnows and other floating baits.

Hot weather sends the fish deep, and the best catches occur along the old river channel between the dam and the US 421 bridge. Dusk to dawn is the best timeslot from mid-June through early October. Live baits such as nightcrawlers, spring lizards and big creek minnows inched along 5-to-15-foot drop-offs account for a large number of trophy smallies. Deep-water jigging with ⅜-to-¼-ounce spider jigs tipped with Uncle Josh's 101 pork rinds is lethal here, with brown, blue and black being the top colors. During the autumn "turnover," spinnerbait and crankbait fishing is good along main channel points from the dam to the Avens Bridge.

Bigmouth bass fishing is better at South Holston than many would think a cool lake could provide. Winter angling is nil, but by mid-March good catches can be made in the back of major feeder creek embayments, especially at Fishdam and Jacob creeks. Slow-wobble, deep-running crankbaits are the most effective offering, followed by strawberry-colored worms and live minnows. Spring fishing activity centers off sloping gravel and mud points and creek meander drop-offs. Spinnerbaits and worms are the best bets at this time. Spawning occurs in these same general areas, as well as around flooded greenery. The best tactic then is to rip baits through such likely areas.

Hot-weather bassin' is good in the very early morning hours, but like just about everywhere else in the TVA system, the best largemouth bass fishing at this time occurs under the cloak of darkness. Main channel points where small streams enter the lake or old building foundations are always worth investigating at this time. Jig'n'pigs are effective at this time, along with live bait and purple, motor oil and black firetail plastic worms. Bass scatter in early October, and can be found almost anywhere bait fish can be located. Shad-mimicking crankbaits and chartreuse-skirted spinnerbaits are the top producers until mid-December, when catch rates drop.

South Holston Lake enjoys an excellent reputation as a rainbow trout hot spot. Its tailrace rates among the finest producers of trophy brown trout in the eastern United States. Trout were first stocked in the lake in 1959. The TWRA stocks rainbow trout, as does the Virginia Commission of Game and Inland Fisheries. There is very little natural reproduction, although during late fall big trout are sometimes found in some mountainous feeder streams. Most fish planted here are fingerlings, but a number of creel-size fish (9 to 12 inches) are also put into the lake. Because the lake holds a large number of shad, trout growth rates are good.

Although winter trout fishing at this lake can be very good, remarkably few endure the season's rigors to take advantage of it. During December through early March these fish can be taken casting the shoreline with 2-to-3-inch-long shad-style crankbaits or on nightcrawlers. Creek mouths on the lake's eastern shoreline are particularly good at this time.

When water temperatures climb into the high sixties, it's a safe bet these fish are on their way to 15-to-25-foot depths. Trolling crankbaits and live minnows works well during the daylight hours until June. Hot weather sends these fish another 15 to 25 feet deeper and concentrates them down the lake between the dam and the Little White Oak Recreation Area. At this time serious trout fishing on South Holston Lake becomes a nocturnal affair. The best method is to mark these fish with an electronic depth finder and then locate above them. Vertical jigging with spoons or live bait is good, especially under a lantern.

Crappie fishing at this lake is also better than many outsiders might suspect, although admittedly it is spotty and some years are markedly better than others. White and black crappie are about equally represented. Those taken here are nice, usually over 1½ pounds, and when things are "hot," catches of up to 50 per angler in a day are not uncommon.

Winter calico fishing is not well developed, but come late March, the slabside fleet can be expected to sail in force. Natural cover for spawning, such as stick-ups or deadfalls, is virtually nonexistent; however, the lake sports quite a number of TVA fish attractors. One bonafide hot spot for spring crappie action is the Jinkerson Branch embayment, which sports a cluster of shallow brush piles for these fish to home in on.

Calico nesting activity usually commences in mid-April. Feeder creek embayments are heavily utilized at this time. Bobber fishing with minnows and flies is the most common technique, followed by trolling these same offerings. Following the spawn, crappie fishing success plummets, for this is a deep lake with loads of drop-offs that make it difficult to locate scattered fish. Fall crappie fishing can be pretty good. Again feeder creek areas are the center of crappie feeding activity. At times trolling jigs and minnows or casting the bank will produce good results.

South Holston Lake boasts a very good white bass fishery, although it wasn't planned. They were stocked during the 1950s by some unknown "Johnny Appleseed"–style white bass fan. Fishery biologists would probably not have placed these fast-growing, prolific fish here, but that's beside the point now because they're permanent fixtures.

White bass fishing is a three-part game here. Early spring finds these fish finning up the lake in large numbers to spawn between Avens Bridge and the forks of the river (the Middle and South forks of the Holston). Excellent catches of fish up to three pounds are made casting the current with Roostertails and flies. White bass stay in the headwaters spawning well into May. The stripe's return to the lake signals the beginning of first-class top-water action using smaller spinners and shallow-diving top-water plugs. Later in the summer around July 4th, very good twilight action can be found throughout the lake fishing under lanterns with minnows.

Sauger were stocked in South Holston Lake in 1963, although they are indigenous to the South Fork of the Holston River. Today they are available in limited numbers, although this fishery never really panned out. Most late winter and spring catches are made incidentally by white bass anglers fishing the headwaters. Crappie fishermen also occasionally pick up rattlesnake fish when trolling, as do trout anglers.

Catfish are abundant in South Holston Lake. Flathead and channel cats are the primary fare here, followed by a few big-growing blues. Virginia's state record flathead catfish, a 57 pounder, was taken here in 1957. Serious whiskered-fish chasing doesn't begin here until fair weather is well established, but it lasts until well into autumn. Spring catches are best along the main river channel between Jinkerson Branch and Sullivan County park. Hot weather finds these fish taking refuge in back coves and feeder creek embayments.

South Holston Lake is a typical bluegill lake. Like the catfish-catching clan, the 'gill's fans don't get started until it's comfortable outdoors. Spawning, which is concentrated in backwater areas throughout the lake, takes place in May and June. Following the spawn the numerous bluffs bordering the lake are always good bets for action. Traditional hot spots include the Knobs stretch above the dam and around Friendship Dock. Fly rodders can have a bushel of fun popping bugs where overhanging trees shade the water.

Watauga Lake

SIZE: small

ACCESSIBILITY: good, fair in winter; few marinas

LOCATION: Tennessee (Johnson and Carter counties)

PRESSURE: moderate

PRIMARY GAMEFISH: crappie, bluegill, smallmouth and largemouth bass, walleye

SECONDARY GAMEFISH: white bass, rainbow trout, ohrid trout, catfish

BEST MONTHS: April, May, June, July, September, October

BEST BAITS: live minnows, hair jigs, spring lizards, pig'n'jig, nightcrawlers, deep-diving crankbaits, plastic worms

BEST BET: night fishing for walleye using nightcrawlers along the lake's bluffs in June

Tennessee's mountain lakes are jewels that must be seen and fished to be appreciated. Watauga Lake in upper East Tennessee is one such highland beauty. Its emerald-green water and lofty, well-forested shoreline combine to make it one of the most scenic Volunteer State lakes. It is located in the heart of Tennessee's earliest pioneer settlements. The historic Sycamore Shoals area, where the Overmountain Men mustered before the Battle of Kings Mountain, is only a few miles downstream. It is also the birthplace of the famous Watauga Association, the first Anglo frontier self-government.

Watauga is a storage–flood control–power production lake formed by the impoundment of the Watauga and Elk rivers. Each begins in western North Carolina's highlands. At full pool the lake covers 6,430 surface acres and its elevation is 1,975 feet above sea level. It extends 16 miles and has 106 miles of shoreline. Full pool is usually achieved by June, and there is a 50-to-60-foot drawdown each fall.

Constructed in 1948, Watauga Dam is still considered an engineering wonder. Water from the lake is channeled through a mammoth tunnel carved through the center of the adjacent mountains to the Watauga Powerhouse. From there it enters the headwaters of little Wilbur Lake, which predates Watauga by a third of a century. Watauga is an earth-filled dam wedged into a great gap in the Iron Mountains; it stands 318 feet high and 900 feet wide. The famed Appalachian Trail passes over the dam.

Watauga is a deep, steep-walled lake sporting little natural cover other than rocks and sandbars 50 to 60 feet deep at full pool. When the lake was initially flooded, timber was left standing below that level. Steep drop-offs, rocky points, cove mouths and deeply cut creek and river channel meanders are key gamefish cover here. The water quality is excellent; most of the time the bottom is visible in depths of up to 10 to 15 feet.

Pond Mountain is located to the south and to the north rise the lofty Iron Mountains, over which the Appalachian Trail also passes. Much of the property bordering this lake is under the stewardship of Cherokee National Forest. The lake is bounded to the north by Johnson County and to the south by Carter County. Elizabethton, Bristol and Mountain City are the closest towns. US 321 traces alongside much of Watauga's southern banks, and TN 67 crosses at river mile 43.

Watauga has six boat docks and five public launch ramps. There are six U.S. Forest Service recreation sites along the lake: Rat Branch, Shook Branch, Carden's Bluff, Watauga Point, Little Milligan and Sink Mountain. All except the Rat Branch and Little Milligan facilities offer overnight camping. Camping is also permitted at TVA's Watauga Dam Reservation.

Fishing Information

This is a typical mountain lake, with warm-, cool- and cold-water fisheries. Excellent smallmouth bass and walleye populations exist here, as does good fishing for rainbow and ohrid trout, redeye and largemouth bass, and bluegill. White bass and crappie are available, while angling for channel catfish, Watauga's dominant whiskered fish, can be good at times.

The lake's gin-clear water is aesthetically grand, but it holds relatively few nutrients upon which to build a forage base. In addition, Watauga is too cold for threadfin and suboptimum for gizzard shad. Populations of walleye, white bass, smallmouth and largemouth bass and rainbow trout—all topflight predators—have long dwelt here. The fact that food was scarce reduced the likelihood of Watauga Lake's reaching its potential.

Watauga Lake offers great scenery and outstanding fishing. TVA photo.

In 1977 the Tennessee Wildlife Resources Agency released 2,000 alewives in Watauga in an effort to provide a broader food base. By the eighties these bait fish occupied the entire lake. Improvement in the number and size of bass, walleye and trout was seen. The average Watauga smallie now weighs over 2 pounds.

The introduction of the alewives also brought about significant changes in local angling strategies. Alewives dwell in cooler and generally deeper water than shad. They also tend to move and feed in shallow reaches at night. This also affects the behavior of the predatory fish that stalk them for dinner.

The smallmouth bass is Watauga's best-known gamefish representative. Two pounders are often culled, and four pounders don't raise an eyebrow. Winter smallmouth bass fishing here is not as well developed as it is on some of the East Tennessee lakes. Between February and early April, deep-water tightlining with crawfish or minnows along creek channels works fairly well, as do fly and rind combos. Throughout the year above-average water clarity dictates the use of lighter lines in the 6-to-10-pound-test class.

Spawning occurs in May and lasts about one month. Mating occurs at 5-to-15-foot depths off points with sloping gravel bases. At this time live creek minnows and crawdads are top producers, followed by crawdad-style crankbaits and Model A Bombers. May also produces first-class top-water bass action. Floating 3-to-5-inch-long, gold or silver Rebels worked parallel to points and brush can produce heart-stopping strikes.

Postspawn smallie action quickly becomes a nighttime only affair. Be forewarned, Watauga rates among the deepest and most challenging brown bass fishing anywhere, but the rewards can easily make up for the effort required. Under cover of darkness big bass stalk points and deep drop-offs. Live baits, particularly spring lizards, are super offerings, while white, black and chartreuse spinnerbaits tipped with pork rind trailers are dynamite. During late summer through October, pig'n'jigs are recommended.

During the hot-weather night-fishing season, smallie holding depths vary considerably between 5 and 25 feet. Top locations for night smallie action include the steep bluffs between Lakeshore and Deer Spring docks, Deer Lick Hollow and the points near the confluence of Roan Creek and the Watauga River.

Watauga gets little attention as a largemouth bass lake, but if you're a skeptic, go to any of the local bass club's tournament weigh-ins. You'll quickly discover the green bass is remarkably well represented here. Largemouth benefited from the stocking of alewives and the institution of a minimum-size limit. Three pounders from Watauga are respectable, and anything over five pounds is considered a real prize.

Like tangling with cold-weather brown bass, winter largemouth bass angling revives slowly here. Mid-April finds these fish concentrated in headwater embayments like Doe and Roan creeks. Waves churned up by the wind beat clay points into a "cloudy" condition, creating great springtime bass fishing opportunities. Fly and rind jigs and spinnerbaits in white, yellow or chartreuse are good bets.

When looking for Watauga hawgs, stay alert for muddy or colored water. True, they avoid extremely muddy water, but they are fond of prowling the edges of colored-water sites. Also, if you motor into a cove or embayment with dingy water, don't limit your efforts just to the color line at the front of the cove; explore its back side, too. Mountain thunder showers, which muddy coves, quickly run off. When water at the rear of a cove is clear, it indicates a topflight largemouth bass fishing spot.

During the summer largemouth bass fishing is primarily a nighttime affair. Rule number one on Watauga lake is that largemouth bass are always scattered during hot weather. Rule number two is that you can use any lure you'd like as long as it's a brownish-orange jig. The deep-water coves in the lake's lower two-thirds provide the best night summertime action.

Autumn bass fishing can be good. River channel points with a little dingy color are excellent starting points. Crawfish or big shiners are excellent choices, along with red and motor oil plastic worms.

Watauga Lake's walleye fishery was another beneficiary of the increased forage base resulting from the introduction of alewives. Marble-eye size and number have increased in recent years, as has angler interest. Walleye can be taken year-round from this lake. Late evening and early morning winter action in the vicinity of Pioneer Landing and around the mouths of the Elk River and Roan Creek is excellent through early March. Casting to or from the shoreline is productive, along with trolling green or orange quarter-ounce, minnow-tipped jigs anywhere moving water can be found. At this time some do well suspending lanterns over creek mouths and jigging dollflies and minnows underneath.

Mid-spring signals the marble-eye's return to Watauga's main body. During the daytime they "lay low" deep in the old river channel, atop bars and off of points. Holding depths of 40 feet are not uncommon, and downriggers are necessary for deep-water trolling. Sunset brings a radical change, though. During the spring when surface water temperatures are under 70 degrees, Watauga walleye move right in against the shoreline in 2-to-5-foot-deep water to prey upon spawning shad. Then jigs or small, shallow-diving crankbaits worked parallel to the banks are effective.

Hot weather brings out the night-fishing marble-eye clan in large numbers. Walleye are now ambushing alewives at the mouths of coves and feeders, plus points and drop-offs. At night during the summer surface feeding sometimes occurs, but these fish are usually found 8 to 20 feet deep. Electronic depth finders are essential for locating Watauga's summertime fish. Trolling medium-depth-running crankbaits or jigs works well, as does positioning a light over the water and jigging minnows below it. This fishing pattern holds well into cold weather.

Trout fishing was once Watauga's mainstay, although no species is native here. Stocked rainbows of 8 to 10 pounds are relatively common, and the newly introduced ohrids may surpass this if natural reproduction occurs. Occasionally, large brown trout are also caught.

Several years ago there was a much-heralded run of rainbow trout reproducing in the Doe Creek watershed. From the late fifties to the early seventies, extremely large 'bows swam miles up this crystalline rill to spawn. At the height of the run in December and January, limits consisting of 5 to 8 pounders were common. We made several trips there, but never caught a trophy trout, although everyone accompanying us did. On a couple of occasions we hooked fish in the 5-pound class, but they were all treated to LDRs (Long-Distance Releases).

Today the legendary Doe Creek run has nearly disappeared. Streamside construction was a big factor in its demise, as perhaps was Watauga's walleye population explosion or over-fishing of the run itself. It is as much a mystery why the big trout no longer run upstream here as it is why this unusual spawning event occurred in the first place.

Cold-weather trout fishing is still very popular and productive here. In the winter trout station at the mouths of Doe and Roan creeks and the Elk and Watauga rivers. The cold surface temperatures are within the trout's tolerance range, and they can be caught in 5-to-8-foot-deep water. Silver, orange or red medium-depth-running crankbaits are excellent choices, followed by small Mepps or Panther Martin–style spinners. Such baits as salmon eggs, sweet corn or nightcrawlers are always productive.

In March trout scatter to ply the lake's cold depths 40 to 60 feet deep. Locating this quarry now requires an electronic depth finder. Ideal starting points include bluffs that taper off with sloping gradients and creek mouths located in the lower one-third of the lake. Downrigger trolling with spoons or shad-type plugs is the best avenue to daytime trout fishing success. At night, fishing under lanterns is effective, particularly around the dam. It's as simple as falling off a log; just drop a hook baited with a minnow or corn 25 feet deep, sit back and wait for a big trout to slam by.

Panfish angling is modestly productive at Watauga, and those caught are usually large. Bluegill are the top panfish representatives, followed by crappie, and white bass. During the summer, locating a shaded bluff is the key to first-class bluegill action at 8-to-12-foot depths. Prior to this, fishing for fish bedding in or around man-made brush piles and in shallow, "bowl-shaped" back coves can be torrid. Crickets, meal worms, and red wigglers are the best offerings.

Crappie are not plentiful in Watauga Lake, except for about a two-week period each year (usually in mid-May) when the calicos are bedding.

During early spring white bass can be found in good numbers in the lake's headwaters. Dollflies and Roostertail spinners are the best lures. Later in the year these fish can be found surface feeding throughout the lake.

Watauga has good, but limited Mr. Whiskers fishing. Jug fishing is growing in popularity here. Channel cats up to 10 pounds are taken during the summer, with the Roan Creek and Pierce Branch embayments being the top spots.

Lake Facilities Guide

Legend

	Y: Yes, this particular service is available.
Dock	A marina or dock with gas, oil, live baits, and miscellaneous fishing tackle
Food	S: Snack foods are available. M: Hot meals are available.
Lodging	Overnight lodging in a furnished room or cabin
Ramp	A boat-launch ramp is available at this location. It may or may not be a fee launch site.
Camping	This listing shows the general availability of campgrounds. These vary widely from free or fee public campsites, to commercial tent sites and full hook-up trailer sites. T: Tent camping available TR: Trailer camping available

Note: Most TVA recreational facilities are managed through field offices, which may be as much as 50 miles from the site. However, these are the best sources of information for those facilities.

	Dock	Food	Lodging	Ramp	Camping
Apalachia Lake					
None; see Hiwassee Lake for nearest facilities.					
Boone Lake					
Jay's Boat Dock, Rt. 4 Jonesboro, TN 37659 615-282-0844	Y	S		Y	

240

	Dock	Food	Lodging	Ramp	Camping
Boones Creek Marina Rt. 4 Jonesboro, TN 37659 615-282-2052	Y	M		Y	
The Pier Rt. 11 Kingsport, TN 37663 615-323-5073	Y	M		Y	
Tri-Cities Boat Dock Rt. 1 Piney Flats, TN 37686 615-323-7524	Y			Y	
Sportsman's Dock Rt. 1 Piney Flats, TN 37686 615-538-7517	Y	S		Y	
Davis Dock Rt. 2 Blountville, TN 37617 615-323-8467	Y	S		Y	

Calderwood Lake

None; see Fontana and Tellico
   lakes for nearest facilities.

Chatuge Lake

Jackrabbit Mountain Recreation Area Box 731 Asheville, NC 28802 704-837-1783				Y	T, TR
Chatuge Cove Complex Box 198A Hayesville, NC 28904 704-389-6155	Y	S		Y	
Towns County Recreation Area Box 381 Hiawassee, GA 30546 404-745-6928				Y	T, TR

	Dock	Food	Lodging	Ramp	Camping
Lazy Acres Camp Rt. 1 Hiawassee, GA 30546 404-896-2257	Y		Y	Y	
Kerr's Lakeside Cottages Rt. 1 Hiawassee, GA 30546 404-896-2251	Y		Y	Y	
Mountain View Cottages Rt. 1 Hiawassee, GA 30546 404-896-3550	Y	S	Y	Y	
Shady Rest Cabins Rt. 1 Hiawassee, GA 30546 404-896-2240			Y		
Robertson's Cabins Rt. 1 Hiawassee, GA 30546 404-896-4413			Y		
One Stop Marina Hwy. 76 Hiawassee, GA 30546 404-896-4349	Y	S		Y	T, TR
Towns County Park Box 381 Hiawassee, GA 30546 404-896-4191	Y		Y	Y	
Boundary Waters Resort & Marina Hiawassee, GA 30546 404-896-2530	Y		Y	Y	
Lake Chatuge Recreation Area Box 643 Gainesville, GA 30501 404-745-6923				Y	T, TR
Dyers Cabins Hiawassee, GA 30546 404-896-3943		S	Y		

	Dock	Food	Lodging	Ramp	Camping
Cheoah Lake					
None; see Fontana Lake.					
Cherokee Lake					
Cherokee Dam Reservation 2611 W. Andrew Johnson Hwy. Morristown, TN 37814 615-587-5600				Y	T, TR
Mossy Creek Dock Rt. 1 Jefferson City, TN 37760 615-475-5431	Y	S		Y	
Black Oak Dock Rt. 1 Jefferson City, TN 37760 615-475-3063	Y	M	Y	Y	
Cedar Hill Dock Rt. 2 Talbott, TN 37877 615-581-1148	Y	S	Y	Y	T, TR
May Spring Recreation Area 2611 W. Andrew Johnson Hwy. Morristown, TN 37814 615-587-5600					T, TR
Wa-Ni Village Rt. 3 Rutledge, TN 37861 615-828-5547	Y	M	Y	Y	T, TR
Panther Creek State Recreation Park Morristown, TN 37814 615-581-2623		S			T, TR
Southern Dock Rt. 3 Rutledge, TN 37861 615-828-5300	Y	M	Y	Y	T, TR

	Dock	Food	Lodging	Ramp	Camping
Gilmore Brothers Dock Rt. 2 Rutledge, TN 37861 615-767-2177	Y	S	Y	Y	T, TR
German Creek Dock Rt. 1 Bean Station, TN 37708 615-767-2550	Y	M	Y	Y	T, TR
Cherokee Park Morristown, TN 37814 615-586-2532				Y	T, TR
Hamblen Dock 910 W. Main, Box 1162 Morristown, TN 37814 615-586-2939	Y	S			
Cornette's Dock Rt. 2 Bean Station, TN 37708 615-586-9941	Y	M	Y	Y	
Fall Creek Dock Rt. 1 Russellville, TN 37860 615-586-4701	Y	S	Y	Y	T, TR
Fall Creek Recreation Area 2611 W. Andrew Johnson Hwy. Morristown, TN 37814 615-587-5600				Y	T, TR
Cherokee Boat Dock Rt. 2 Mooresburg, TN 37811 615-272-6120	Y	S		Y	T, TR

Chickamauga Lake

	Dock	Food	Lodging	Ramp	Camping
Chickamauga Marina Box 5063 Chattanooga, TN 37406 615-622-0821	Y	S		Y	

	Dock	Food	Lodging	Ramp	Camping
Gold Point Marina Box 252 Hixson, TN 37343 615-877-2501	Y	S	Y	Y	
Booker T. Washington State Park Rt. 2, Box 369 Chattanooga, TN 37416 615-894-4955	Y	S		Y	T, TR
Big Ridge Marina Box 26 Hixson, TN 37343 615-842-5828	Y		Y	Y	
Loret Resort Villas Rt. 1 Harrison, TN 37341 615-344-8331	Y	M	Y	Y	
Harrison Bay State Park Rt. 1 Harrison, TN 37341 615-344-6214	Y	M	Y	Y	T, TR
Chester Frost County Park Rt. 3 Gold Point Circle Hixson, TN 37343 615-842-0177		S		Y	T, TR
Lakesite Marina Box 99 Hixson, TN 37343 615-842-0431	Y	S	Y	Y	
Shady Grove Boat Harbor Rt. 2 Soddy, TN 37379 615-332-5613	Y	S		Y	T
Pine Harbor Boat Dock Rt. 2 Soddy, TN 37379 615-332-3963	Y	M		Y	T, TR

	Dock	Food	Lodging	Ramp	Camping
Chickamauga Lake, continued					
Highway 58 Boat Dock Big Spring, TN 37323 615-334-9879	Y	M		Y	
B & B Marina Rt. 2 Charleston, TN 37310 615-336-2341	Y	M		Y	
Dayton Boat Dock Dayton, TN 37321 615-775-2795	Y	S		Y	
Blue Water Resort Rt. 1, Box 496 Dayton, TN 37321 615-334-9928	Y	S		Y	T, TR

Chilhowee Lake

None; see Fontana and Tellico
lakes for nearest facilities.

Douglas Lake

Douglas Dam Reservation 2611 W. Andrew Johnson Hwy. Morristown, TN 37814 615-587-5600				Y	T, TR
Douglas Boat Dock Rt. 1 Sevierville, TN 37862 615-397-3321	Y	S		Y	
Sportsman's Shop Dock Rt. 3 Dandridge, TN 37725 615-397-3250	Y	S		Y	T, TR
Shady Grove Dock & Resort Rt. 3, Box 208 Dandridge, TN 37725 615-397-3372	Y	S	Y	Y	

	Dock	Food	Lodging	Ramp	Camping
Stumpy Cove Motel Rt. 3 Dandridge, TN 37725 615-397-3347		S	Y	Y	
Inspiration Point Rt. 3, Box 14-0 Dandridge, TN 37725 615-397-2116	Y	S	Y	Y	T, TR
Smokey View Campground Rt. 3 Dandridge, TN 37725 615-397-7202		S		Y	T, TR
Terry Point Campground Rt. 3 Dandridge, TN 37725 615-397-7928		M		Y	T, TR
Dandridge Municipal Park & Dock Rt. 2 Dandridge, TN 37725 615-397-7420	Y	S	Y	Y	T, TR
Indian Creek Dock Rt. 2, Indian Creek Rd. Dandridge, TN 37725 615-397-7286	Y	S	Y	Y	T, TR
Swann's Boat Dock Rt. 2 Dandridge, TN 37725 615-397-2185	Y	S	Y	Y	T, TR
Fancher's Willow Branch Rt. 2 Dandridge, TN 37725 615-397-3510		S		Y	T, TR

Fontana Lake

| Fontana Dam Reservation
Box 606
Athens, TN 37303
615-745-1783 | | | | | T, TR |

	Dock	Food	Lodging	Ramp	Camping
Fontana Village Fontana Dam, NC 28733 704-498-2212	Y	M	Y	Y	T, TR
Crisp Dock Almond, NC 28702 704-479-3214	Y	S	Y	Y	
Panther Creek Dock Star Route Bryson City, NC 28713 704-456-9870	Y	S		Y	
Greasy Branch Dock Rt. 2 Bryson City, NC 28713 704-488-6753	Y	S		Y	
Alarka Dock Rt. 2 Bryson City, NC 28713 704-488-2602	Y	S		Y	
Almond Dock Hwy. 28N, Box 1 Bryson City, NC 28713 704-488-6423	Y	S	Y	Y	

Fort Loudoun Lake

	Dock	Food	Lodging	Ramp	Camping
Fort Loudoun Dam Marina 130 Lee Dr. Lenoir City, TN 37771 615-986-5536	Y	M		Y	
Bakers Boat Dock Rt. 2 Friendsville, TN 37737 615-986-9203	Y				
Smokey Landing Boat Dock Rt. 2 Friendsville, TN 37737 615-995-2375	Y	M		Y	
Choto Marina Rt. 2 Concord, TN 37922 615-966-5472	Y	S		Y	

	Dock	Food	Lodging	Ramp	Camping
Concord Boat Dock Box 145 Concord, TN 37922 615-966-5831	Y	M		Y	
Fox Road Boat Dock 1110 Fox Road Concord, TN 37922 615-966-9422	Y	S		Y	
Louisville Boat Dock Rt. 2 Louisville, TN 37777 615-984-9001	Y	S		Y	
Duncan Boat Dock Duncan Rd. SW Knoxville, TN 37919 615-588-9127	Y	S		Y	

Fort Patrick Henry Lake

	Dock	Food	Lodging	Ramp	Camping
Warrior's Path State Recreation Park Box 5026 Kingsport, TN 37663 615-239-8992	Y	M	Y	Y	T, TR

Guntersville Lake

	Dock	Food	Lodging	Ramp	Camping
Honeycomb Creek Recreation Area 170 Office Warehouse Annex Muscle Shoals, AL 35660 205-386-2223				Y	T, TR
Honeycomb Boat Dock at Snug Harbor 1202 Clinton Ave. E. Huntsville, AL 35801 205-536-3113	Y			Y	T, TR
Street Bluff Boat Dock Rt. 3 Guntersville, AL 35976 205-582-6453	Y	S		Y	

	Dock	Food	Lodging	Ramp	Camping
Guntersville Boat Mart Rt. 1 Guntersville, AL 35976 205-582-2038	Y	S		Y	
Beech Creek Boat Dock Rt. 1 Guntersville, AL 35976 205-582-3153	Y	S	Y	Y	T, TR
Alfred Marine & Repair Base Rt. 6 Guntersville, AL 35976 205-582-4400	Y			Y	
Guntersville Marina Guntersville, AL 35976 205-582-6867	Y	M		Y	
Vaughn's Recreation Area Rt. 2 Guntersville, AL 35976 205-582-4821	Y	M	Y	Y	TR
Lake Guntersville State Park Star Rt. Guntersville, AL 35976 205-582-3666	Y	M	Y	Y	T, TR
Claysville Boat Dock Rt. 6 Guntersville, AL 35976 205-582-5517	Y			Y	TR
Riverbend Marina Scottsboro Hwy., Rt. 6 Guntersville, AL 35976 205-582-6857	Y	S		Y	
Ossawintha Rt. 6 Guntersville, AL 35976 205-582-4592	Y	S	Y	Y	T, TR
Turner Marina Box 102 Guntersville, AL 35976 205-582-4709	Y	S	Y	Y	T, TR

	Dock	Food	Lodging	Ramp	Camping
South Sauty Creek Boat Dock Rt. 1 Langston, AL 35755 205-582-3367	Y	M	Y	Y	TR
Bucks Pocket State Park Rt. 1 Grove Oak, AL 35975 205-569-2000	Y	S		Y	TR
North Sauty Marina Scottsboro, AL 35768 205-574-3762	Y	S		Y	
Goose Pond Colony Scottsboro, AL 35768 205-259-1808	Y	S		Y	T, TR
Scottsboro Municipal Park Scottsboro, AL 35768 205-259-0999	Y			Y	
Jackson County Park Scottsboro, AL 35768 205-259-6617	Y	M		Y	T, TR
Comer Bridge Boat Dock Section, AL 35771 205-228-3008	Y	S		Y	
Mud Creek Boat Dock Rt. 1 Hollywood, AL 35752 205-259-5517	Y	M	Y	Y	T, TR
Stevenson Municipal Park City Hall Main St. Stevenson, AL 35772 205-437-2123	Y			Y	

Hiwassee Lake

Bear Paw Resort Rt. 4 Murphy, NC 28906 704-644-5451	Y	M	Y	Y	

	Dock	Food	Lodging	Ramp	Camping
Hiwassee Hide-Away Rt. 5 Murphy, NC 28906 704-837-5049	Y	S		Y	
Hanging Dog Recreation Area Box 731 Asheville, NC 28802 704-837-5152		S			T, TR

Kentucky Lake

	Dock	Food	Lodging	Ramp	Camping
Guinn's Boat Dock Rt. 1 Gilbertsville, KY 42044 502-362-4671		S			T, TR
VanWinkle Boat Dock Rt. 1, Box 23 Gilbertsville, KY 42044 502-362-9967		S			T, TR
Kentucky Dam Boat Dock Gilbertsville, KY 42044 502-362-9914	Y		Y		
Kentucky Dam Marina P.O. Box 9 Gilbertsville, KY 42044 502-362-8500	Y	S		Y	
Kentucky Dam Village St. Resort Gilbertsville, KY 42044 502-362-4271	Y	M	Y	Y	T, TR
Grand Rivers Municipal Park Grand Rivers, KY 42045 502-362-8201	Y	S		Y	T, TR
Moor's Resort, Inc. Rt. 2 Gilbertsville, KY 42044 502-362-8361	Y	M	Y	Y	T, TR
Ellenberger's Resort Rt. 4, Box 156 Benton, KY 42025 502-354-6628	Y	S	Y	Y	T

	Dock	Food	Lodging	Ramp	Camping
Malcolm Creek Dock Rt. 4, Box 161 Benton, KY 42025 502-354-6496	Y	S	Y	Y	T, TR
Big Bear Resorts, Inc. Rt. 4, Box 156 Benton, KY 42045 502-354-6414	Y	M	Y	Y	T, TR
King Creek Resort Rt. 4, Box 129 Benton, KY 42045 502-354-8268	Y	S	Y	Y	T, TR
Bee Springs Lodge Rt. 4 Benton, KY 42045 502-354-6515	Y	M	Y	Y	T, TR
Southern Komfort Rt. 4 Benton, KY 42045 502-354-6422	Y	M	Y	Y	T, TR
Hester's Spot-in-the-Sun Rt. 4, Box 244 Benton, KY 42045 502-354-8280	Y	S	Y	Y	TR
Shawnee Bay Resort Rt. 4, Box 253B Benton, KY 42045 502-354-8360	Y	S	Y	Y	T
Cozy Cove Resort Rt. 5 Benton, KY 42045 502-354-8168	Y	S	Y	Y	
Hickory Hill Resort Rt. 5, Box 385 Benton, KY 42045 502-354-8207	Y	S	Y	Y	
Lakeside Campground Rt. 5 Benton, KY 42045 502-354-8157	Y	S	Y	Y	T, TR

	Dock	Food	Lodging	Ramp	Camping
Kentucky Lake, continued					
Cedar Knob Resort Rt. 5, Box 166 Benton, KY 42045 502-354-6998	Y	S	Y	Y	T
Sportsman's Marina Rt. 5 Benton, KY 42045 502-354-6568	Y	S	Y	Y	TR
Pirate's Cove Resort Rt. 1 Hardin, KY 42048 502-354-6377	Y		Y	Y	
Town & Country Resort Rt. 5 Benton, KY 42045 502-354-6587	Y	S	Y	Y	T, TR
Kenlake State Resort Park Rt. 1 Hardin, KY 42048 502-474-2211	Y	M	Y	Y	T, TR
Paradise Resort, Rt. 6 Murray, KY 42071 502-436-2767	Y	S	Y	Y	
Little Oaks Resort Rt. 6 Murray, KY 42071 502-436-5533	Y			Y	
Lynhurst Resort Rt. 6 Murray, KY 42071 502-436-2345	Y	S	Y	Y	
Irvin Cobb Resort Rt. 6 Murray, KY 42071 502-436-5811	Y	S	Y	Y	
Blood River Dock Rt. 5 Murray, KY 42071 502-436-5231	Y	S		Y	

	Dock	Food	Lodging	Ramp	Camping
Some Other Place New Concord, KY 42076 502-436-5519	Y	S	Y		T, TR
Lakeview Cottages New Concord, KY 42076 502-436-5876	Y	S	Y	Y	T, TR
Cypress Springs Resort New Concord, KY 42076 502-436-5496	Y	M	Y	Y	
Cypress Bay Resort Rt. 2 Buchanan, TN 38222 901-232-8221	Y	S	Y	Y	T, TR
Shamrock Resort Rt. 2 Buchanan, TN 38222 901-232-8211	Y	M	Y	Y	T, TR
The Overlook Rt. 1, Box 56 Buchanan, TN 38222 901-642-1281	Y	S	Y		
Paris Landing State Resort Park Rt. 1 Buchanan, TN 38222 901-642-2360	Y	M	Y	Y	T, TR
Oak Haven Lodge Rt. 1, Box 23 Buchanan, TN 38222 901-642-1550	Y	S	Y	Y	
Eagle's Nest Marina Rt. 1 Buchanan, TN 38222 901-642-6192	Y	S		Y	
Buchanan's Resort Rt. 1 Buchanan, TN 38222 901-642-2828	Y	M	Y	Y	T, TR

	Dock	Food	Lodging	Ramp	Camping
Kentucky Lake, continued					
Mansard Island Resort Rt. 1 Springville, TN 38256 901-642-5590	Y	M	Y	Y	T, TR
Pleasant View Resort Rt. 1 Springville, TN 38256 901-593-5511	Y	M	Y	Y	TR
Country Junction Rt. 2 Springville, TN 38256 901-593-3662		S		Y	T, TR
781 Boat Dock Rt. 2 Dover, TN 37058 615-232-7371				Y	
Driftwood Dock Rt. 2, Box 176B Dover, TN 37058 615-232-6121	Y	S		Y	T, TR
Brownfield Resort Rt. 2, Box 79 Dover, TN 37058 615-232-6070	Y	S		Y	T, TR
Granny's Branch Dock Rt. 2 Big Sandy, TN 38221 901-593-3295		S	Y	Y	T, TR
Leatherwood Resort Rt. 2 Dover, TN 37058 615-232-5137				Y	T, TR
Leatherwood Kentucky Lake Resort Rt. 2 Dover, TN 37058 615-232-7550	Y	M	Y	Y	T, TR

	Dock	Food	Lodging	Ramp	Camping
Sandy's Camp Rt. 2 Big Sandy, TN 38221 901-593-3328			Y		
Whitie's Resort Rt. 2 Big Sandy, TN 38221 901-593-5557			Y		
Southernaire Resort and Dock Rt. 2 Stewart, TN 37175 615-721-3321	Y	M	Y	Y	TR
Cane Creek Dock Rt. 2 Stewart, TN 37175 615-721-3483	Y	S	Y	Y	TR
Bass Bay Resort Rt. 2 Big Sandy, TN 38221 901-593-3239	Y	M	Y	Y	T, TR
Randy's Camp Rt. 2 Big Sandy, TN 38221 901-593-3200			Y		
Turkey Creek Dock Rt. 2 Waverly, TN 37185 615-297-3825	Y	S	Y	Y	T, TR
Harmon Creek Dock Star Route Eva, TN 38333 901-584-5484		S		Y	T, TR
Clydeton Dock Rt. 2 Waverly, TN 37185 615-296-2211	Y	S	Y	Y	
Noble's Dock 4620 Tara Drive Nashville, TN 37215 615-296-4633	Y			Y	

	Dock	Food	Lodging	Ramp	Camping
Kentucky Lake, continued					
Denver Dock P.O. Box 74 Denver, TN 37054 615-535-2199		S		Y	T, TR
Beaver Dam Lodge Rt. 4, Box 219A Camden, TN 38320 901-584-3963	Y	M	Y	Y	TR
Anchor Inn Marina New Johnsonville, TN 37134 615-535-2995	Y	M	Y	Y	T, TR
Birdsong Resort Rt. 2 Camden, TN 38320 901-584-7880	Y	S	Y	Y	T, TR
Crooked Creek Sports Marina Rt. 1 Lobelville, TN 37097 615-593-2112	Y	S	Y	Y	T, TR
Ponderosa Dock Sugar Tree, TN 38380 901-847-2525	Y	S		Y	
Cherokee Heights Dock Star Route Sugar Tree, TN 38380 901-847-2874	Y	S		Y	
Perryville Marina Box 97 Perryville, TN 38364 901-847-2444	Y	S		Y	
Lost Creek Dock Rt. 2 Decaturville, TN 38329 901-852-4221	Y	S		Y	
Cypress Creek Dock Rt. 6 Linden, TN 37096 901-847-7549	Y	S	Y	Y	

	Dock	Food	Lodging	Ramp	Camping
Cedar Creek Dock Rt. 6 Linden, TN 37096 615-589-5394		S	Y	Y	
Clifton Boat Harbor Clifton, TN 38425 615-676-5278	Y	S	Y	Y	
Saltillo Marina P.O. Box 141 Parson, TN 38363 901-847-2638	Y	S	Y	Y	
Bellis Botel Rt. 4 Savannah, TN 38372 901-925-4787	Y	M	Y	Y	
The Wharf Rt. 4 Savannah, TN 38372 901-925-9485	Y	M		Y	

Melton Hill Lake

	Dock	Food	Lodging	Ramp	Camping
Melton Hill Dam Reservation 2611 W. Andrew Johnson Hwy. Morristown, TN 37814 615-587-5600					T, TR
Oak Ridge Marina Melton Lake Drive Oak Ridge, TN 37830 615-482-6538	Y	M		Y	

Nickajack Lake

	Dock	Food	Lodging	Ramp	Camping
Nickajack Dam Reservation Box 606 Athens, TN 37303 615-745-1783				Y	T, TR
Hales Bar Resort & Marina Box 247 Guild, TN 37340 615-942-5573	Y	S		Y	T, TR

	Dock	Food	Lodging	Ramp	Camping
Ross's Landing Park 100 Riverfront Pky. Chattanooga, TN 37401 615-756-7618	Y	S		Y	

Norris Lake
*(on the Clinch River
    Embayment)*

	Dock	Food	Lodging	Ramp	Camping
Norris Dam State Park Box 27 Norris, TN 37828 615-426-7461		M	Y	Y	T, TR
Sequoyah Lodge and Marina Rt. 1 Box 194A Andersonville, TN 37705 615-494-9920	Y	M	Y	Y	T, TR
Rainbow Marina & Resort Box 88 LaFollette, TN 37766 615-562-2720	Y	M	Y	Y	T
Star Dust Dock Rt. 1, Box 149A Andersonville, TN 37705 615-494-9997	Y	M	Y	Y	T, TR
Big Ridge State Park Maynardville, TN 37807 615-992-5523	Y	M	Y		T, TR
Hickory Star Resort Rt. 1, Box 119 Maynardville, TN 37807 615-992-9186	Y	M	Y	Y	T, TR
Lakeview Dock P.O. Box 2014 Maynardville, TN 37807 615-278-9593	Y	S		Y	
Seymour's 33 Bridge Marina Rt. 3, Box J Maynardville, TN 37807 615-992-3091	Y	S		Y	T, TR

	Dock	Food	Lodging	Ramp	Camping
Claiborne Boat Dock, Inc. Rt. 4 New Tazewell, TN 37825 615-278-3131	Y	S	Y	Y	T, TR
Straight Creek Boat Dock Rt. 1, Box 173 New Tazewell, TN 37825 615-562-2368	Y	M		Y	
Lone Mountain Boat Dock Rt. 3, Box 238 Tazewell, TN 37879 615-626-9437	Y	S		Y	
(on the Powell River Embayment)					
Shanghai Resort Rt. 2, Box 337 LaFollette, TN 37766 615-562-7651	Y	S	Y	Y	
Springs Dock Rt. 4 LaFollette, TN 37766 615-562-2405	Y	S	Y	Y	
Powell Valley Resort and Marina Rt. 1, Box 287 LaFollette, TN 37766 615-562-5975	Y	M	Y	Y	T, TR
Larry's Flat Hollow Marina Rt. 2 Speedwell, TN 37870 615-562-8314	Y	M	Y	Y	
Blue Springs Hollow Dock Rt. 2 Speedwell, TN 37870 615-562-9953	Y	S	Y	Y	
Straight Branch Boat Dock Rt. 3 Speedwell, TN 37870 615-626-5826	Y	M	Y	Y	T, TR

	Dock	Food	Lodging	Ramp	Camping
Nottely Lake					
Terry's Boat Dock Box 675 Blairsville, GA 30512 404-745-4268	Y	S	Y	Y	
Lake Cove Lodge Rt. 4 Blairsville, GA 30512 404-745-6223	Y	M	Y	Y	
Leisuretime Lodge Rt. 4 Blairsville, GA 30512 404-745-5110	Y		Y	Y	
Pickwick Lake					
Pickwick Dam Reservation TVA 170 OS WHA Muscle Shoals, AL 35660 205-386-2223				Y	T, TR
Pickwick Landing State Resort Park Pickwick Dam, TN 38365 901-689-5175	Y	S	Y	Y	T, TR
Pickwick Cove Marina Rt. 4 Iuka, MS 38852 601-667-3192	Y	S		Y	
Goat Island Marina Rt. 4 Iuka, MS 38852 601-423-5810	Y	S		Y	
J. P. Coleman State Park Rt. 4 Iuka, MS 38852 601-423-6515	Y	M	Y	Y	T, TR
Eastport Dock Iuka, MS 38852 601-423-6972	Y	M	Y	Y	

	Dock	Food	Lodging	Ramp	Camping
Colbert County Park Colbert County Board of Revenue Tuscumbia, AL 35674 205-360-2764				Y	T, TR
Mill Creek Boat Dock Iuka, MS 38852 601-423-6129	Y	S	Y	Y	T, TR
Threet's Smokehouse Restaurant P.O. Box 218 Florence, AL 35630 205-764-1441	Y	M		Y	T, TR
Colbert Ferry Park Natchez Trace Parkway National Park Service P.O. Box 948 Tupelo, MS 38801 205-359-6372	Y			Y	
McFarland Bottoms Park Florence, AL 35630 205-766-5611			Y		T, TR

South Holston Lake

	Dock	Food	Lodging	Ramp	Camping
Lakeview Boat Dock Rt. 4, Box 10 Bristol, TN 37620 615-878-4331	Y	S	Y	Y	
Little Oak Mountain Recreation Area Elizabethton, TN 37643 615-587-5600				Y	T, TR
Friendship Dock Rt. 4 Bristol, TN 37620 615-878-5547	Y	M	Y	Y	
Laurel Boat Club Rt. 1, Box 894 Bristol, TN 37620 615-878-3721	Y	S			

	Dock	Food	Lodging	Ramp	Camping
Jacob's Creek Recreation Area Elizabethton, TN 37643 615-587-5600				Y	T, TR
Sportsman's Marina, Inc. Box 1183 Bristol, VA 24201 703-628-2850	Y	S		Y	TR

Taccoa (Blue Ridge) Lake

	Dock	Food	Lodging	Ramp	Camping
Blue Ridge Marina Star Route 11 Blue Ridge, GA 30513 404-632-2618	Y	S		Y	
Morgantown Point Recreation Area Box 643 Gainesville, GA 30501 404-632-3031				Y	T, TR
Blue Ridge Recreation Area Box 643 Gainesville, GA 30501 404-632-3031				Y	T, TR

Tellico Lake

	Dock	Food	Lodging	Ramp	Camping
Lotterdale Cove Recreation Area Rt. 2, Box 301 Vonore, TN 37885 615-856-3832				Y	T, TR
Notchy Creek Recreation Area Rt. 2, Box 301 Vonore, TN 37885 615-884-6280				Y	T, TR
Toqua Recreation Area Rt. 2, Box 301 Vonore, TN 37885 615-884-6498				Y	

	Dock	Food	Lodging	Ramp	Camping
Tims Ford Lake					
Holiday Marina P.O. Box 1593 Awalt Road Tullahoma, TN 37388 615-455-3151	Y	S	Y	Y	T, TR
Watauga Lake					
Watauga Dam Reservation 2611 W. Andrew Johnson Hwy. Morristown, TN 37814 615-587-5600				Y	T, TR
Fish Springs Dock Rt. 2, Box 142 Hampton, TN 37658 615-768-2336	Y	S		Y	TR
Hank's Boat Dock Rt. 2 Butler, TN 37640 615-768-2353	Y	S		Y	
Larsen's Landing Rt. 3, Box 180 Butler, TN 37640 615-768-2270	Y	M	Y	Y	T, TR
Midway Dock Rt. 1, Box 252 Butler, TN 37640 615-768-2677	Y	M		Y	
Watts Bar Lake					
Watts Bar Resort Watts Bar Dam, TN 37395 615-365-9595	Y	M	Y	Y	
Piney Point Resort Rt. 1, Box 279 Spring City, TN 37381 615-365-6262	Y	S	Y	Y	

	Dock	Food	Lodging	Ramp	Camping
Watts Bar Lake, continued					
Shep's Holiday Resort Rt. 3, Box 395 Spring City, TN 37381 615-365-6218	Y		Y	Y	TR
Rhea Harbor Rt. 2, Box 402 Spring City, TN 37381 615-365-6851	Y	S	Y	Y	
Toestring Cottages & Campground Rt. 3, Box 465 Spring City, TN 37381 615-365-5712	Y	S	Y	Y	T, TR
Stump Hollow Campground Rt. 1 Spring City, TN 37381 615-365-6192	Y	S		Y	T, TR
Sam's Boat Dock Rt. 1, Box 423 Ten Mile, TN 37880 615-334-5620	Y	S	Y	Y	T, TR
Euchee Boat Dock Rt. 1 Ten Mile, TN 37880 615-334-5343	Y	S	Y	Y	T, TR
Campground on the Lakeshore Rt. 2 Ten Mile, TN 37880 615-334-4284				Y	TR
Red Cloud Campground Rt. 1 Spring City, TN 37381 615-365-5572	Y			Y	T, TR
Eden of the Lake Resort Rt. 1, 234 Lakeview Dr. Spring City, TN 37381 615-365-6929	Y	S	Y	Y	T, TR

	Dock	Food	Lodging	Ramp	Camping
Terrace View Marina & Resort Rt. 1 Spring City, TN 37381 615-365-5238	Y	S	Y	Y	
Bill's Pier Rt. 1, Box 254W Spring City, TN 37381 615-365-4431	Y	S	Y	Y	
Arrowhead Resort Rt. 1 Spring City, TN 37381 615-365-6484	Y	M	Y	Y	T, TR
Eagle Lodge Resort Rt. 4, Box 325 Rockwood, TN 37854 615-354-0202	Y	S	Y	Y	T, TR
Newport Resort Rt. 1, Box 126A Spring City, TN 37381 615-365-9521	Y	S	Y	Y	T, TR
Blue Springs Marina Rt. 2, Box 324 Ten Mile, TN 37880 615-376-7298	Y	M	Y	Y	T, TR
Bayside Marina Rt. 2, Box 404 Ten Mile, TN 37880 615-376-7031	Y	M	Y	Y	T, TR
Harbor Point Rt. 4, Box 267 Rockwood, TN 37854 615-354-2974	Y	M	Y	Y	T, TR
Caney Creek Marina Rt. 8, Box 123 Harriman, TN 37748 615-882-1996	Y	M		Y	
Watts Bar Lake Rt. 1 Kingston, TN 37763 615-376-5880	Y			Y	T, TR

	Dock	Food	Lodging	Ramp	Camping
Watts Bar Lake, continued					
Long Island Marina Rt. 2, Box 386 Kingston, TN 37763 615-376-6288	Y	S		Y	
Interstate Camper's Resort Rt. 2, Box 348 Lenoir City, TN 37771 615-376-9017		S			T, TR
Wheeler Lake					
Wheeler Dam Reservation TVA 170 OS WHA Muscle Shoals, AL 35660 205-386-2223				Y	T, TR
Joe Wheeler State Park Wheeler, AL 35678 205-247-5466	Y	M	Y	Y	T, TR
Elk River Lodge Rt. 5 Athens, AL 35611 205-729-8228	Y	S	Y	Y	
Elk River Rest Area P.O. Box 610 Florence, AL 35630 205-247-5466	Y	S		Y	
Limestone County Park Limestone County Park Commission Athens, AL 35611 205-232-1320				Y	T, TR
Mallard Creek Recreation Area TVA 170 OS WHA Muscle Shoals, AL 35660 205-386-2223				Y	T, TR
Round Island Recreation Area TVA 170 OS WHA Muscle Shoals, AL 35660 205-386-2223				Y	T, TR

	Dock	Food	Lodging	Ramp	Camping
Lake Shore Marina Box 1786 Decatur, AL 35601 205-353-2615	Y			Y	
Point Mallard Park P.O. Box 1865 Decatur, AL 35601 205-350-3000		S			T, TR
Huntsville/Madison County Marina Hobbs Island Rd. Huntsville, AL 35803 205-536-4666	Y	S		Y	

Wilson Lake

	Dock	Food	Lodging	Ramp	Camping
Wilson Dam Reservation TVA 170 OS WHA Muscle Shoals, AL 35660 205-386-2223				Y	T, TR
Point Park Recreation Dept. 2500 Chisholm Rd. Florence, AL 35630 205-766-5233					T, TR
Marina Mar Rt. 7 Florence, AL 35630 205-757-1122	Y	M	Y	Y	
Lakeview Inn P.O. Box 726 Florence, AL 35630 205-757-2167	Y	S	Y		
Emerald Beach Marina Rt. 2 Killen, AL 36645 205-757-9086	Y	S		Y	TR
Fisherman's Resort Rt. 2 Town Creek, AL 35672 205-685-2114	Y	M	Y	Y	TR

Index

About the Authors

Joann and Don Kirk live in Morristown, Tennessee, between Cherokee and Douglas lakes. As well as fishing the lakes of the TVA system, they travel the world together in search of outdoor study material.

Joann is a well-known outdoor photographer. During the past decade her work has graced the covers and inside pages of most fishing and hunting magazines. She is also an avid angler who finds equal joy in boating either a frisky bluegill from the lakes near her home, or a heavyweight Atlantic salmon from a wilderness river in Quebec.

Don is a lifelong outdoorsman. He is a prolific and accomplished writer; over 1,500 of his stories have appeared in most sporting publications. An expert angler, Don is best known among trout fishermen, but he delights in catching all species of fish found in North America.

―――― Other Menasha Ridge Press Guidebooks

A Hiking Guide to the Trails of Florida, Elizabeth F. Carter

The Squirt Book: The Illustrated Manual of Squirt Kayaking Technique, James E. Snyder, illustrated by W. Nealy

Chattooga River Flip Map (Section IV), Ron Rathnow

Nantahala River Flip Map, Ron Rathnow

New River Flip Map, Ron Rathnow

Ocoee River Flip Map, Ron Rathnow

West Branch of the Penobscot and the Kennebec Gorge Flip Map, Ron Rathnow

Youghiogheny River Flip Map, Ron Rathnow

Kayak: The Animated Manual of Intermediate and Advanced Whitewater Technique, William Nealy

Kayaks to Hell, William Nealy

Whitewater Home Companion, Southeastern Rivers, Volume I, William Nealy

Whitewater Home Companion, Southeastern Rivers, Volume II, William Nealy

Whitewater Tales of Terror, William Nealy

Carolina Whitewater: A Canoeist's Guide to the Western Carolinas, Bob Benner

A Paddler's Guide to Eastern North Carolina, Bob Benner and Tom McCloud

Wildwater West Virginia, Volume I, The Northern Streams, Paul Davidson and Ward Eister, with Dirk Davidson

Wildwater West Virginia, Volume II, The Southern Streams, Paul Davidson and Ward Eister, with Dirk Davidson

Diver's Guide to Underwater America, Kate Kelley and John Shobe

Shipwrecks: Diving the Graveyard of the Atlantic, Roderick Farb

Boatbuilder's Manual, Charles Walbridge, editor

272

Smoky Mountains Trout Fishing Guide, Don Kirk

A Guide to the Backpacking and Day-Hiking Trails of Kentucky, Arthur B. Lander, Jr.

A Fishing Guide to Kentucky's Major Lakes, Arthur B. Lander, Jr.

A Canoeing and Kayaking Guide to the Streams of Florida, Volume I, North Central Peninsula and Panhandle, Elizabeth F. Carter and John L. Pearce

A Canoeing and Kayaking Guide to the Streams of Florida, Volume II, Central and South Peninsula, Lou Glaros and Doug Sphar

Appalachian Whitewater, Volume I, The Southern Mountains, Bob Sehlinger, Don Otey, Bob Benner, William Nealy, and Bob Lantz

Appalachian Whitewater, Volume II, The Central Mountains, Ed Grove, Bill Kirby, Charles Walbridge, Ward Eister, Paul Davidson, and Dirk Davidson

Appalachian Whitewater, Volume III, The Northern Mountains, John Connelly and John Porterfield

Northern Georgia Canoeing, Bob Sehlinger and Don Otey

Southern Georgia Canoeing, Bob Sehlinger and Don Otey

A Canoeing and Kayaking Guide to the Streams of Kentucky, Bob Sehlinger

A Canoeing and Kayaking Guide to the Streams of Ohio, Volume I, Richard Combs and Stephen E. Gillen

A Canoeing and Kayaking Guide to the Streams of Ohio, Volume II, Richard Combs and Stephen E. Gillen

A Canoeing and Kayaking Guide to the Streams of Tennessee, Volume I, Bob Sehlinger and Bob Lantz

A Canoeing and Kayaking Guide to the Streams of Tennessee, Volume II, Bob Sehlinger and Bob Lantz

Emergency Medical Procedures for the Outdoors

Guide and Map to the Uwharrie Trail, Nick Hancock

Harsh Weather Camping, Sam Curtis

Modern Outdoor Survival, Dwight R. Schuh

Quantity Sales

Most Menasha Ridge Press books are available at special quantity discounts when purchased in bulk by corporations, organizations, and special-interest groups. Custom imprinting or excerpting can also be done to fit special needs. For details write: Menasha Ridge Press, P.O. Box 59257, Birmingham, Alabama 35259-9257 or call 800-247-9437, Attn: Special Sales Dept.

Individual Sales

Are there any Menasha books you want but cannot find in local stores? If so, you can order them directly from us. You can get any Menasha book in print. Simply include the book's title, author, and ISBN number, if you have it, along with a check or money order for the full retail price plus $2.00 to cover shipping and handling. Mail to: Menasha Ridge Press, P.O. Box 59257, Birmingham, AL 35259-9257.

Note to our readers

Your comments, corrections, and any information you have about material contained in this book would be greatly appreciated. Please feel free to write us or the authors care of Menasha Ridge Press, Post Office Box 59257, Birmingham, AL 35259-9257.